I0796542

Grant's Enforcer

GRANT'S ENFORCER

TAKING DOWN THE KLAN

Guy Gugliotta

The University of Georgia Press
Athens

Athens, Georgia 30602
www.ugapress.org

Designed by Melissa Buchanan
Set in Kepler Std
Printed and bound by Sheridan Books

The paper in this book meets the guidelines for permanence and durability of the Committee on Production Guidelines for Book Longevity of the Council on Library Resources.

Most University of Georgia Press titles are available from popular e-book vendors.

Printed in the United States of America
25 26 27 28 29 C 5 4 3 2 1

EU Authorized Representative
Easy Access System Europe—Mustamäe tee 50,
10621 Tallinn, Estonia, gpsr.requests@easproject.com

Library of Congress Cataloging-in-Publication Data
Names: Gugliotta, Guy, author.
Title: Grant's enforcer : taking down the Klan / Guy Gugliotta.
Description: Athens : The University of Georgia Press, [2025] | Includes bibliographical references and index.
Identifiers: LCCN 2024048187 (print) | LCCN 2024048188 (ebook) | ISBN 9780820373362 (hardback) | ISBN 9780820373379 (epub) | ISBN 9780820373386 (ebook)
Subjects: LCSH: Ku Klux Klan (1915–) | Racism—United States—History. | Hate groups—United States—History. | United States—Race relations—History.
Classification: LCC HS2330.K63 G84 2025 (print) | LCC HS2330.K63 (ebook) | DDC 322.4/20973—dc23/eng/20250203
LC record available at https://lccn.loc.gov/2024048187
LC ebook record available at https://lccn.loc.gov/2024048188

CONTENTS

PROLOGUE

Night Riders

MARCH 5, 1871

Jim Williams rode down Yorkville's main street and parked his mule in front of Rose's Hotel. It was late Sunday afternoon, the end of "sales day," and the town was still packed with merchants, bankers, drummers, and shoppers—men, women, and children, black and white—from all over York County, South Carolina.

Yorkville, a few miles south of the North Carolina border, was a pretty little town with wide, tree-lined streets, small shops, and a considerable number of richly appointed homes spreading out from the town center. Rose's Hotel was a local showpiece—three elegant stories with a massive front porch and broad balconies on the upper floors.

Jim Williams was not there for the accommodations. He was a black captain in South Carolina's state militia, and the militia had its headquarters in the hotel. For what he had to say he needed some friendly faces at his back. Yorkville was a mostly white town, and it was also a stronghold of the Ku Klux Klan.

Ever since the end of the previous year bands of disguised Ku Klux had ravaged York County, rousting black families in the middle of the night, beating men and women, raping mothers and older daughters, and in a few cases murdering those who provoked particular animosity.[1]

Many of the men and some of the women were so scared that they were hiding in the woods at night—"laying out" is what they called it—to escape the night riders. Jim Williams wasn't scared; he was angry, and people knew it. Yorkville's black citizens looked up to him; the whites resented him.[2]

Jim Williams was well known enough so he had no trouble drawing a crowd. There is no record of how long he spoke or his exact words. Long afterward, Klan member Milus Smith Carroll wrote that Williams threatened the Klan: if they ever decided to come into his militia territory on the southern edge of York County, "very few would return to their homes."[3]

Whatever Williams said, reports traveled fast. By nightfall, maybe forty white men were gathered at the Brier Patch, a stretch of empty ground near the Harkness place five miles west of Yorkville. It was a cool, humid night. Spring was coming up fast. Rufus McLain's Black Panthers were there, along with Will Johnson's Rattlesnakes, Chambers Brown's Broad Rivers Klan, and the Yorkvilles of Dr. J. Rufus Bratton.[4]

Bratton, a former Confederate army surgeon, was the overall leader. He was a severe, icy zealot battling what he believed to be an existential threat to the white people of South Carolina. "There can be no doubt," Bratton said later, "that the hostility between the races is bitter and universal, and is permanent."[5]

Most of the Brier Patch riders didn't know what they were doing that night. Those who spoke about it later said they thought the idea was to seize whatever guns they could find from York County's blacks—militiamen or civilians, it didn't matter—and scare the men who owned them so they wouldn't vote for Republicans—"Radicals," as they were more commonly known.

That was certainly part of the plan, but Dr. Bratton had another idea, shared with a few trusted colleagues. With his Sunday speech in Yorkville, Jim Williams had defied York County's white establishment once too often.[6]

JIM WILLIAMS had been born Jim Rainey on Dr. Samuel Rainey's York County plantation southeast of McConnellsville, near the southern edge of York County. Julia Rainey, the doctor's widow, knew him "very well," she said later, and saw him often, both as a boy and after he grew up. Her husband "treated him very kindly," she said. "There was always a great deal of politeness between us."[7]

That was about all anyone said about the first part of Jim Rainey's life. The second part began in 1864, after he ran off to become a Union soldier and join General Sherman in Georgia. When he returned to York County a year later, he was Jim Williams—taking the surname of his biological father.[8]

By all accounts, Williams lived a peaceful postwar life. The Williams home, a country cabin he shared with his wife Rose and their children in the woods ten miles south of Yorkville, was equidistant from McConnellsville and Brattonsville, the ancestral home of Dr. Bratton's family. Williams had "lived among the Yankees" but didn't like them, Williams once told a white neighbor. He "liked his own people," the neighbor said.[9]

He was a careful, forthright man who never swore, frequently dropped in for visits at the Rainey plantation, and moved easily among his neighbors, black and white—an "upright gentleman in every respect," according to another white neighbor.[10]

Things changed in 1870. South Carolina governor Robert Scott, a Republican from Ohio, recruited and deployed state militiamen in midyear, ostensibly to keep the peace prior to the fall election—in which he was running for a second term.

White South Carolinians would not serve alongside black soldiers. As a consequence, despite a smattering of northern whites in leadership positions, the overwhelming majority of the militiamen were black recruits. Jim Williams, because of his wartime experience, was an obvious choice to lead one of the companies.

Scott outfitted the militiamen with .58-caliber Remington muskets that had been converted to breechloader rifles.[11] Fitted with bayonets, these were formidable military weapons, and the militiamen were well aware of it. They infuriated South Carolina's white citizens by holding political rallies, drilling and marching through upcountry towns. The whites, virtually all of whom were Democrats, were convinced that Scott had armed the militia as a political ploy to intimidate the opposition and enable him to win reelection in October. Which he did. Soon after, Scott moved to disband the militia, sending emissaries across the state to collect their weapons, with some success.

But Jim Williams demurred. He alone of York County's militia leaders refused to disarm his company, undoubtedly convinced that the county's all-white law enforcement system would neither protect black citizens from the Ku Klux Klan nor punish the Klan even if they were caught.

The Williams company had ninety-six men, most of whom farmed shares, leased smallholdings on nearby plantations, or worked as hired labor.[12] They had not drilled since the previous year, and they were barely soldiers. The Williams militia had neither beaten nor killed anyone.

Jim Williams, with his stature as a local leader and his refusal to turn in the company's arms, became an increasing focus for white animosity. According to local gossip and rumor, he was looking to intimidate—or, worse, provoke confrontations with—the white community.

Like his men, however, Williams had harmed no one, and he did what he could to calm things down. A short time before his Rose's Hotel speech he had assured John L. Lowry, a white neighbor, that Lowry "need feel no uneasiness," and that Williams did not "intend to hurt them."[13]

But Williams had no compunction about speaking his mind about politics and current events, not only with his black followers but with whites as well. This was not normal behavior in York County. During the 1870 campaign, Williams had approached another white neighbor whom he had known for years and asked him to vote Republican. It was an amiable conversation, the neighbor later said, or at least it started out that way. He told Williams he was a Democrat and would vote the Democratic ticket. Not Williams. "I would see them in hell," he replied.[14]

Then there was the time a drunken white landowner stumbled into a Williams company muster and attacked one of the militiamen. The drunk was subdued, arrested, and held overnight. White York County did not like it when former slaves manhandled former masters.[15] Dr. Bratton may have used disarmament as an excuse for his night riders, but his main interest was to put an end to black political activism. Ku Klux riders had murdered at least two blacks already and had beaten countless others since the elections. Now there was Jim Williams.

The Brier Patch crowd set off a bit after eight o'clock, riding south. Quite a number wore dark, calf-length gowns—black or maybe red, impossible to know in the dark—and others wore white. Most of the riders also had hoods, some stitched up with cloth ears or with real horns attached. Others wore everyday clothes and false faces or pullover oilcloth masks with eyeholes.

Some of the horses were draped in blankets. The reason for this was open to debate. Some Ku Klux apparently thought costumed horses helped them look more like the avengers from hell they aspired to be. Others claimed that blacks were simple people, terrified of the supernatural and easily frightened. Still others admitted implicitly the opposite. They disguised their horses so their prospective victims wouldn't know who they were by identifying their favorite mounts.[16]

That the latter reason had some truth to it was supported by another rule broadly followed by the mounted riders. No names. Instead, everyone had a number. The man giving the orders that night was "Number Six." Probably Dr. Bratton.[17]

THE NIGHT RIDERS, reinforced by several dozen Ku Klux who had met them along the way, numbered around sixty men by the time they reached Joe Moore's mill, about seven miles south of Yorkville. It was about midnight, and they were looking for Gadsden Steel, a freedman who lived next door to Joe Moore. Steel was twenty-six and worked for Moore at the mill. He was supposed to know where to find Jim Williams.

Steel's wife awakened him when she heard the Ku Klux approaching, and he had just pulled on his pants when several Klan members broke down his door and asked him where he kept his guns.

He didn't have any, he said.

They pushed him outside. He was surrounded by costumed horsemen.

One of them gun-whipped him "three licks over the head," Steel recalled later, and slashed him twice, near one of his eyes and next to his mouth. Other riders went next door to roust Moore, his white boss, and haul him outdoors.

Is Steel a bad boy? asked his principal tormentor.

"A very fine boy," Moore said.

How did he vote? asked the tormentor.

"Republican," replied Moore.

The tormentor turned back to Steel: "Goddamn you, I'll kill you for that."

Steel was brought before Number Six, sitting astride his horse.

"How do you do?" Number Six said. He leaned over and jabbed Steel sharply in the chest with horns about two feet long. Steel jumped back. Several men punched him.

"Stand up to him, goddamn you, and talk to him," said one.

Number Six asked who had guns. A lot of people had them, Steel replied, but not now. They turned them in.

"Well, ain't Jim Williams got the guns?" somebody asked.

Steel said he had heard this but didn't know.

"We want you to go and show us the way to Jim Williams's house."

"I've never been there," Steel said.

"We want you to go and show us to where his house is; if you don't show us to where his house is, we will kill you."

Then one of the men looked up at the moon. "Don't tarry here too long with this damned nigger; we have to get back to hell before daybreak."[18]

CHAPTER ONE

The Georgia Question

Amos Tappan Akerman, a slim, slightly built man of medium height, appeared before the House of Representatives Committee on Reconstruction on December 19, 1868, to testify about Georgia's efforts to be readmitted to the Union after three years of provisional governments, military occupation, and martial law.[1] It was not going well.

The forty-seven-year-old lawyer from Northeast Georgia's Elbert County was a rarity among southern white men. He had been born and raised in New Hampshire, he told the lawmakers, but had lived for the past twenty-five years in Georgia "all my mature life."[2]

Akerman considered himself a Georgian. He had been a slave owner and had served in the Confederate army. In the war's aftermath, he was barred from holding any office in state or federal government unless Congress voted to lift these "disabilities."

It was unclear whether the committee knew any of this, but it did not matter. Akerman had embraced the Republican Party at war's end, had become a fierce advocate for the civil and constitutional rights of Georgia's former slaves, and had actively campaigned for General Ulysses S. Grant, who had just won the U.S. presidency the previous month. This was why Congress had summoned him.

Akerman's ostensible purpose was to support Georgia's reentry to the Union, but he had much more on his mind. He was deeply involved in the vicious and often violent politics that engulfed Georgia and the rest of the former Confederacy. Southern blacks wanted the rights the war had won for them. Whites clung fiercely to a way of life that had been upended by the same war.

Whites' fear and hatred stalked the Reconstruction South. States manipulated their institutions to deny the rights of blacks. If that didn't work, they called on the Ku Klux Klan for intimidation, bullying, threats, and—if all those didn't work—terrorism.

Akerman had seen it firsthand. He had been threatened, heckled in public, sworn at, spat at, snubbed, and ridiculed in print and on the stump. This was nothing compared to what Georgia's blacks had endured, but it matched or exceeded anything Washington's white committee members had seen.

AKERMAN KNEW his home state was a shambles. Congress had readmitted Georgia to the Union earlier in the year, but subsequent sins had put the wisdom of that decision in doubt. The state had voted in November's general elections—for the Democrats—but the House was reluctant to seat Georgia's delegation until some serious "irregularities" were resolved. This was what the committee was now attempting to do. Without sworn congressmen, Georgia was still not part of the Union.[3]

Northern newspapers described all this as "the Georgia Question."[4] The readmission process, as laid down by Congress, had begun in April during Georgia's elections for governor and the state legislature. Large numbers of white Democrats chose to boycott the balloting, refusing to take an oath of loyalty to the United States, a precondition for the franchise in the former Confederacy.

As a consequence, the Republicans swept into power, winning the governorship and both houses of the legislature. The winners included twenty-five black assemblymen and three black state senators. And, shortly after taking their seats, the legislators ratified the Fourteenth Amendment, another congressional prerequisite for readmission. This law, a momentous guidepost in constitutional jurisprudence from the day it took effect, guaranteed citizenship and equality before the law for "all" persons—no other adjectives—born or naturalized in the United States.

Georgia's defeated Democrats were not cowed. In a series of legislative challenges and rulings from a sympathetic state judiciary, they managed over the next several months to stand the Fourteenth Amendment on its head.

State courts agreed that under the new amendment states could not "abridge," "deprive" or "deny" the rights and privileges of citizens, but black Americans before ratification had neither citizenship nor rights. The Fourteenth Amendment thus did not apply to the blacks, because they had nothing to be taken away. Akerman had argued in court on behalf of the banished lawmakers, but to no avail. The legislature, still dominated by whites, voted to oust all its black members and replace them with whites.

The votes were lopsided: 82–23 in the state legislature and 24–11 in the senate. Those numbers meant that significant numbers of white Republicans voted with the majority. Although apparently comfortable with slavery's departure, these Georgians were not prepared to embrace racial equality.

That was in September.[5] Next came the presidential campaign. The 1868 election marked the first time blacks were allowed to vote for the U.S. president, and virtually to a man they firmly allied with the Republicans, the party of the martyred Lincoln.

Once again, many Democrats refused to take the loyalty oath, and once again this decision should have produced an easy Republican victory. This time, however, whites decided to improve their chances by bullying and terrorizing black voters to keep them from the polls. Mild tactics involved catcalls at Republican gatherings, linking arms to prevent black voters from approaching ballot boxes, and warnings that a vote for Grant would mean the loss of a job, if not permanent unemployment.[6]

As the year wore on, however, whites raised the stakes. After nightfall during the fall, gangs of costumed riders roamed the countryside, invading the homes of some white, but mostly black, Republicans. Frequently these raids were accompanied by beatings, robberies, rapes, or even murder.

These night riders were newly minted members of the Ku Klux Klan, which had sprung up a couple of years earlier in Tennessee before spreading suddenly and dramatically into Georgia and across the rest of the South.

These tactics worked. Democratic presidential candidate Horatio Seymour won Georgia by fourteen points. As Baptist pastor Henry M. Turner, one of the ousted black lawmakers, put it wryly in his own Washington testimony: "I must say, so far as I have learned from letters and from persons I have seen . . . with bullets in their legs, bullets in their sides, and bullets in their heads, the evidence is very strong that the election did not pass without great outrages being committed."[7]

Georgia's electoral abuses had no practical effect on the outcome of the general election—Grant won handily, but, along with the earlier statehouse purge, the fall campaign had further damaged the state's efforts to portray itself as "reconstructed" and worthy of readmission to the Union. Georgia got little sympathy in the northern press: "A perfect reign of terror has been brought on by the whites by means of their organizations of Ku-Klux-Klans, and frequent murders have been committed," the *Philadelphia Inquirer* reported after the first week of Reconstruction Committee hearings.[8]

The committee also had little sympathy for Georgia. This was the era of "Radical Reconstruction." Longtime Reconstruction Committee chairman and firebrand abolitionist Thaddeus Stevens had died in August, but he was replaced ten days before Akerman's testimony by George S. Boutwell of Massachusetts, another Radical Republican. The Georgia Question hearings marked Boutwell's debut.

Even worse, perhaps, for Georgia's prospects, the committee was in post-election lame duck session. It was the Christmas season, and the vast majority of lawmakers and staff had already left town for the holidays.

Akerman was sworn in on a beautiful, late autumn Saturday morning. The

Washington, D.C., *Evening Star* urged readers to try a walk along the Potomac wharves to watch small steamers get underway for holiday voyages to Norfolk, Baltimore, Philadelphia, and the eastern shore of the Chesapeake.

At the National Theater, Agatha States was appearing as Leonora that night in the final pre-Christmas performance of Verdi's *Il Trovatore*. The previous evening, the Army Medical Museum—the recast Ford's Theatre—had treated lingering lawmakers to a demonstration of the "power and usefulness of the microscope in distinguishing the very minute and at times imperceptible . . . objects or substances which make up the animal, mineral and vegetable kingdom."

Thomas Russell & Co., at "the sign of the golden eagle" on Pennsylvania Avenue, displayed several classic whiskeys for the Christmas connoisseur—including rye, "Irish, scotch and Old Bourbon, the Milk of Kentucky." A few doors away the Hudson Taylor Bookstore was offering twenty-four volumes of Dickens for $90 and Shakespeare in fourteen volumes for $40.[9]

Meanwhile, Akerman and the Reconstruction Committee were stuck in a drafty committee room in the Capitol listening to Ku Klux horror stories from Reverend Turner and other witnesses.

Congress was considering two possible ways to answer the Georgia Question. Lawmakers could ignore the ouster of the black legislators and readmit Georgia by seating its white congressional delegation, a tacit acknowledgment that political manipulation—and terrorism—were permissible and productive. But after resounding victories in both the U.S. House and Senate, with Grant coming to the White House for at least the next four years, and with Boutwell trying to live up to Stevens's standard, the Republicans were not inclined to look the other way.

The second option was simply for Congress to refuse to seat the delegation. By doing so, Georgia would return to the postwar political wilderness. This solution had its own drawbacks, however, chief among them the prolongation of an expensive and nationally unpopular military intervention and the white resentment that accompanied it.

The U.S. Army had had a 270,000-man occupation force in the South in June 1865, but six months later that number had shrunk to 88,000. By the time Akerman appeared before Congress, there were approximately 20,000 troops in the former Confederacy, and as many as half of these were in Texas guarding the frontier.[10] Congress wanted to suppress Klan violence but did not want to pay for a massive army presence to do the job.

Akerman had another idea, but he chose a roundabout, hackneyed way of conveying it. He began his testimony by admitting how unrepentant much of confederate Georgia remained, and how Georgia's difficulties arose from white dissatisfaction with the results of the war, "of which the prime was emancipation." He often treated northerners, even House committee members with decades of antislavery activism, as if they had no understanding of the depths of bitterness that consumed the white South.[11]

Violence had peaked during the election campaign, Akerman said, but a "partial subsidence" had occurred in subsequent weeks. A "considerable portion" of the state's Democrats "disapproved of the violence," and disapproval was increasing.[12]

For this, however, he presented no evidence. He instead recounted his efforts to lead perhaps 400 black voters to the polls on election day, only to have them repeatedly blocked, insulted, chased away, and pursued by a stone-throwing white mob. By the time the polls closed, Akerman said, 798 Democrats and 21 Republicans had voted.[13]

Asked about Georgia's justice system, Akerman damned it with faint praise. The law is "as well administered as it ever was," Akerman said, then explained that justice had never been administered particularly well.[14]

He recounted the story of a drunken Elbert County overseer who had shot a black child for no reason. The child recovered, but when prosecutors brought the case before a grand jury, they could not get an indictment for assault with intent to commit murder because "the offense charged was too high," Akerman said, adding that he could not recollect any occasion when a white person had been convicted of a crime against a black person.[15]

"I think the disposition to suppress disorder is increasing," he said, despite all these shortcomings and again having cited no evidence to support his view of ostensible progress. "My impression is that any action of Congress restoring military government and overthrowing the reconstruction which had been supposed to be perfected in Georgia would be most pernicious."[16]

Akerman's endorsement of Georgia statehood ended here, probably leaving the committee befuddled. He said he wanted Georgia to rejoin the Union, yet it was clear that he had no faith in the white-dominated status quo. Who was this bumpkin?

But then he turned his attention to the weakness of Congress's two options. Georgia's Democrats were bitterly opposed to black rights and reconstruction. This could not be ignored. Acceptance of the status quo was impossible.

But denying statehood and reimposing military rule was counterproductive because it simply gave Georgia's whites a target for their resentment and an excuse to avoid taking responsibility for their state's affairs.

"In my judgment anything like a proconsular government . . . will only postpone to a future day the troubles which we now have in Georgia," he told the committee.[17] Instead, Akerman continued, try something different: readmit Georgia, let the discontent play out, but use law enforcement to quell the major abuses.

But what if the law was not working?

That was the key question, and Akerman had come prepared to answer it.

Send cases to federal court, he said. Specifically, use the Fourteenth Amendment—ratified only months earlier—whenever it could be shown that because of race, color, or "political sentiments," a victim could not "go into the state courts and obtain impartial justice."[18]

Congress could use the amendment to enforce civil rights—to ensure that the Georgia legislature allowed blacks to hold elective office. All lawmakers needed to do was pass a law to cover a specific case—or any similar case. There was no need for military government. The Fourteenth Amendment could be applied to any state that resisted its intent and reach.

"With all due deference," he told lawmakers, "the Amendment provides that no state shall deny to any person within its jurisdiction the equal protection of the law."[19] And, by implication, he said, the same procedure could be used in any state to overrule any legislature on any issue.

Did he mean, asked an incredulous Fernando Beaman, one of the founders of the Republican Party, that Congress, if it chose, "could pass a law to assemble a convention in the state of Massachusetts and correct any wrong existing there?"

"Undoubtedly," an unruffled Akerman replied.[20]

With that answer, the seated congressmen went from incredulous to intrigued.

Suddenly, Akerman had the committee's full attention. This was a provocative and even presumptuous argument for an obscure Georgia lawyer to make before the U.S. Congress. Federal interference in the affairs of individual states—trampling on the canon of states' rights—was a transgression to be undertaken only in the gravest of circumstances.

The Civil War had been such a circumstance, but wholesale military intervention was no longer politically feasible by the time Akerman spoke, nor was it desirable, in Akerman's view. Akerman was offering another option: instead of targeting entire states, target individual offenders and set an example by trying them in federal court and sending them to jail.

How could it be done? It was not as if Congress in 1866 had failed to consider the dramatic expansion of federal power embodied in the Fourteenth Amendment.[21] The potential danger to states' rights was a serious sticking point during floor debate in both the Senate and House. So too were provisions forbidding any state "to abridge the privileges or immunities" of citizens or "deprive any person of life, liberty or property, without due process of law."[22]

And both Akerman and the committee members—many of whom were attorneys—also knew that ratification alone did not mean that the Fourteenth Amendment could automatically be applied however and whenever Congress or the president wished to do so. Additional laws had to be crafted to interpret and describe how and when the amendment would be used, how it would be enforced, and what penalties would be exacted for violations. Akerman was suggesting that this "enabling legislation"—authorized in Section 5 of the amendment—be crafted to expand the reach of the Fourteenth Amendment to whatever degree necessary.

So Akerman was no bumpkin. In the intricate and lengthy legal discussion that ensued that December morning, it quickly became clear that he believed that the Fourteenth Amendment could resolve the Georgia Question by federal fiat but without recourse to martial law. Violate the Fourteenth Amendment, he suggested, and federal authorities could step in whenever and wherever they wished to prosecute crimes deliberately aimed at black victims as civil rights violations.

And that was not all. If, for instance, the Ku Klux Klan broke into a man's house, horsewhipped him, raped his wife, and stole his money, the offenders could be tried in federal court for violating the victim's Fourth Amendment protection against "unreasonable searches and seizures" This was a truly radical idea, as Akerman and the committee members certainly knew, because it meant that the Fourteenth Amendment would give prosecutors the power to treat common crimes as violations of constitutional rights—specifically those enumerated in the Bill of Rights—and try the cases in federal court. This concept had also provoked considerable argument during the 1866 debate.[23]

Akerman understood that such a sweeping assertion would undoubtedly be tested in court, but, he told the committee, he welcomed the challenge. "I have no doubt of the fact that Congress possesses such power under that amendment of the Constitution."[24]

Akerman thus proposed to use the Fourteenth Amendment to radically reinterpret the Bill of Rights. The first ten amendments to the Constitution were intended to protect states and individuals from the tyranny of the federal government. But the Fourteenth Amendment, Akerman contended, gave the federal government license to use the Bill of Rights to protect individuals from the tyranny of the states.

Committee members hammered Akerman on this point, but he held his ground. And instead of the rambling monologue that had marked his earlier testimony, he responded with sharp, detailed answers to questions he had clearly mulled for some time. His closing argument was clear: the Civil War had proved the primacy of the federal government over states' rights. You have the power, he told his interrogators. Now use it.

On March, 4, 1869, President Grant was inaugurated, and the Forty-First Congress was sworn in—all but Georgia's delegation, which was not allowed to sit. Fifteen months later Grant appointed Amos T. Akerman attorney general of the United States.

CHAPTER TWO

The Grand Wizard

APRIL 2, 1868

The Ku Klux Klan announced its arrival in York County with a paid advertisement in the *Yorkville Enquirer*, a conservative weekly whose measured and generally careful coverage was as good as any in South Carolina's upcountry, if not the entire state:

"K.K.K. DEAD-MAN'S HOLLOW SOUTHERN DIV. Midnight, March 30."

"*General Order No. 1.*"

"REMEMBER the hour appointed by our Most Excellent Grand Captain-General. The dismal hour draws nigh for the meeting of our mystic Circle. The Shrouded-Knight will come with pick and spade; the Grand Chaplain with the ritual of the dead. The grave yawneth, the lightnings flash athwart the heavens, the thunders roll, but the Past Grand Knight of the Sepulcher will recoil not.

"By order of the Great Grand Centaur SULEYMAN, G.G.S."

This mix of menacing gibberish and intimidation had marked the Klan's progress for weeks as it began its rapid spread across the former Confederacy in early 1868. It was a crucial year. General Ulysses S. Grant, no friend of the former Confederacy, was the likely Republican candidate for president; the Fourteenth Amendment was headed for ratification in July; freedmen would be allowed to vote for the first time in their lives in November elections; and a month after that Amos T. Akerman would tell the House Committee on Reconstruction that violations of civil rights ought to be tried in federal court. What did the Klan intend?

The *Enquirer*'s editors were skeptical. "We can believe no good can result from such organizations," they wrote.[1]

York County, on the border with North Carolina, was probably the last stop on a three-week journey by former Confederate general Nathan Bedford Forrest, who had arrived in Atlanta in early March as a director and "General Traveling Agent" for the Southern Life Insurance Association. Forrest was said to be the national leader of the Ku Klux Klan, its "Grand Wizard."[2]

By mid-March, short news stories, posters, and paid newspaper advertisements not unlike the one in the *Enquirer* started appearing in Georgia cities, heralding the arrival of the "Mystic Order of the Ku Klux Klan," and effectively announcing the establishment of the Klan's Georgia chapter.[3] The announcements did not say who was in charge, but knowledgeable Georgians regarded former Confederate general John B. Gordon as the state's Klan leader.[4] He was one of Forrest's principal Georgia contacts and was just beginning a long political career that would include the Georgia governorship and two terms as a U.S. senator. Like Forrest, he was a Southern Life executive making the substantial sum of $5,000 per year.[5]

Georgia's gubernatorial and state legislative elections were only weeks away. General Forrest, perhaps, was helping make sure that white Georgians—most of whom were refusing to vote—had allies ready and able to protect their interests.

He toured the state for most of March as the Klan's chief proselytizer, and dens sprang up behind him in Macon, Columbus, Milledgeville, and Augusta. The *Augusta Chronicle*, unlike the *Enquirer*, welcomed the "mystic brotherhood," noting that "the faithful" were meeting nightly: "Success say we to the Ku Klux!"[6] Then he moved on, probably crossing the border into South Carolina to meet with Wade Hampton, who, like Forrest and Gordon, was a noted Confederate commander, an important postwar political figure, and an executive of Southern Life.[7]

About a week after Forrest left Georgia, a mob of Klan members broke into the Columbus home of white Republican activist George Ashburn and shot him three times in the head, once in the abdomen, and once in the leg as he lay in bed. He died instantly. The incident caused outrage throughout the North and even in the South. Political murder—of white people—was an uncommon event. The coroner ruled that Ashburn had been killed by "persons unknown."

"All were well-dressed gentlemen," a witness later recalled in the *Buffalo (N.Y.) Express*, in an interview apparently reprinted from the Columbus, Georgia, *Sun*. "They were nice, dandy young gentlemen."

The *Express* in a scathing accompanying commentary, however, noted the "curious" justification for the assault put forth by the Georgia paper: "It absurdly struggles to lay the crime at the door of Ashburn's friends, the negroes, and charges these same negroes with a concerted effort to implicate 'some of the best and most exemplary young men in our city.'"[8]

The Ashburn murder, and the effort to shift blame for horrific crimes elsewhere, was a look toward the Klan's future, not only in Georgia but also throughout the South. In Alabama, the *Selma Messenger* of April 18 quickly adopted this approach, dismissing Ashburn as a "notorious, unscrupulous incendiary," blaming Georgia's outrages on black transgressions and denouncing one "Black fiend" who "ravished the person of a young white lady." Another southern account claimed Ashburn was murdered in a brothel. What did he expect? Blaming the victim soon became another Klan favorite.[9]

As time passed, Ku Klux sympathizers found other ways to justify the crimes: pernicious black political activism; provocations by black militias; black and white corruption in Radical state governments; and blacks' innate lawlessness, manifested in everything from alleged assaults on white women to robbery and arson.

FOR GENERAL FORREST, the southern pilgrimage was the beginning of what was turning out to be a fine year. The Civil War may have been over, but the former Confederacy still revered him as "the Wizard of the Saddle," a self-taught Tennessee volunteer who became a Confederate cavalry commander without peer.

The North, by contrast, reviled him as "the Butcher of Fort Pillow." On April 12, 1864 at Fort Pillow, Tennessee, Forrest's men massacred nearly three hundred Union soldiers, most of them black. Many had already surrendered.[10]

Still, Forrest's unsavory past did not cause him particular discomfort, while his stature had undoubtedly enhanced the legitimacy of the Ku Klux. Moreover, in the months following his journey on behalf of Southern Life, his postwar fortunes reached apogee. He was forty-six years old, "rather a handsome man," as one visitor described him, a bit over six feet tall, 185 pounds, "with broad shoulders, a full chest, symmetrical muscular limbs; erect in carriage; . . . dark gray eyes, dark hair, mustache, and beard worn upon the chin, a set of regular white teeth, and clearly cut features."[11] The war had forced him to abandon his antebellum profession as a millionaire Memphis slave trader, but he had apparently made a nice transition. Along with his job at Southern Life, he was the boss of a pair of Memphis-based railroad companies and a significant player in Tennessee's Democratic Party.

In the summer of 1868, a few months after the southern tour, President Andrew Johnson, a fellow Tennessean, pardoned Forrest for his wartime transgressions, and Tennessee Democrats sent him as a delegate to the party's national convention at New York's Tammany Hall. There his friend Frank Blair Jr. was nominated as Horatio Seymour's vice presidential running mate for the upcoming presidential race.

Perhaps it was the pardon, perhaps the success of his southern travels, perhaps the rising influence of his friends and his fellow Confederate officers, but on August 28, apparently feeling magnanimous, Forrest welcomed a reporter from the *Cincinnati Commercial* to his Memphis office to talk about state and national affairs.

"Mr. Woodward"—no more is known about him or his career—may have spent some time reviewing Forrest's recent achievements, but his dispatch said little about them beyond noting that "the southern people have elevated him to the position of their great leader and oracle."[12]

What interested Mr. Woodward most deeply was Forrest's role as the purported leader of the Ku Klux Klan. The brazen murder of George Ashburn had greatly increased the country's interest in this mysterious organization, and by late August the Klan's night riders were spreading mayhem throughout the South.

It was not as if postwar racial violence in the former Confederacy had sprung up overnight. As Amos T. Akerman later related to Congress, frequent and often brutal attacks by disaffected southern whites against their black neighbors had arisen virtually from the moment of surrender at Appomattox. In late 1866 the Freedmen's Bureau reported thirty-three murders of freedmen in Tennessee since the end of the war. Arkansas had twenty-nine murders, South Carolina twenty-four, and Kentucky nineteen. Louisiana had seventy, according to U.S. Army figures, along with 210 beatings and other assaults.[13]

The occupation soldiers did what they could, but with steadily dwindling forces these efforts fell short, and when the Ku Klux arrived, they found fertile ground. Klan violence waxed and waned in individual states depending on local politics, the strength and zeal of the U.S. Army, the level of white bitterness, and the Klan leaders' ability to exploit it. In this regard, as Akerman had observed, 1868 was Georgia's year.

THE KLAN, however, was not an outgrowth of southern rage—at least not initially. According to memoirs, interviews, diaries, and periodicals that only came to light much later, the organization was the inspiration of six young, idle, bored, and not particularly motivated former Confederate officers in Pulaski, Tennessee, in late 1865. At first the founders regarded their social club as something of an outrageous practical joke, beginning with the name, derived from the Greek "*kuklos*" ("circle" or "band") and "Klan," a redundancy with nice alliteration. Otherwise, as its chief chroniclers, John C. Lester, one of the six original members, and Daniel Love Wilson wrote much later, the name was "absolutely meaningless," at least in the beginning. Its leader was known as the "Grand Cyclops."[14]

The early Klan served as a vehicle for ridiculous rituals, dress-up parties, costumed night riding and lots of drinking. From the beginning, members insisted on secrecy, both to fascinate the locals and promote exclusivity. Besides that, the chief occupation of the organization, Lester and Wilson wrote, was "mirth."[15]

After a couple of months of debauch, however, as Pulaski itself started to lose interest, country people began to seek membership, and new "dens" were established outside of town. The organization also expanded still further by initiating travelers, who carried the message home to found out-of-state dens.

As the organization spread, it also began to change, evolving by the spring of 1867 into something akin to the prewar "slave patrol"—a chain of loosely connected neighborhood organizations dedicated to keeping blacks off the street and out of mainstream society. The Pulaski Klan soon discovered that their secrecy and rituals were, as Lester and Wilson asserted, "the most powerful devices ever constructed for controlling the ignorant and superstitious [blacks]."[16] The Klan clearly was no longer a social club.

Lester and other members of the original Pulaski six remained in the Klan, but it became apparent that the organization's geographical expansion and its evolving focus was increasingly driven by new members who were older, far more political, and far more discontented with the post–Civil War order.

Chief among these were former Confederate generals John C. Brown and George W. Gordon, a Pulaski attorney and no relation to Georgia's Gordon. George Gordon is regarded as the author of the first Ku Klux "prescript"—the manual and bylaws, which prescribed "the supreme penalty of the law"—death—for anyone who betrayed its secrets.[17]

Tennessee's Gordon was probably key in recruiting Forrest to the cause. Most accounts agree that Forrest, perhaps escorted by Gordon, arrived in Nashville in midyear 1867 on the day of a Klan meeting at the Maxwell House Hotel. There he took the oath and was immediately elected the Ku Klux national leader, the only "Grand Wizard" the Klan ever had.[18]

The next year the Klan massively expanded. The most likely reason was the Reconstruction Act of March 2, 1867, passed by the Republican-led Congress over Johnson's veto. The law listed the requirements for readmission to the Union for the former Confederate states—all but Tennessee, which had already been readmitted. Aspirants had to draft new constitutions to be approved by a majority of voters, including black voters. Then legislatures had to ratify the Thirteenth and Fourteenth Amendments. The law also divided the South into five military districts, each with its own commander.

The net effect of the new law was to erase whatever room for maneuver the former Confederacy thought it had in trying to escape the heavy hand of the victorious federal government. Not only would there be no slavery. There would be equal rights. Blacks would vote. The U.S. Army would enforce compliance.

Memphis memoirist Lee Meriwether described how the new law might have convinced his father and other prominent Memphis citizens—including Forrest—to embrace the Klan. During gatherings at the Meriwether house, Forrest and others routinely worried about how to save the South from "ignorant ex-slaves" and carpetbaggers (transplanted northerners seeking wealth and prosperity in the defeated South). They determined that there was only one way. "It was agreed," Meriwether wrote, "that the Ku Klux Klan by midnight parades as 'Ghosts,' and by whipping and even by killing Negro voters" would drive them from the polls and ensure victories for white Democrats.[19]

As became obvious when his interview with Forrest was published, Woodward was no amateur. His format was question-and-answer, and he prefaced the interview by assuring Forrest: "I will publish what you say, and then you cannot possibly be misrepresented." He began by asking whether there really was a Ku Klux Klan. Or, as some northerners suspected, was it simply "an organization which existed only in the frightened imaginations of a few politicians?"

Forrest took the bait: "Well, sir, there is such an organization, not only in Tennessee, but all over the South, and its numbers have not been exaggerated." In Tennessee, he said, the Klan had over 40,000 members. Altogether, he added, acolytes had enlisted "about 550,000 men" throughout the former Confederacy and beyond.

There was more. Right at the moment, Forrest said, he was principally concerned with Tennessee's Republican governor, William G. Brownlow, and his plans to activate the state militia to quell Klan violence. Brownlow was an unwavering enemy of Forrest, who returned the sentiment. It was Brownlow's newspaper that first branded Forrest as the Butcher of Fort Pillow.

Forrest told Woodward he did not regard the Brownlow government as legitimate. "If the militia are simply called out, and do not interfere with or molest anyone, I do not think there will be any fight," he said. "If, on the contrary, they do what I believe they will do, commit outrages, or even one outrage upon the people, they and Mr. Brownlow's government will be swept out of existence."

Forrest described the Ku Klux as "a protective, political, military organization." He was not a member, he said in reply to a direct question, but he was "in sympathy and [would] cooperate with them."

He opposed enfranchising the blacks, but his interest in vengeance, at least as reported to Woodward, lay elsewhere. "I have no powder to burn killing negroes," he said. "[Should violence break out] I intend to kill the Radicals.

I have told them this and more. There is not a Radical leader in this town that is not a marked man, and if a trouble broke out, not one of them would be left alive."[20]

The *Commercial* published the interview on September 1, 1868, and it was widely reprinted. At that moment Forrest's words were the only authoritative public source of information about the Ku Klux Klan.

On September 3, two days after publication, Forrest wrote a letter to the *Commercial*, revising his remarks, perhaps realizing that he had talked too much and that some of what he had said could be construed as treason.

He used all the stratagems of a seasoned political waffler. He took refuge in the passive voice: It "was reported" that there were forty thousand members in Tennessee, he wrote. He hedged, saying he believed there were many more Klan members throughout the South. And he said that he had misspoken: the Klan "would obey all state laws." He did not, however, disavow what he had told the *Commercial* about the ubiquity of the Klan.[21]

Many contemporary accounts contended that Forrest only served as Grand Wizard for a year before stepping down, purportedly because he opposed the Klan's predilection for violent crime. These same accounts hold that he had already departed when he was interviewed by Woodward.

The truth of these assertions cannot be ascertained, but there appears to be little doubt that Forrest used his wizarding time, however brief, to spread the Ku Klux gospel well beyond the borders of Tennessee—at least as far as York County, South Carolina. And whatever Forrest's level of comfort with violence, which at least when it came to the Radical Republicans was considerable, his imprimatur gave legitimacy and credibility to the terrorist organization that he helped birth.

Three years after Forrest spoke with Woodward, with Klan violence rampant in York County and throughout much of the South, the general was called to testify before a special congressional committee investigating Klan activities in the former Confederacy. At that point, perhaps believing that enough time had elapsed for readers to forget the block quotes Woodward had used, he denied virtually everything he had told the *Commercial*.

Woodward had made up the 550,000-membership figure, he said. Forrest had never been a member of the Ku Klux Klan, he had only spoken with the reporter for five minutes, he was not feeling well the day of the interview, and he had been misquoted. The committee pushed him hard, trying to get him to divulge details of the organization—the nature of the prescript, its scope and its reach. Throughout, Forrest professed total ignorance. This, once again, was standard practice when Ku Klux members or leaders were questioned, even under oath. It was clear that the committee did not believe his disclaimers, but Forrest did not waver.[22]

Forrest was, however, candid in expressing his bitterness and his dread about what was happening around him. It was a terrible time, and southern whites were terrified of blacks, he testified. "The great fear of the people" was a race war—that southern whites, like the French in Haiti seventy years earlier, "would be dragged into a revolution" and massacred.[23] Forrest may have been renowned for his bravery, but his remarks spoke to the paranoia that consumed the whites of the postwar South. General Forrest was scared.

CHAPTER THREE

The Outsider

Amos T. Akerman arrived in Washington on June 23, 1870 with impeccable, if unintentional, timing. He strode onto the Senate floor only an hour after senators had confirmed him unanimously as the new attorney general of the United States. He introduced himself around.

He apparently made a good first impression. The *New York Times* described a "spare" man, "scrupulously neat in his personal appearance." "He has an affable manner, with a quiet self-possession, which make him at the same time easy of approach and dignified of demeanor." He was the first and would turn out to be the only southerner ever to serve in a Reconstruction cabinet.[1]

The novelty wore off quickly, however, and official Washington, after a few days, had adopted a cautious attitude toward the new arrival. The confirmation fight predicted by newspapers—both Republican and Democratic—never materialized. But political tension was readily apparent—a bipartisan ambivalence that could never be overcome. The *Chicago Tribune* observed that some Republicans in Congress "and the whole class of extreme and implacable men" were "baying on his track because he was at one time a minor officer in the rebel army." The paper added, "More amenable and considerate persons rejoice that the president moves toward a day of general reconciliation by such a gracious act."[2]

Back in Georgia, the *Atlanta New Era*, the state's establishment Republican organ, called Akerman's appointment "a fitting tribute to the merits of that gentleman as a jurist and as a man." Democrats disliked him, the *New Era* said, because his "enlarged and liberal views" did not please "the hidebound, provincial 'Democracy'" represented by "mentally constipated, provincial journals."[3]

The Democratic press, dominant in Georgia, did not, however, dismiss Akerman out of hand. His appointment spoke to one of the South's basic postwar grievances: the North had imposed a Radical dictatorship in the former Confederacy, leaving the South with its paltry congressional minority—mostly carpetbaggers, scalawags (southerners who allied themselves with reconstruction), and blacks—as its only voice in the federal government. Now suddenly there was Akerman.

"We suppose that the nomination will be ridiculed by many, and it may be defeated as there are many congressmen who will avail themselves of any pretext to prevent even a quasi-representation of the South in the cabinet, the *Daily Columbus* (Ga.) *Enquirer* wrote. "But we have no ridicule for the event. We believe that Akerman is fully up to the average standard ability of the present Federal Executive Government, and we are not aware that he has ever been accused of any act of dishonesty or corruption."[4]

President Grant said nothing publicly about why he had chosen Akerman, and there was no one else of stature in Washington to vouch for him. The northern Republicans did not know much about their southern cousins, so Grant's endorsement would have to suffice.

And it did. "The people who trust and believe in the President must accept Mr. Akerman on the faith of the few who do know him," the *New York Times* wrote when he was appointed.[5] A few days later, the *Times* informed readers that "Akerman" was spelled without a "c" and that his name was pronounced with a long "a": "ACHE-erman."[6]

In the eighteen months since his testimony before the House Reconstruction Committee, much had happened to Akerman. Early in 1869, newly inaugurated President Grant had tried to appoint him U.S. Attorney for Georgia—the top federal lawman in what was still an occupied state. But Akerman's revered Fourteenth Amendment barred anyone, including himself, who had participated in "insurrection" by serving in the war as a Confederate official or an officer in the Confederate Army from getting a job in the postwar federal government. Only Congress could lift the prohibition.

This setback, however, did not shake Akerman's beliefs in both the rectitude and potential reach of the Fourteenth Amendment or in its power to trump state law in advancing the cause of civil rights, and he proved his point before the Georgia Supreme Court shortly after his federal appointment was denied.

Richard W. White, elected in 1868 as clerk of the Superior Court of Chatham County, Georgia, had been ousted from office on grounds that as a mixed-race man he was ineligible to hold public office under state law.

In district court, White had unsuccessfully contended that he was not mixed-race. Akerman in his appeal, however, did not bother with this defense. This was a Fourteenth Amendment case.[7]

Under Georgia's new constitution, he told the court, anyone guilty of felony, treason, corruption, dueling, or embezzlement, among other sins or shortcomings, could not hold public office, but "black and white are not words found in the instrument." Black citizens were citizens. They had the right to hold public office. "[Slavery is gone, so] let us give it up totally," Akerman said. "Shall a dead institution forever haunt us?" The court ruled 2–1 in favor of White. It was a landmark decision.

At the end of the year Akerman successfully petitioned Congress to have his "disabilities" removed, and on December 22, almost exactly a year after his House testimony, Grant duly appointed him Georgia's U.S. Attorney.[8] At that point he was generally regarded as the ablest Republican in the Georgia bar.[9]

Despite his politics and his civil rights agenda, Akerman up to that time had enjoyed respect across partisan lines. Friends in high places, chief among them former Whig allies and U.S. congressmen Alexander Stephens and Robert Toombs, screened him from the worst outrages of the Georgia disaffected. Stephens had left Washington in 1861 to become the vice president of the Confederacy, and Akerman had served during the war under Toombs, who led Georgia's Home Guard. Both men—now Democrats—remained important political players in Georgia's postwar politics.[10]

By 1870, however, the Reconstruction Acts and the Ku Klux Klan had made political accommodation virtually impossible. A Republican lawyer in private practice might be left alone, but Akerman had now joined the federal government, and his one-time avocation as a civil rights activist had become his job. He had chosen sides. He soon learned what that meant.

He spent the first half of 1870 riding the circuit in Georgia, chasing smugglers, jailing moonshiners, and learning more about the bands of murderous whites who roamed the countryside, assaulting their former slaves and stalking anyone—black, or white—who was allied with the Yankee government.

Georgia had a new military occupation headed by General Alfred Terry, a trusted Grant protégé and civil rights hardliner whose job was to restore order. Terry purged the elected legislature of former Confederates, replaced them with the mostly Republican runners-up, and restored to their seats the elected black legislators (all Republicans) who had been ousted in 1868.[11]

White bitterness and frustration, as Akerman had predicted the previous year, knew no bounds. Nobody dared challenge Terry and his bluecoats, but Akerman was a different story.

On the road, innkeepers frequently refused him lodging, and once, when they did not, Akerman checked out of his hotel only to find out that his horse had been shaved and painted with black and white zebra stripes. That was not his horse, he said, and he refused to mount up. Later he learned that a gang of Ku Klux had planned to ambush and perhaps kill him. They had painted the horse so they could identify him as he rode out of town.[12]

And when his wife Matty fell ill for twelve weeks, living alone and caring for an infant son, her "friends" all but ignored her. During her convalescence only one neighbor bothered to look in on her.[13]

AKERMAN WAS born poor in Portsmouth, New Hampshire, February 23, 1821, the ninth of twelve children in a farming family of staunch Congregationalists who revered education. His mother died when he was thirteen. He graduated from high school with distinction and was able to enter Dartmouth College as a sophomore, but only with the help of $700 in loans from relatives, neighbors, and especially the family of one of his high school classmates. He graduated Phi Beta Kappa from Dartmouth in 1842.[14]

He wanted desperately to get out of debt, and diary entries from his early adult years indicate that becoming solvent was his principal—and perhaps even his only—goal. "I could not bear the thought that he [his principal benefactor] should be the loser through kindness to me," he wrote later.[15]

To earn the money he needed, Akerman headed south, first to North Carolina and then to Georgia, spending most of the next seven years either teaching in private schools or home-tutoring the children of the southern rich.

Pedagogy was not an uncommon vocation for bright but impoverished college graduates without political or business connections. What was unusual in Akerman's case was that he chose to ply the trade in the South, far from family and anything he had experienced among the New England yeomanry.

In interviews decades later, his sons explained that a swimming accident as a youth had caused hemorrhaging in their father's lungs. He moved south because he needed a warmer climate.[16] In an interview in the *Buffalo Morning Express* following his confirmation as attorney general, one of Akerman's childhood friends described this ailment as a "consumptive tendency."[17] Whatever the cause, the condition was real, lasting, and recurrent.

His enthusiasm for teaching was sporadic. At the end of the 1846 school year, he sent his young charges on their way with the accompanying diary entry: "May God bless them forever!"[18] Days later, heading off to a tutoring job in Savannah, Georgia, he hoped for brighter lights: "I find that I lose temper in school more frequently than formerly," he wrote. "I fear that I may be provoked to excessive violence by dull pupils."[19]

In Savannah he moved into the home of John M. Berrien, who had served as President Andrew Jackson's attorney general, initially to tutor Berrien's young children. It was one of the important decisions of Akerman's life, but he did not realize it at first.

He had misgivings about Savannah because of his respiratory problems. "[These] incline me to quit sedentary . . . pursuits," he wrote in his diary. He always felt better in the open air, he frequently noted, but he agreed to work for Berrien on the understanding that he could leave in the fall should he have a relapse.[20]

Akerman lived at the Berrien home without interruption for two years, then sporadically for three more. At some point he began to read law with Berrien as his mentor, and in 1849 he went north for several months to see his family in Portsmouth, visit a high school friend, and then travel west to stay with his sister in Peoria, Illinois, where he worked briefly for a Whig newspaper. He returned to Georgia late in the year, convinced, apparently, that the North offered him neither professional opportunity nor good weather. In October 1850 he was admitted to the Georgia state bar. He would live in Georgia for the rest of his life.[21]

Akerman's key early attribute was self-confidence, which was linked somewhat oddly to a remarkable lack of ambition. He paid off his last debt in 1845, and, after returning to Georgia in 1849, he bought a farm in Northeast Georgia and commuted to Savannah until he became a lawyer. When one of his high school benefactors expressed disappointment that his investment had led him to become a farmer, Akerman shrugged.

"All that I mean to say is that it is no disgrace to have lived without distinction, when distinction is no certain sign of merit," he wrote. He liked farming, he said, and was in fantastic health from being constantly outdoors. "I cannot doubt that if I can better pass my earthly sojourn in other employments, I shall in good time be led to them providentially."[22]

He continued to farm and opened a private law practice but struggled until he moved sixty miles south to Elbert County in 1856 to team up with a former judge. The partnership was an immediate success, and Akerman by the beginning of the war was worth about $15,000—moderately wealthy for the time and place.

He kept the farm, mostly for health purposes, bought slaves—eleven of them, eventually—and earned a reputation for acuity and integrity. He became part of Georgia's Whig establishment. He had been interested in politics ever since his Dartmouth days, but he did not seek an active role in public service. In a letter to a friend, however, he said he would not turn one down, should an opportunity arise.[23]

In general, his views conformed to those of his adopted South. He had abandoned Congregationalism to became a Carolina Presbyterian. He went to church twice on Sundays, he believed a woman's place was in the home, he distrusted Catholicism, and he was disturbed that he could not always reconcile science and the Bible. He had no particular quarrel with slavery, writing in his diary that "no great blessing is bestowed on the Africans by keeping them at home [because] most of them are slaves in Africa." Those brought to America might, he wrote, "in the end become more elevated than their brethren in Africa by association with a superior race."[24]

In all, the prewar Akerman came across in his writings as resolute and honest but also something of a pedant and a bore. He was clearly someone who needed more human contact. "Why are not more of our ministers metaphysicians?" he wrote one Sunday in 1846 when he was barely twenty-five years old. "How can men rightly persuade the soul without knowing something of the soul?"[25]

In Akerman's defense, he came to understand how tiresome he could be. After ending his early diary in 1846, he did not try again until 1855—at thirty-four. "I am prone to mount a stilt when I take up a pen," he told the reader—himself—by way of introduction. "Careless writing for my own eye only may correct this fault. No one struts when there is no one to admire his gait."[26]

In one respect, however, Akerman's politics were unusual and atypical for his time, in an environment where states' rights were sacrosanct. "I want a strong government," he said in an 1846 diary entry, "but I want it to be administered by a strong man."[27] He was not talking about state government.

"I was a Union man until the North seemed to have abandoned us," he wrote to a friend in 1874. He recalled how in early 1861 the administration of President James Buchanan had sent the civilian steamer *Star of the West* to Charleston to resupply Fort Sumter, besieged by South Carolina secessionists. The captain abandoned his mission when South Carolina military cadets opened fire on the ship.

Two weeks after that, Akerman wrote, Georgia militiamen seized the federal arsenal near Augusta. Neither incident provoked a response, Akerman wrote. "Not caring to stand up for a government which would not stand up for itself, and viewing the Confederate government as practically established in the South, I gave it my allegiance."[28]

He signed up with the Georgia Home Guard and was in uniform and drilling by mid-July 1861. He was not an enthusiastic volunteer, remarking in his diary after the South's July 21 victory at Bull Run, "In a few days we shall learn whether this event will speedily end this miserable war."[29]

Akerman spent the early part of the war mustering, marching, and "busy writing wills." He had no desire to fight but helped with recruiting and clerking for his Elbert County militia commander. On June 12, 1861, with characteristic humorlessness and attention to detail, he outlined his typical day: "meals, 2 hrs.; exercise 2 hrs.; reading 30 mins.; afternoon siesta 1.5 hrs.; church 1 hr.; reading law and dealing w/law matters, 8 ½ hrs." His conclusion: "less indolence than I apprehended."[30]

In mid-1863 Akerman's Home Guard regiment was called up and sent to Athens as would-be dragoons—mounted infantry. Akerman was "ordnance officer," still clerking, but apparently only having to worry about guns and ammunition.

Sometime during the next several months, however, he met Martha Rebecca Galloway, "Matty," an Athens schoolmistress and preacher's daughter with a background similar to his own. Raised in Princeton, New Jersey, she attended Mount Holyoke College with the help of loans from friends, and upon graduation she settled in Athens to run a girls' school in tandem with the boys' school that her uncle, Alexander Scudder, had just opened. Like Akerman, she settled her debts out of her own pocket.[31]

Akerman, smitten, planned his courtship like a military campaign, first ascertaining that he had no other serious competitors (Matty was twenty years younger), then making his move. On May 28, 1864, the couple married in a private ceremony at the home of "Uncle Alex," and Akerman immediately departed for Atlanta where the militia was getting ready to confront Sherman's Georgia invasion.[32]

Akerman's morose self-absorption disappeared instantly. He noted with great glee that his marriage had become the talk of Athens because he and Matty had hardly told anyone beforehand. It may have been the first naughty thing he had done in years, and he confided to Matty how tickled he was that the "busy bodies" never found out.[33]

"The first letter I ever received from my wife . . . has been read twice and is now in my pocket," he wrote on June 4. She should write long or short, he told her. "But tell me anything, little and great." His enthusiasm for the war, never profound, vanished altogether. "All I want is to do my simple duty to the country, and if life is spared through that, to get home and spend the rest of my days on the farm and in the profession, in the society that is dearest to me."[34]

Six weeks later Atlanta's post office closed, and Akerman's Civil War correspondence ended. Sherman was closing in on Atlanta, and looting was rampant. The regiment stayed in place until September, then began a journey to Griffin, Macon, Griffin again, Lovejoy's Station, Albany, Thomasville, Savannah, and Hardeeville in Georgia, and Hamburg, South Carolina. Then on to Augusta and Mobley's Pond, back to Hamburg, then back to Macon, and finally to Milledgeville, where he mustered out.[35] Akerman never saw action during the war.

Akerman's postwar conversion to Republicanism was total and immediate. This decision appeared to have had several causes, most of them articulated only years after the fact.

In July 1870, just after being nominated for attorney general, he wrote his "dear sister" (he had more than one) a long letter. He said, "I felt that our [the Confederate] surrender ought to be complete; that the political ideas of the conquering party ought to be the basis of Reconstruction." Slavery was gone, and its "adjuncts" should "be dismissed."[36]

Discarding the Old South was easier for someone not imbued with it in the first place. It was time to move on, and his analysis of what happened after the surrender was concise and prescient. "There was a choice between acting in politics upon ideas which had prevailed in the war and upon the ideas which had been overcome," he wrote to a friend in 1871. "The former, I thought, was the part of wisdom, and honor, too."

It turned out, however, that southerners "were not equal to the occasion." Instead, he wrote, "they consulted the past rather than the future, and were moved in politics by resentment rather than by reason."[37]

Finally, and perhaps most importantly, Akerman, as his early writings had shown, was a lifelong believer in federal power and strength. The South, he wrote in 1876, had paid too much attention to military swagger, "forgetting that those who leave it to the law to avenge their wrongs are from that very disposition the more efficient soldiers when the law calls them to the field."[38] Ulysses S. Grant, mud-spattered, unassuming, and relentless, was the epitome of federal implacability. Akerman's admiration for Grant was unwavering and absolute.

By the end of the war, Akerman's net worth had shrunk to $1,500, but with the goodwill of Stephens, Toombs, and others he handily resuscitated his legal practice and, in the process, won statewide respect for integrity and incorruptibility. His rebuke of an aspiring superior court judge in 1868 for swindling a war widow earned him fulsome praise from the *Atlanta Constitution* as "the honest and talented Akerman."[39]

In late 1867 the Republicans chose him as a delegate to Georgia's constitutional convention, which finished in early March 1868. Akerman missed the final vote, apparently abandoning the gathering because he opposed making relief payments not just to the truly destitute but also to well-to-do landowners seeking to write down debts. "There is an alarming amount of selfishness here," he wrote to Matty in early February.[40]

Akerman survived the convention and remained in the Republican limelight. In July he was a candidate for the U.S. Senate but finished as a distant also-ran. When the state supreme court threw out the black lawmakers that same month, Akerman argued unsuccessfully for their reinstatement.

Later that year, undaunted, he became a regular pro-Grant speechmaker and organizer of black voters during the presidential campaign. He persevered even as Klan-inspired intimidation and terrorism grew throughout the state.

His campaign ended on Election Day with the vicious rock-throwing melee he described before Congress at the end of the year.

BY THE TIME he arrived in Washington in mid-1870 he had plodded undaunted through five postwar years of violence with steely resolve. Akerman hated bullies, and, with the exception of President Grant, he hated having people tell him "this is how we do things" in Washington or anywhere else. He may have been soft-spoken, but he was not malleable. He may have had regrets, but he never let them show.

"If . . . I had foreseen the strength of the prejudices to be encountered," he wrote much later, "[I might not have had] the courage to enter the field on the side which I believed both expedient and right." But "having entered," he continued, his obstinacy prevailed. "I was not disposed to recede, though hard-pressed by my adversaries."[41]

Official Washington had the bare outlines of Akerman's biography when he was appointed but knew nothing about his strengths, his weaknesses, his legal record, or his character. Two puzzling questions immediately arose: Why did Grant choose him? And how did Grant find him?

The White House offered no help, but an explanation soon arose. It contained some fact, some rumor, and much conjecture—plenty of ammunition for critics to question both Grant's judgment and Akerman's qualifications.

Washington insiders theorized that Akerman's arrival was a two-step process. Political custom in mid-nineteenth century Washington discouraged presidents from having two cabinet members from the same state. Akerman was succeeding Ebenezer Rockwood Hoar, a lion of the Boston bar with impeccable establishment connections.

Hoar had been recommended to Grant by Massachusetts congressman Boutwell, the chairman of the Reconstruction Committee during Akerman's 1868 testimony. When Grant's first choice for Treasury secretary could not be confirmed, he appointed Boutwell instead. Hoar, already installed as attorney general, had volunteered to resign. Grant had demurred then but now had apparently changed his mind.

But why pick a southern nobody? Eventually the theory arose that Akerman, rather than having been selected in spite of being a southerner, had instead been appointed *because* he was a southerner. The Civil War had been over for five years, and Grant had decided that diversity was a good idea. It was time to bring the prodigals back into the fold. Appointing Akerman, as the *Chicago Tribune* had asserted, was Grant's "gracious act."[42]

CHAPTER FOUR

Disorder in the Upcountry

AUGUST 22, 1870

Judge Richard Carpenter came to Yorkville on August 22, 1870, a Monday. He was the South Carolina gubernatorial candidate of the Reform Party, an ad hoc amalgam of Democrats and disillusioned Republicans hoping to unseat Radical incumbent Robert Scott and return "good government" to the state.

The judge had opened his upcountry campaign the previous week. It had been an unnerving experience. Instead of crowds of supporters eager to welcome him on his quest, there were "armed companies" of black state militiamen everywhere, he recalled later, "with ammunition distributed, as was understood, as if on the eve of battle."[1]

The militiamen were a new phenomenon. Recently armed and activated by Governor Scott, ostensibly to maintain order during the campaign, there were twelve thousand of them statewide and four companies in York County.[2] The militia was composed largely of black troopers, with a smattering of white carpetbagger and scalawag officers. Black Union army veteran Jim Williams, who captained the McConnellsville company in southern York County, was an exception.

Yorkville was nervous. The county as a whole had a population of twenty-four thousand, evenly divided between blacks and whites, but Yorkville's fifteen hundred residents were overwhelmingly white.[3] John Moroso, covering the campaign for the *Charleston Courier*, had been in Yorkville for three days before Carpenter's arrival and had noticed "a great deal" of unease because of "reports of the negro militia coming into town."[4]

BEFORE 1870, whites' mistrust of blacks in York, as in most of South Carolina, had focused on the Union League. Originally established in the North during the war to promote the federal cause, it had evolved in the Reconstruction South into a quasi-secret arm of the Republican Party—with overwhelmingly black membership. In South Carolina the league probably included virtually every voting-age Radical in the upcountry.[5]

At one York County Union League gathering, as Yorkville businessman Joseph Herndon later recounted, "it was said" that prominent Scott ally and

State Comptroller John Neagle—a white Radical—had confided to black listeners that "matches were cheap." Herndon recalled black militiamen marching up and down "with fifes and drums and making threats." Asked to describe the warnings, he responded: "I understood that the threats were to burn up our little village." And now there was the prospect of armed black militiamen marching into town with fixed bayonets, catcalling the bystanders and threatening arson.[6]

It was possible that the Union League's secrecy, symbols, and rituals suggested to Herndon and others of the Yorkville gentry that the league was the black equivalent of the Ku Klux Klan, but there is little evidence that its members ever plotted the assaults and murders of upcountry whites. The league's purpose was to promote political education and solidarity among southern freedpeople.[7] It was enough for whites, however, that the league *seemed* like the Ku Klux, and everybody in the upcountry knew what the Ku Klux could do.

The only militiamen who showed up in Yorkville that Monday morning, however, were five mounted state constables carrying Winchester rifles. They came into town before the Reform rally began and rode up the main street to militia headquarters at Rose's Hotel. Two men were in the yard out front beating on a kettle drum and a bass drum as the Reformers gathered about fifty yards away. "I heard white people expressing much anger at the attempted interruption," Moroso said.

The constables eventually dismounted and started holding an impromptu rally of their own, but both events ended shortly. The noise was just too much. "A riot was imminent," Moroso recalled. "How it was prevented I do not know."[8]

Carpenter didn't make it to the podium in Yorkville, but, hoarse and exhausted as the campaign proceeded, he persevered.[9] He had found rough going before, especially when he attempted to speak at any gathering with a large contingent of blacks. Yorkville was one more indignity. He had seen worse.

Despite repeated setbacks, however, the Reformers continued to believe their own propaganda. South Carolina's white-owned newspapers lambasted the Scott administration and constantly exaggerated Reformer strength, claiming that black voters were flocking to their standard, even though there was little evidence of this. The *Charleston Daily News* reported that a July 27 rally in Anderson, in the northwestern part of the state, drew a crowd of twenty-five hundred, including "fully" one thousand blacks. This was a much larger number, the paper said, "than attended a Radical mass meeting at the same place the Friday night previous."[10]

These reports were seldom anything other than hearsay or wishful thinking. No reporter had ever had a serious interview or even a fleeting conversation with a black voter. In effect, South Carolina opinion-makers were pretending that blacks didn't exist, except as platoons of ill-mannered, rifle-wielding thugs.

Flare-ups, as they occurred, were laid at the Radicals' feet. The *Charleston Daily News* accused white Radicals of keeping blacks from attending Reform events by telling them that the Reformers intended to poison them at barbecues.[11] Carpenter later told congressional investigators that whites on "several occasions" were shot by blacks on rally days and that two blacks wanting to attend a Reform event were killed in Barnwell County by other blacks. In several places he said he had heard that if any black voted for a Democrat, the Union League would order him shot. He described an instance where a black jury acquitted two blacks accused of cattle rustling when the evidence was clear, after which the accusers were indicted for false imprisonment.[12]

The irony of his own remarks escaped Carpenter. If his stories were true—by no means a sure thing—they showed that blacks apparently had learned well their lessons from their former owners—well enough to be accused of the same outrages that the whites had inflicted upon them for centuries.

The Reformers' main enemy, however, was not Radical violence. It was simple arithmetic. South Carolina in 1870 had ninety thousand black voters and sixty thousand white voters; it was the only state in the country besides Mississippi with a majority black population. Democrats, champions of slavery and secession, were looking at years, perhaps decades, of political exile.

The Ku Klux had tried to help during the 1868 general elections, using strong-arming and threats to discourage blacks from voting and in one instance ambushing and murdering a black state senator on a railroad platform in Abbeville, on the Georgia border.

That didn't work well. Blacks were voting for the first time in 1868, and white Democrats—as in Georgia—were either barred from the polls for their Confederate past or were refusing to vote because they disdained the election. This had allowed Scott to win the governorship handily, and Republicans also won both houses of the state legislature. General Grant won the state on his way to the presidency.[13]

The Klan lay dormant for the next two years but remained vigilant, especially in upcountry counties like York. Far from the massive black populations on the cotton coast, the upcountry had nothing to fear from a black uprising. The even split in York County's population would give the whites an easy upper hand in a fair fight, if violence was the yardstick.[14] The Klan had large numbers of Confederate veterans in its ranks. The militia were amateurs.

Now, with Scott running for reelection in 1870, the Klan lay low. Things were different in Washington than they had been two years earlier. President Grant, unlike the departed Andrew Johnson, could count on overwhelming Republican support in both houses of Congress. He had little desire to placate former Confederates and had purged top generals for being too conciliatory, replacing them with hard men like Alfred Terry, the military governor in neighboring Georgia. And with Amos T. Akerman in his cabinet he had a militant radical as the nation's top lawman. Grant, as the South already knew well, was not someone to be taken lightly.

By the time Carpenter reached Yorkville, South Carolina, like Georgia, was simmering with fear and resentment. The state was sorted into two hostile camps. Whites were almost all Democrats and had almost all of the money. Blacks were almost all Radical Republicans and had the votes. If the yardstick was the ballot box, the election was for the Radicals to lose.

Undoubtedly realizing that they faced another uphill electoral battle, white South Carolina was betting on the Reformers, who included virtually all of the state's Democratic voters and some high-visibility white Republicans like Carpenter, a Kentucky transplant. If the Reformers could attract enough blacks to their cause, maybe they could tip the balance.

They focused their campaign on Governor Scott, and he was a big target—at least for white voters. After two years he and his Radical cronies in the "Scott Ring" had buried the state in corruption and incompetence.

A former Union general of volunteers who had come to South Carolina after the war with the Freedmen's Bureau, Scott had resigned in 1868 to run for governor.[15] A large, well-built, substantial man, he was forty-four in 1870. The *New York Times* described him as "pleasant and entertaining," as well as "affable, kind-hearted and well-meaning," while noting that he was also "sometimes forgetful and ineffective."[16] Some of his disconnectedness may have been caused by chronic back pain that Scott controlled by dosing himself with opium.[17]

Scott's image had fared badly after he spent nearly $8 million in state money on the Blue Ridge Railroad Company to build a North–South route from Cincinnati (in his home state) southeast through South Carolina to Augusta, Georgia. He made money, but there was no railroad. Also during his tenure, South Carolina had a bonded debt of $5.4 million and nothing in the bank, so the legislature raised taxes on large landowners. These white gentlemen, virtually all of them Democrats, were not pleased.

Finally, there was the so-called Land Commission, set up by Scott to buy unwanted real estate and resell it in small parcels to freedmen and poor whites. This immediately became a vehicle for white landowners to unload useless property. By the time the 1870 campaign opened, the commission had spent twice its appropriation and had added another $700,000 to the state debt.[18]

With Scott providing the bull's-eye and South Carolina's mostly Democratic press cheering the Reformers on, Carpenter and his backers looked toward the October election with optimism. Carpenter insisted it had "nothing to do" with racial politics.[19]

This was absurd. "Good government" might have served as a rallying cry for the white voters of antebellum South Carolina, but the war was over. South Carolina politics in 1870 were all about race, and blacks had no stake in a white-dominated Reform government. Before the war they were enslaved and maltreated. They could not seek justice for the abuse they suffered; they could not leave the property of their white owners; they could not own guns, own a business, work for money, or get a basic education. Anyone caught teaching a black person to read faced a fine of $100.

After the war, blacks were free. They could vote, own property, send their children to school, travel anywhere they wanted, and serve in the government. These provisions had been on the public record since 1868, when a constituent assembly, composed mostly of black Republicans (most whites refused to participate), wrote a new state constitution. It asked for nothing special, only that all citizens, regardless of color, enjoy the same rights.

The new constitution apportioned representation by population, not by population and wealth as had previously been the case. It mandated universal male suffrage regardless of race and independent of property ownership. It made free education mandatory for all citizens, lifted racial restrictions on the use of public facilities, and gave women the right to divorce and own property. Anyone violating the anti-segregation provisions could be fined $1,000 and jailed for up to five years. The constitution was approved by referendum in April 1868, and it was a public document.[20]

Scott knew all this and certainly understood the advantage he held when the 1870 campaign began. He didn't even bother to campaign. Bad government did not necessarily mean bad politics.

But Scott also had no hesitancy using racial tensions to enhance his advantages. These, in turn, widened the schism between whites and blacks, and, no surprise, made the Reformers' task even more difficult.

After the legislature had authorized him to form a militia in 1869, Scott bought five thousand obsolete muskets from Remington, then sent them to New York to be converted into breech-loading rifled muskets—very modern small arms.[21] The vast majority of South Carolina's whites would not serve with blacks in a mixed-race militia, something Scott certainly would have known. He filled the ranks with black volunteers.

By deploying the militia in the middle of the campaign, Scott effectively destroyed whatever chance the Reformers had to cast the election as a referendum on his stewardship. Instead, he had deliberately redefined it in racial terms. He aligned himself closely with black political activists. Black state representative Alonzo Ransier was his running mate for lieutenant governor. And Scott pardoned hundreds of criminals—most of them black—so they could vote.[22]

Only one prominent Democrat tried seriously to tell the truth about what was happening. Former governor James L. Orr had a long and unstinting record as a supporter of slavery and states' rights. He had served ten years in the U.S. Congress, rising to become Speaker of the House from 1857 to 1859. He had fought briefly with Confederate volunteers at the outset of the Civil War before joining the Confederate Senate. After the war he won a virtually uncontested whites-only election to the South Carolina governorship during the Johnson administration in 1865 and served until 1868. He did not run against Scott.[23]

On August 17, a letter written by Orr appeared in the *Charleston Daily Courier*. Orr agreed that Scott's state government badly needed cleaning up and that many office holders were incompetent or corrupt and ought to be "driven from the places they occup[ied]." But if the Reformers wanted real reform, he urged them to follow his example: join the Republican party and make it happen.

Then he wrote this extraordinary paragraph:

> The colored vote is . . . nearly a unit for the Republican party, and have they acted unwisely or unpatriotically in their ardent devotion to the Republican party? Suppose our conditions, the white race, were reversed—that we and our ancestors had been slaves for 200 years—that a party had made war to give us freedom—that it had succeeded—that the same party had periled its own supremacy by guaranteeing to us our civil rights—and that above all, the ballot, the effectual weapon of preserving those rights, had been secured to us by solemn constitutional enactment by the same party, and we were in the face of all this appealed to by those who had opposed all these great boons, to join with them in overthrowing the party of our deliverance and redemption. Would any white man for a moment tolerate with patience any such a proposition?[24]

Orr was universally damned as a traitor by white South Carolina for this heresy, and it was not difficult to understand why. On one level his epistle was simple truth-telling: the Reformers did not have the votes and thus were doomed—something the Reformers persisted in denying.

The underlying message, however, was terrifying, for Orr had written that blacks, like whites, voted their own self-interest. Blacks, like whites, had a legitimate point of view. Blacks, his approach suggested, were just like whites, an apostasy that categorically dismissed the prevailing white view that blacks were ignorant, superstitious, unruly, and, if properly handled, malleable. Carpenter, who claimed to be a thoughtful man who wanted to "harmonize" the races, later told Congress that he regarded South Carolina's blacks, "in point of intelligence," as "just as slightly removed from the animal creation as it is once believable for a man to be." Yet he expected blacks to vote for him.[25]

CARPENTER'S UPCOUNTRY campaign opened on August 19, three days after the Orr letter appeared. His first stop was a rally in Chester just south of York County on the Charlotte–Augusta Road, about ten miles south of McConnellsville and twenty-two miles south of Yorkville.[26]

This rally, unlike the Yorkville affair the following Monday, had something of a debate format, with speakers alternating between Reformers and Radicals. Former Confederate general Matthew Butler, the Reform candidate for lieutenant governor, and then Carpenter, would close. The Radical stump was left to surrogates and the Republican undercard, chief among them state attorney general Daniel H. Chamberlain, a Harvard- and Yale-educated carpetbagger who had accomplished the astounding triple feat of aligning himself with black aspirations, profiting from the Scott railroad schemes, and managing at the same time to earn the respect of white Democrats as an impartial arbiter of disputes.

Accounts of these campaign encounters were episodic and, as a rule, infrequent. The Reformers tended to report only good news. Moroso, the *Courier* correspondent, only told the story of the Yorkville incident in court testimony much later, after having written nothing about it when it occurred. The few Radical papers tried to be statesmanlike and dignified.

The Chester rally offered neither good news nor dignity, but at least one attendee, who identified himself only as X, sent a detailed description of it in a letter to the editor of the Winnsboro, South Carolina, *Fairfield Herald*, and the *Herald* printed it.

The town square gathering began inauspiciously when black Radicals accosted a black Reformer at the Chester train station to keep him from speaking, but a phalanx of whites kept the jostlers at bay, X wrote. The rally itself opened quietly. The crowd was apparently predominantly black but listened without disruption to Radicals and Reformers alike. Prior to the debates, both parties had agreed that there would be no interruptions and no interventions until the individual speakers had finished their presentations.

Then it was Carpenter's turn. He spoke for about five minutes before referring to a remark made by one of the earlier speakers, Lucius Wimbush, a black state senator from Chester. The letter did not describe the substance of the remark, but X wrote: "Wimbush was standing behind the speaker's stand, and was heard to say 'it's a d_____d lie.'" Someone suggested that Wimbush circle the speakers' stand and face Carpenter. He did so, then asked a question that Carpenter answered. A furious Wimbush called Carpenter "a damned liar." Wimbush presumably had little love for the Reformers. As a youth he had accompanied Matthew Butler to college as his manservant.

Wimbush asked Carpenter another question, and Carpenter apparently reminded him that speakers were not to be interrupted. Wimbush replied using "worse language than before," X wrote. At that point, one of the white listeners approached Wimbush and laid a hand on his shoulder "to quiet him," X continued. The crowd apparently thought the would-be peacemaker had struck Wimbush and started heaving rocks at Carpenter and the other Reformers. One bystander near Carpenter was knocked down and badly injured. "This affair would have terminated seriously but for the forbearance of the whites," X concluded.[27]

Much later Alexander Wylie, a Chester physician, described the incident in more detail. Wimbush was browbeating Carpenter about whether Carpenter believed a black woman could sue a white man for "bastardy"—fathering her child out of wedlock. Wylie described Wimbush as a "yellow man," suggesting he may have been thinking of his own father. The crowd—both whites and blacks—were becoming more upset the longer the interchange continued. Finally Wylie, respected by both whites and blacks in Chester, approached Wimbush—one of his patients—and laid a hand on his shoulder. "For God's sake, stop this!" he said, and the stone-throwing began.[28]

Carpenter spoke without incident the next day in Carmel Hill, a tough town outside of Chester, then headed north to Yorkville where he was drummed off the podium.

Yorkville residents, upset that racial animosity had disturbed their town after the near riot in Chester, had had enough.[29] Shortly after the aborted rally, the *Yorkville Enquirer* endorsed the formation of white militias to counter Scott's militia regiments. This announcement was greeted with amazement—perhaps feigned—by Comptroller Neagle, who told a Yorkville audience in September that "considering the good feeling between the races," whites should feel perfectly safe "with an armed guard of colored men to preserve law and order."

The *Enquirer* accepted the fantasy that there was good feeling between the races—"hitherto"—but said "the arming of one [race] exclusively must create ill-will." Whites could not regard this as "anything but an insult," since it either implied that whites were "not to be trusted" to maintain law and order or that blacks had to have weapons "to preserve their rights."

The main difficulty, however, was something else entirely, the *Enquirer* continued. "The colored militia have been privately informed that the object of their organization is to scare and keep down the white people." The only answer to this challenge was "a counter organization [to] satisfy the militia that the white people are *not scared*."[30] The *Enquirer*'s impartiality was starting to fray.

The Ku Klux was not visibly on hand at that moment, but Carpenter told congressional investigators it was active in at least ten South Carolina counties, among them York and other upcountry counties like Chester, Union, Spartanburg, and Laurens. The Klan was a response to the Scott administration and the woeful "condition of things," he said. "I think there were a great many respectable people and well-meaning men who were engaged in it."[31]

Dr. J. Rufus Bratton, one of Yorkville's "best people," could attest to that. He had spent 1868 preparing for the inevitable race war and had helped York County's white citizens come to what he later described as "a little agreement," to arm themselves with pistols and to patrol and protect private property. By late 1870 he was able to say that virtually every York County landowner participated.[32] Lines had been drawn.

CHAPTER FIVE

Grant

In June 1870 President Ulysses S. Grant had been in office for a bit over a year. He enjoyed tremendous personal popularity—at least in the North—as the everyman general who had saved the Union. He had handily won election in 1868 by campaigning on the slogan "Let us have peace."

It was a worthy suggestion but so far had proved to be an elusive goal. Republicans dominated both houses of Congress, and had passed the Fourteenth and Fifteenth Amendments with the aim of granting blacks full citizenship—to include both civil rights and the franchise.

This Radical agenda was anathema to white southerners, and the national Democrats embraced the southerners' cause, demanding an end to reconstruction and the restoration of the rights of states—to determine who could vote, who could hold office, and who could own property.

This chasm could not be bridged, but Grant, once in office, had little interest even in trying. He had handpicked the generals he wanted as district governors, but if he deemed them too soft he replaced them with like-minded acolytes like General Terry in Georgia.[1] As an advocate for the fortunes of freedpeople and civil rights, Grant in 1870 was as single-minded as any congressional Radical.

Grant also soon found out, however, that his Republican colleagues did not all share his views. The Radicals, ascendant since 1866, wanted the South to toe the line on reconstruction and black rights and, like Grant, were willing to use the federal government to force compliance. Moderates wanted conciliation—bring former Confederates back into government and seduce the renegade states with the promise of postwar prosperity.

Personal animosities also divided the Republicans. The party had held power for nearly a decade, long enough to cultivate jealousies, hold grudges, and create byzantine alliances and rivalries that newcomers—and Grant, despite years in the public eye, was a newcomer—were at pains to deconstruct and cope with.

Grant's inner circle had two factions of its own to help decipher—or deepen—these divisions. The first was composed of professional politicians and policy makers with long resumes. Its unquestioned leader was Secretary of State Hamilton Fish, a former New York governor and U.S. senator.[2]

The second group consisted of military comrades and protégés who had accompanied Grant to Washington. Their initial leader was Secretary of War John Rawlins, Grant's close friend and a devoted former staff officer who knew all of the president's foibles—his naïveté, his awkwardness, his sometimes-misguided loyalties, and his drinking. Grant had battled alcoholism throughout his adult life.[3]

Rawlins had served as Grant's gatekeeper, protector, and, when the drinking got bad, his guardian. But Rawlins died of tuberculosis in September 1869, only six months after Grant's inauguration. Without him Grant was left unprotected from myriad questionable characters, the "cronies" who came to define the corruption that engulfed his presidency in its later years.[4]

The most authoritative account of the administration's inner workings is the diary of Secretary Fish, who stayed with Grant throughout his presidency. Fish's observations, sympathetic to Grant but not blind to his faults, describe a socially reticent man. He was not a natural politician and disliked the glad-handing and horse-trading needed to build consensus in a devilishly complex political world. At times, Grant could be indecisive and easily led, and he was especially impressed by rich businessmen seeking favors. He was fiercely loyal to his friends, frequently unwisely so. When challenged, especially by those who had not earned his trust, he was stubborn and resentful. And he held grudges.[5]

By 1870 the Washington establishment was well aware of these shortcomings. Republicans were publicly supportive and, in the case of Fish and other admirers, fiercely loyal and protective. Democrats were critical but deferential. It was not a good idea to offend a national icon.

In private, however, there was always an undercurrent of doubt—a feeling, even among Republican stalwarts, that the war hero was not quite up to the job. He had limited political skills and poor political judgment. He followed bad advice and made questionable, sometimes bewildering decisions.

Amos T. Akerman, through no fault of his own, epitomized these misgivings when he arrived in the capital June 23, 1870, aboard the "Potomac Boat."[6] His appointment was unusual and controversial. He had never worked in Washington, he had no national reputation, and he was a former slaveholder and former Confederate army officer. What was Grant thinking?

Grant, never much interested in explaining himself, said nothing. And Akerman appeared just as mystified as the rest of official Washington. He had been on the job as U.S. Attorney for Georgia for barely six months when to his "great surprise," he later wrote, Grant put him in the cabinet.[7]

Just like that. Neither Grant nor anyone in his administration had reached out to Akerman to ask if he wanted the job, and it took four days to find him after the White House announced his nomination June 17.

It was General Terry who finally tracked him down. On June 18 Terry wired Grant to tell him he could not reach Akerman at his home in Elberton and had sent a "special messenger by train." Three days later, after the messenger had presumably spoken to Matty, he wired Grant again: "Mr. Akerman not at his home. Supposed to be in Savannah."

Terry wired Savannah: "[Find Akerman], and tell him the President wishes him to come to Washington immediately." Akerman, it turned out, was in Athens. On June 21 Terry wired Savannah again: "Tell me what he says."[8] Akerman said yes and headed north.[9]

Akerman gave Grant's critics a perfect cover. The new attorney general was a nonentity and a complete stranger, neither a high-visibility political veteran nor a crony, and news of his nomination immediately triggered speculation that a misguided Grant had simply made a mistake.

This could be quickly rectified, the *New York Times* suggested, by withdrawing Akerman's name and offering the job to Republican senator George H. Williams of Oregon. The *Times* admitted this was unlikely but noted "a very general feeling" that Williams in the cabinet "would be received with great satisfaction."[10] But whose satisfaction? Most likely Williams's: he was a lame duck from a Democratic state who was looking for a job. The *Times* soon backtracked, however. There was "no foundation" for the Williams theory, it reported. Williams, perhaps, had had his knuckles rapped, but his name kept reappearing whenever Akerman's fortunes seemed to be dimming.[11]

The *Chicago Tribune* gave Akerman a modest boost June 25, noting accurately that his views "on the validity, scope and force of the Fourteenth and Fifteenth Amendments" were "as far advanced and as broad" as anyone's.[12] Two weeks later, however, it was time for the *Tribune* to second-guess Grant's "unfortunate" choice. Because he was an unknown, he did "not command the confidence of the party which [was] responsible for the administration." Since Akerman had voluntarily held a commission in the rebel service, the paper said, he was "offensive" in his elevation to the post."[13] He was a political and institutional orphan.

Akerman offered little to clear the fog. The day after his Senate confirmation he remained in "his rooms" receiving callers, the Philadelphia *Evening Telegraph* reported.[14] The *New York Herald* spoke to him briefly when he went to meet his fellow cabinet secretaries at the White House. He told the *Herald* that southern states had "broken down" governments. They needed to be rebuilt, using "the legislation of the national government." His views on federal primacy had not changed in the eighteen months since his appearance before the House Reconstruction Committee.[15]

Grant's silence continued, and the Washington press filled in the blanks with the preferred early story—that it was time to get rid of Hoar, the redundant Bostonian, and time to reconcile with the Confederacy by nominating a southerner. This narrative would have to suffice, even though it never won complete acceptance.

What came to be regarded as the definitive account only surfaced decades later in a memoir written for the *Atlantic Monthly* by Jacob Cox, Grant's former interior secretary. Akerman's nomination, according to Cox, was the byproduct of another unusual Grant initiative—his effort to sign a treaty to purchase the Dominican Republic—more commonly known at the time as Santo Domingo—in hopes of annexing it as a state.

There were a number of reasons to undertake this project. The navy wanted a coaling station at Samaná Bay; annexation would put a damper on the bloody unrest in nearby Cuba where Spain was struggling to hold on to one of its last colonies; a new state at the entryway to Latin America would remind Europe of the Monroe Doctrine—no poaching allowed in the New World without U.S. permission. Also, Santo Domingo, sparsely populated at the time, might serve as a multiracial sanctuary for former slaves, a magnet powerful enough, perhaps, to induce southern whites either to stop persecuting their black neighbors or lose their labor force altogether.[16]

Finally, Santo Domingo was thought to be immensely wealthy in natural resources. This was the pitch private secretary Orville Babcock, an Army protégé in the process of turning crony, made in October 1869—a month after Rawlins's death—when he returned from a junket to Santo Domingo with mineral samples, souvenirs, and other island exotica he displayed for the cabinet, along with a draft annexation treaty—which he had no authority to negotiate.[17]

Neither Fish nor Cox nor anyone else in the cabinet or Congress had much interest in Santo Domingo, and, after Babcock made his pitch and left the room, Fish and Cox decided to kill the plan by pretending it did not exist, perhaps deciding to protect Grant from himself.

Except that Grant wanted to go forward, and at the next cabinet meeting he told Fish to draft a formal treaty and present it to Congress. An incredulous Cox asked Grant, "[Do] we *want* to annex Santo Domingo?" Grant's face turned red, but he said nothing, and he never raised the subject again before the entire cabinet.

Fish wrote the formal treaty, and Grant signed it November 29 and sent it to the Senate early in December. Grant had nowhere near the two-thirds Senate majority he needed for ratification. He needed to bargain for votes—a task for which he had neither the inclination nor the requisite talent.

One way to win support was to lobby the carpetbag Republican senators in the South, Cox wrote. The sticking point here was the southerners' reluctance to incur the wrath of Senator Charles Sumner, the Senate's leading Radical. Sumner fiercely opposed the treaty as little more than a scheme to enrich American and Dominican fortune-hunters. Grant, who had counted on Sumner's support, believed he had been double-crossed. He never forgave the perceived betrayal.

Sumner, however, had enormous cachet with black voters, and his endorsement was critical to southern Republicans' political survival. A possible way out of the dilemma, the senators told Grant, was to put a southerner in the cabinet—one who would give them consideration for patronage jobs. "Reciprocity was necessary," Cox wrote. To take a vote in favor of the Santo Domingo treaty, the southerners needed something they could show their constituents.

"When asked in what departments they found a lack of consideration, the Attorney General's was named," Cox said. Hoar was hiring U.S. attorneys to staff the brand-new Justice Department, to be created in early 1870. These positions were patronage plums, but Hoar hated patronage and wanted the best candidates available—like Akerman.

Senators and House members had railed against Hoar for months for refusing to name their favorites, Cox wrote. Grant, meanwhile, had been interested in getting rid of Hoar for some time, Cox claimed, intimating that Hoar's refusal to play the patronage game was the reason. Cox in his memoir described the southern Republicans pejoratively as a "different" class of politicians, connivers trying to bamboozle Grant.[18]

In early December 1869, Grant nominated Hoar to fill a vacancy in the Supreme Court. The nomination reached the Senate at virtually the same moment as the Santo Domingo treaty. This was no accident, Cox wrote: "It is fair to regard it, in part, as an attempt to conciliate adverse influences." Get Hoar out of the way, hand out patronage, and win on Santo Domingo.[19] The Senate refused to confirm Hoar—the Radicals saw him as no friend to reconstruction—leaving him to languish in the cabinet for six more months.[20] On June 15, 1870, Grant asked Hoar to resign. He gave no reason.

Hoar immediately complied, and on June 16 Grant told Hoar that he "had been thinking of Mr. Akerman, of Georgia," as his replacement, Cox wrote. Hoar replied that "he believed Mr. Akerman to be an honest man and a good lawyer," but he did not endorse Akerman or offer an opinion on his fitness for the job. On June 17 Grant formally nominated Akerman and sent his name to the Senate.[21]

It was all for naught. On June 30 the Senate emphatically refused to pass the Santo Domingo treaty. The vote was 28–28.

COX DID NOT reveal who told him about the Santo Domingo machinations, but he probably had the information when Akerman took office or shortly afterward. The timing is important, for if Cox and the rest of the Cabinet knew at the time about the southern carpetbaggers, their opinion of their new colleague, probably tepid to begin with, undoubtedly would have nosedived. Not only was Akerman an outsider and a nobody, he was also a handpicked yes-man, if Cox's story was the last word. This was a heavy burden for Akerman to carry.

But, while Cox's account is plausible, it has serious weaknesses. First and obvious, Georgia in mid-1870 was not a state, had no senators, and therefore had no treaty votes on offer. Basic politics should have directed Grant to ask a wavering but influential senator from a southern voting state to put a favorite son in the Cabinet.

Second and perhaps unknown in Washington: Akerman was incorruptible. Everyone in Georgia knew it. The *Atlanta Constitution*, no friend of Republicans, on June 21 noted, "[Akerman's] private character is beyond reproach. Even his political opponents concede this."[22] If Grant wanted to cajole southern senators by hiring a lackey, Akerman was not only from the wrong place. He was the wrong man.

A third shortcoming of the Cox account is that both he and Fish were focused almost exclusively on the insider politics of the moment—doing damage control for the perceived Santo Domingo adventure.

Grant resented this. With only two weeks left before the July 1 treaty ratification deadline, he complained to Fish that Cox, Hoar, and Treasury Secretary George S. Boutwell were not "sustaining his views" on Santo Domingo.[23] He fired Hoar two days later. Cox, like Hoar, an enemy of the patronage system and a moderate on civil rights, was gone at the end of October. Boutwell, with solid credentials as a Radical, served to the end of Grant's first term. Fish was indispensable, regardless of his views.

What Fish and Cox had forgotten was that while Grant might have been naïve and perhaps unduly influenced by a crony like Babcock on Santo Domingo, he was rock-solid on matters of reconstruction and civil rights, and he was ruthless in his pursuit of justice for the South's newest citizens.

This, perhaps, was the true underlying reason for getting rid of Hoar, and, if so, then Grant could not have made a better choice to replace him. It is impossible to know whether Grant intended to pick Akerman all along, but there are many hints that he was aware of Akerman's career in Georgia and may even have known him personally.

Gossipy newspaper accounts linking Grant and Akerman surfaced shortly after Akerman's appointment and periodically in the following months and years. The origin of most if not all of them appears to have been Buffalo lawyer E. Carleton Sprague, one of Akerman's high school classmates and a lifetime friend and correspondent. All of the accounts centered on Grant's interest in Akerman because of either a letter Akerman had written or a speech that he had given or perhaps both.

An account in the *Chicago Tribune* described a winter gathering early in 1869 attended by then–president elect Grant and Sprague at the Milwaukee home of a West Point classmate of Grant's. Sprague read a letter from Georgia that "struck Grant profoundly, and he inquired all about Akerman," the *Tribune* said. "He was sorely puzzled to obtain good office-holders in the South."[24]

Another version appeared in the *Buffalo Morning Express and Illustrated Buffalo Express*. Written just after Akerman's appointment, it quoted an unnamed source (undoubtedly Sprague) who suggested that Grant's attention "was drawn" to Akerman after reading a letter published in Georgia during the presidential campaign in which Akerman explained his support for Grant. "Early after his inauguration," the *Express* wrote, Grant "sought the acquaintance of Mr. Akerman and . . . has frequently counseled with him since."[25]

A simpler but perhaps more convincing account appeared in the July 1, 1870, *New-York Tribune*. The letter that had impressed Grant discussed reconstruction and had been printed in Atlanta's Republican paper the *New Era* "a year or two since," the *Tribune* wrote. Grant "somehow got hold" of it, and, when Akerman came to Washington, he visited Grant "at his house," and "the interview resulted in mutual satisfaction and good will."[26]

The *New-York Tribune* version is significant because it suggests Akerman could have met with Grant during Akerman's visit to testify on Georgia—after the election but before inauguration. Akerman visited Grant "at his house" rather than at the White House.

This was possible. Grant returned to Washington from a rail trip to Chicago early the morning after Akerman's congressional testimony. He may have summoned Akerman for a meeting. Akerman never mentioned such an encounter, but soon after Grant was inaugurated he—or Hoar, perhaps at Grant's bidding—made the first attempt to appoint Akerman U.S. Attorney for Georgia.[27]

That there was a letter seems certain. A lengthy tribute to Akerman written in the 1880s by Georgia memoirist Rebecca Felton remarked that Akerman's 1868 campaign speeches "met the eye of General Grant," leading to his appointment as U.S. Attorney and eventually attorney general.[28] Felton was a neighbor and close friend of Akerman's widow Matty, clearly the principal source for her article. It is clear that the Akermans believed that the speeches or letter (or both) were the catalyst, or it could simply mean that Sprague had told the Akermans what he thought had happened.

Beyond the gossip, however, Akerman had an attribute that would have interested Grant profoundly for policy reasons. Akerman was from Georgia, and Grant, like the Radical Congress, was determined to bring Georgia into line with his reconstruction policies. Could Akerman, with impeccable Radical credentials and twenty years' worth of local political connections, be the solution to the Georgia Question?

Grant publicly singled out Georgia early in his first annual message to Congress on December 6, 1869. He noted with satisfaction the readmission of seven former Confederate states to the Union. But Georgia remained the outlier. He recalled how Georgia had unseated its black legislators and replaced them with former Confederate soldiers and sympathizers who—in violation of the Fourteenth Amendment—were unable to take the loyalty oath.

It would not be wise, he said, for Congress to legislate to return the ousted members to the legislature, and Congress should refuse to seat anyone "ineligible" under the Fourteenth Amendment.[29]

Grant said nothing further about Georgia, and this in itself signaled its importance to him. The Georgia reference was brief—probably inserted late—but it was the first thing he mentioned, and there was no mistaking his intent. Grant had allied himself solidly with Congress's Radical positions on race: equality for blacks, no blanket amnesty for former rebels, and assertion of federal hegemony in matters of civil rights. And find a solution to the Georgia Question.

By the end of the month Akerman had gotten his waiver from Congress and had become U.S. Attorney for Georgia. Grant nominated Hoar for the Supreme Court, and General Terry went to Atlanta to reestablish a military government.

At that point, while Akerman might have been unknown to Washington at-large, Grant could very well have been following his progress. He routinely received private communiqués from trusted wartime subordinates, and Terry was one of these. Akerman and Terry, as the top federal civilian and military officials in Georgia, knew each other, worked together, and were of like mind.

Treasury Secretary Boutwell also undoubtedly knew Akerman. As chairman of the House Reconstruction Committee, then-congressman Boutwell had been the lead questioner during Akerman's 1868 testimony. And Senator Sumner, deeply involved in the debate over Georgia, probably knew of Akerman. He had undoubtedly known Grant for years, and in 1868 and much of 1869 had a cordial relationship with him.

The key player in the political wrangling that ended in Akerman's appointment, however, was quite likely Congressman Benjamin F. Butler, chairman of the House Reconstruction Committee succeeding Boutwell and, since the death of Thaddeus Stevens, the de facto leader of the House Radicals.

Butler, like Hoar, was a successful Boston attorney. He had had a checkered career as a "political general" during the war, and in the process had earned Grant's displeasure and outright enmity. He had rehabilitated himself in Congress, however, serving as a House manager in the 1868 impeachment trial of President Andrew Johnson. In early 1869, with the help of a mutual friend, he and Grant made peace, and Butler soon became a presidential confidant.[30]

Butler and Hoar hated each other. Hoar was an intellectual Boston patrician, while Butler, from industrial Lowell, Massachusetts, was an outspoken, abrasive political manipulator and a champion of the working class. Like Akerman, Butler was an overachiever from a humble background, and Hoar disdained him. The two men were bitter political enemies and lifelong rivals, and it was no secret.

In his 1892 memoir Butler took credit for sabotaging Hoar's Supreme Court nomination because of "public policy and private wishes."[31] The private wishes were obvious. As for public policy, Butler probably wanted Hoar, the moderate on reconstruction, away from the court. He also wanted Hoar out as attorney general. There is no evidence that Grant knew of these efforts.

In these endeavors Butler allied himself with future son-in-law and Mississippi Republican senator Adelbert Ames, a charismatic Union war hero who, like Butler, was determined to build Republican strength in the South.

To do that, they agreed, the federal government had to do more to protect black constituents from Ku Klux predations. This had been the focal point of Akerman's 1868 presentation. It is not known whether Butler was in the hearing room when Akerman testified, but he could easily have found out what happened. He was also in regular correspondence with Georgia Republican governor Rufus Bullock, a leading ally in Butler's efforts to expand Georgia's Republican Party and keep it in power.

Akerman and Bullock were not friends, but they agreed on civil rights, and Akerman, as much as any Republican attorney in the South, was aware of the Klan horrors taking place throughout the region.

Butler urged Ames to seek out other southern senators and get them to lobby Grant to dump Hoar and hire a southerner. Ames probably led the meeting Cox described when he and other southern Republican senators saw Grant on June 15. They discussed not only Santo Domingo but also their wish for a tougher stance on reconstruction from the attorney general. That was the day Grant summarily fired Hoar.[32]

In Ames, young, dashing, and smooth-talking, Butler had made a good choice to lead these discussions. Butler had none of these attributes. He was well aware that many lawmakers in his own caucus resented his strong-arm tactics, his frequent incivility, and his low-brow background.[33]

Cox and especially Hoar disdained Butler for this reason, but this was a grave mistake. Butler was certainly a belligerent, ruthless partisan when he held the winning hand, but he was also a careful deal maker and compromiser when he did not. It also helped that he enjoyed an open door to the White House. Hoar's ouster and Akerman's subsequent appointment spoke loudly to Butler's taste for political intrigue.

Butler said he favored the annexation of Santo Domingo, but for him it was a cost-free position: as a House member he had no vote and could make Grant happy without going on the record. Support for Santo Domingo also may have helped him evade Grant's displeasure while he ruined Hoar's Supreme Court nomination.

Butler spent the first half of 1870 focused on Georgia, which, having earned special mention from Grant, lingered as the most visible offender in the Radicals' efforts to "reconstruct" the South. Like Akerman, Butler wanted to use the Fourteenth Amendment to force Georgia and the rest of the former Confederacy to submit to the federal will. Hoar was a liability.

GRANT'S OWN actions further intensified the Radical cause. In March, three months before Akerman's nomination, Grant sent an unusual special message to Congress, commemorating ratification of the Fifteenth Amendment extending voting rights to freedmen. He described the amendment as "a measure of grander importance than any other one act of the kind from the foundation of our free Government to the present day."[34]

Then, on May 31, Congress approved the Civil Rights Act of 1870, which soon came to be known as the First Enforcement Act. This was, at least in theory, the enabling legislation that Akerman had advocated during his 1868 congressional testimony.

The Enforcement Act's first priority, in keeping with the president's own emphasis, was to bring the wrath of the federal government down on state and local officials who tampered with the voting rights of freedmen.

But the new law also targeted the Ku Klux Klan and kindred organizations, making it a felony—with fines of up to $5,000 and imprisonment for up to ten years—for two or more people to "band or conspire together, or go in disguise upon the public highway, or upon the premises of another with the intent to violate the civil rights of any citizen." Finally, the act reaffirmed the Fourteenth Amendment's prohibition against former members of the Confederate military and political hierarchy serving in any official postwar capacity without a congressional "disability" waiver like the one Akerman had obtained late the previous year.[35]

Grant, despite his discomfort in the limelight, had begun publicly to advertise his intention to bring the South to heel. First had come his annual message the previous December, and now he had marked the landmark significance of the Fifteenth Amendment. As 1870 unfolded, these public observations would become warnings, and the warnings would grow harsher and more ominous as time passed. Klan terrorism was on a massive upswing, and Grant was losing patience. He understood violence as well as anyone then living, and when he named Akerman as his attorney general he picked a man who had as much or more experience with white terrorism as anyone he might have chosen. Whether he knew it or not, Grant had found his enforcer.

CHAPTER SIX

Race Riot

OCTOBER 20, 1870

Erastus W. Everson rode into Laurens County on October 17, 1870, two days before South Carolina's state elections. He was coming from Union County, where he had bought a horse, and he was going home to Anderson. He planned to stay only one night in Laurensville, the county seat, but on the way into town he noticed several bunches of heavily armed horsemen—all of them headed in the same general direction as himself, all of them white. He decided to have a word with the U.S. Army detachment in Laurensville. They were supposed to keep order. Then maybe he would stick around for a bit to see what happened.

Everson was no pilgrim. A seven-times-wounded veteran from Massachusetts, he stayed in the army for three years after the war to hunt down bushwhackers—guerrilla malcontents, Confederate deserters, and scavengers who pillaged the defeated South after the surrender. He finally mustered out in mid-1868 and became an "investigator," first for the Freedmen's Bureau and by autumn 1870 for the Internal Revenue Service. His sudden appearance in Laurens County two days before Election Day may not have been a coincidence. When congressional investigators later interviewed him, they didn't ask, and he didn't say.[1]

Laurens County, like York and the rest of upcountry South Carolina, had been on edge since Governor Scott had called up the state militia. The Ku Klux Klan was ubiquitous, as Judge Carpenter had noted, but inactive, waiting to see if the Reform Party could dislodge Scott and his Radical government. The wait was almost over.

Everson stopped off to visit Colonel Alfred T. Smith, commander of Laurensville's U.S. Army infantry garrison, to tell him about the gunmen he had seen. Then he checked into a local hotel.

Tempers were running high in Laurens—maybe even worse than in the rest of the upcountry—mostly because of campaign rallies organized by county Republican leader Joe Crews, a white rabble-rouser who regularly led marches of armed black militia members through the county's mostly white towns. His brazen provocations had earned him sensational headlines and the loathing of the Democrat-led establishment.[2]

Crews was easy for many whites to hate. Before the war he had been a slave trader, known in part for kidnapping blacks and Indians in the Gulf Coast states and selling them farther north, where prices were higher. He also had a reputation for failing to pay his debts.[3]

After the surrender, he joined the Republican Party, recasting himself as a fierce advocate for freedmen's rights and the Radical cause. As Laurens County's Republican leader he had a virtual monopoly on the loyalties of its 12,600 black residents, who substantially outnumbered the county's white people.[4] He was also a state assemblyman and, more important in 1870, the Laurens County election commissioner.[5]

Finally, as a Scott-appointed lieutenant colonel of militia, he commanded between six hundred and seven hundred militiamen, most of them black. He owned a house in downtown Laurensville and a barn a few blocks away that he outfitted with gunports and trenches—a fortress. He also owned a saw- and gristmill in Clinton, about eight miles southeast of town, where militiamen mustered and bivouacked. He had his Laurensville office in Tin Pot Alley, a large, shabby, vacant store on the town square that he had converted into a militia armory where he was reputed to have over one thousand rifles. On Election Day 1870 he was arguably the most powerful man in Laurens County.[6]

Laurens's politics, with large numbers of black Republicans opposed by economically powerful but embittered white Democrats, were neither better nor worse than those of other upcountry counties. But Crews's willingness to goad whites by playing on their fears of racial unrest made Laurens special, and he gained statewide notoriety as stories of his "incendiary" harangues were printed and reprinted.

As early as mid-April, the *Laurensville Herald* reported on a Republican mass meeting where speakers "proclaimed to the negroes that they would be armed by the next election with rifles that would shoot *thirty times to the minute*."[7]

By August the anonymous "speakers" of earlier accounts had disappeared, and the *Herald* and other newspapers began calling out Crews and other "miserable scalawags" by name. An August 6 rally in downtown Laurensville featured a "procession" of about "500 field hands" and "about an equal number" of elderly black hangers-on. Crews galloped through the streets, leading a unit of "60 black militia in full uniform with fixed bayonets and rifles" marching to the cadence of bass drums. The crowd of onlookers were armed as well, although not as smartly, the newspaper reported, carrying "shot guns, single and double, pistols in belts, old squirrel rifles, bludgeons, sticks, stones, etc., and every fashion of sword and saber."[8]

These dramas, always with Crews as the villain, according to the white establishment, played out every Saturday somewhere in Laurens County, more often as the election approached. The culminating event, in the minds of Laurens's whites, was probably Crews's August 27 speech in Waterloo, ten miles south of Laurensville.

According to the *Charleston Daily News*, Crews told his mostly black listeners that the militia law "had put arms in their hands, and *if they did not defend themselves it was their own fault*." "They had the arms," the report continued, "AND A BOX OF MATCHES ONLY COST FIVE CENTS."[9]

How to explain Crews in Waterloo talking about cheap matches around the same time Comptroller Neagle was making an identical suggestion in a speech before the York County Union League? At this point, less than two months before the election, reporters with an eye for the telling image had created several reconstruction- and campaign-inspired tropes, and the cheap matches reference appeared to be one of them. Its origin, however, was instantly lost in the fog of upcountry folklore.

EVERSON'S HOTEL was catty-corner to Tin Pot Alley on the town square. He spent the evening and most of the next day in and around the hotel, chatting with townspeople and eavesdropping on conversations about the "row" that was liable to occur on Election Day. "Well, if it is to come, it might as well come now as any time," several young men told him. They didn't want to bother the soldiers but would go hard on the state constables, appointed by Governor Scott and sent in to keep order during the voting. These interlopers "had no business" being in Laurensville.[10]

Everson had a room on the hotel's bottom floor with a view overlooking the street. Armed white horsemen took turns riding up and down outside all night. At one point several men came into the hotel and went upstairs to the room above Everson's. He heard them talking about how they planned to seize ballot boxes on Election Day.

He decided to send a message to Crews, whom he knew as a "leader of the colored men."[11] Everson was not particularly fond of Crews—"[his] tastes and mine are a little different," he said later and winced at what he described as Crews's "ill-advised and indiscreet" public remarks. Still, Everson had an instinct for troubled times, and one of those times was at hand.[12]

The danger was real. Everson did not believe the militiamen would hurt anyone "unless they were fired into," but the white gunmen were looking for trouble. "I know these people," he said later. In any kind of a gunfight the militiamen—occasional soldiers with sketchy training—would have no chance against the battle-tested Confederate veterans and their gunslinger allies.[13]

ELECTION DAY dawned with armed men, blacks and whites, eyeing each other uneasily. The hotel plotters' plans to seize ballot boxes never materialized, but the *Laurensville Herald* accused Crews of summoning blacks to perpetrate "bold and infamous frauds," including under-age voting and "repeating." The *Herald* later estimated that there were no more than twelve hundred eligible black voters in town, while nineteen hundred votes were cast for the Radicals, who won easily. It was impossible to know if Crews committed fraud, but as county election commissioner he certainly had the opportunity.

According to the *Herald*, whites in Laurensville were worried throughout the day that Crews would open up his storerooms and start handing out rifles to militiamen and state constables gathered at his house or at his fortress-barn. Crews himself, by all accounts, was nowhere to be seen.

Despite his absence, a "small but compact mass" of white gunmen formed up near Crews's house, prepared to "resist attack" by black militiamen, the *Herald* reported.[14] Men on both sides drew pistols, including one white whom Everson recognized as a hotel plotter from the previous evening.[15]

Colonel Smith did not intervene until a constable warned him that the confrontation was escalating rapidly. Arriving with his troopers, Smith found the militia formed up in Crews's front yard and the whites gathered at the head of the street prepared to charge. The militiamen's white officer was ready and apparently eager to fight. Smith spoke with both sides, telling the whites to cool off and inducing the blacks to lay down their weapons. The whites rode away.[16]

This skirmish seemed to end the Election Day excitement, and Laurensville started to empty out. Some militiamen remained at Crews's barn, others stayed at Tin Pot Alley, and Scott's constables were sleeping in an outbuilding next to Crews's house. The white gunmen, including large numbers of imports from outside the county, were spread over the Laurens countryside, with the biggest group overnighting in Clinton.[17]

COLONEL SMITH and his men left before dawn on October 20, their mission apparently completed with the election's peaceful conclusion. It was a rainy but tranquil Thursday morning.[18]

John A. Leland, the president of Laurensville Female College, a Presbyterian school with primary, secondary, and college curriculums, breathed easier, for his "young ladies once more fearlessly walked through the street, and . . . business everywhere was resumed," he noted in a memoir written years later.[19]

The peace and quiet did not last long. It was "court week" in Laurensville, and by mid-morning the town was bustling with businesspeople, shoppers, officials, and litigants, as well as significant numbers of black and white idlers in the street.

The county courthouse commanded the town square—a substantial space framed by cross streets. Tin Pot Alley fronted the square, facing the courthouse. Everson's hotel was on one of the corners, and late in the morning he walked a block to a barbershop alongside the courthouse. He needed a shave.[20]

Witnesses to what happened that morning quibbled over some of the details, but all agreed on the main points. An undercurrent of tension still rippled through Laurensville. "The armed negroes and constabulary about the lower arsenal at 'Tin Pot' seemed to be exultant," the *Laurensville Herald* reported later, "and some white men were standing about in the square opposite."[21]

Around 11:00 a.m. two white men, one of them a Reformer named Johnson and the other a Radical state constable named Kahlo, got into an argument down in the square, according to William D. Simpson, a prominent Laurensville attorney who saw much of what transpired from a second-floor courtroom where he was trying a case. Johnson accused the constable of calling him a "tallow-faced son of a bitch."[22]

The argument escalated quickly into a fistfight. Passersby gathered around the combatants, who were fifty or sixty yards away from Tin Pot Alley when they started swinging but gradually moved toward the armory's doorway as the constable gave ground.

According to Leland, a friend of Johnson's approached the battle, pistol in hand, to ensure "fair play," but seeing that Johnson was winning moved to holster his pistol when it "accidently discharged."[23]

All the witnesses agreed the gunshot was an accident, but the timing could not have been worse.

"They are firing upon us!" yelled one of the blacks.

By that time Johnson and his opponent had reached the door of the Tin Pot Alley armory, and the beleaguered constable and terrified black bystanders pushed inside. Soon after that, gunfire broke out from second-floor windows. Accounts differed on how many shots were fired, but no one in the square was injured.

White gunmen, spoiling for a fight for several days, immediately returned fire, broke down the armory door, and charged in. The blacks inside fled out the rear door of the building and disappeared in the back streets. Witnesses said the gunfight lasted anywhere from eight to fifteen minutes. Two unidentified blacks died in the initial exchange, and a third, also unidentified, was mortally wounded and died later.[24]

EVERSON HAD no illusions. "I knew they were ripe on both sides," he said later. As soon as he heard the first pistol shot, he leapt from the barber's chair to peek outside. There was a riot brewing, and he knew he would be a target. He was a northerner, and he was wearing a light-colored coat that made him conspicuous.

Everson sat down in the empty courtroom to decide what to do next. Suddenly he heard a loud noise. Looking out the window, he saw a crowd of people—blacks and whites—running up the courthouse steps to get into the building to escape the gunfire. Having no other choice, he descended the stairs and picked his way through the crowd and out the door, unnoticed now in the confusion.

He walked quickly until he got around a corner and out of sight, then sprinted for the woods. He meandered through the trees until he came to the railroad tracks. He knew a handcar carrying mail rumbled by in the afternoon. Could he hitch a ride to Columbia?

About four miles from town, he scaled a high trestle to wait for the postman. This was a mistake. A gang of white gunmen riding toward Laurensville through a nearby cottonfield spotted him and opened fire. Everson crossed the trestle and dropped to the roadbed below, hoping to escape, but a dozen riders immediately surrounded him.

They wanted to shoot him. They didn't believe he was a federal agent and accused him of being a state constable. He told them he was from Trenton, New Jersey. He was a dead man if his captors found out he was from Massachusetts, the cradle of abolitionism. He lived in Anderson, he said, and only wanted to get home.

His captors were unmoved, and they had him cornered. They cocked their pistols. Everson, desperate, had one "last resort." He gave the Masonic sign of distress. The "captain" of the group recognized it and stayed the execution. The men rode on with Everson walking in front. Four more times the captain interceded to save him before finally telling him to walk to "Copeland's." Nobody would bother him, the captain said.

Everson trudged onward, but after ten minutes the gunmen rode him down again. Three more threats, and three more times the captain intervened. Finally they reached the home of George Copeland, a wealthy businessman who lived near Clinton. Everson collapsed by the road.

"I have had seven balls in me," he explained. "I am easily tired out."

No matter. One of the riders told the others he was going to kill Everson and didn't care what his companions thought. Copeland, also a Freemason, joined the captain in pleading Everson's case.

"I know what you think," the gunman replied, "but I am going to shoot him."

Everson climbed to his feet: "If you want to shoot me, shoot. I have a wife and family, and you have probably. If I am to be shot, I can stand it." The gunman, ashamed, backed off. Copeland took Everson into his house.[25]

THE VIOLENCE in Laurensville ended quickly. An exultant Leland noted that every black in town disappeared almost instantly. "As though the earth had opened and swallowed man, woman and child of the race . . . none of them, of any age or of either sex, were seen on the streets for the rest of that day. Old Laurens could boast of at least *one* day, at least, under a white man's government."[26]

District judge Thomas O. P. Vernon ordered county sheriff B. S. Jones to collect the weapons at Tin Pot Alley and at Crews's barn. Jones mustered one hundred "special constables." B. W. Ball, another prominent Laurensville lawyer, deputized for the occasion, confiscated over one hundred rifles at the barn alone.[27] Of Crews, there was still no trace.

According to Simpson, news of the riot spread through the county "worse than a prairie fire," and by nightfall bands of white gunmen were pouring into Laurensville to support outnumbered whites in the race war that apparently had finally arrived. By midnight Simpson estimated the town was hosting twenty-five hundred armed men. He was sure the gunmen had decided to come only after they heard about the riot.[28]

He was wrong. Everson spent the night of October 20 under the protection of Copeland, whose wife had laid out an all-night dinner buffet that was serving one thousand men, most of whom had ridden in from other upcountry counties. This was no disorganized mob.

The gunmen stayed all night. New arrivals reported the capture of Wade Perrin, a just-reelected black state legislator regarded by the whites as a Crews crony and a dangerous agitator.

Everson finally went to sleep at 2:30 a.m. after listening to hours of bitter talk of vengeance. The visitors didn't care about politics or the outcome of the election. They wanted to spread violence, disrupt the peace, and make a mockery of reconstruction, Everson said. The race war, they said, "might as well come now."[29]

The night riders meant what they said. The next day Volney Powell, a white Radical candidate for probate judge, and Bill Riley, a prominent black Radical and a custodian at the Tin Pot Alley armory, were found dead on the Clinton highway about four miles outside of Laurensville, "both with multiple bullet holes in the head and body," Leland later wrote.

Another unidentified black lay "stark and stiff" alongside the same road five miles farther along near Clinton, and Wade Perrin, shot several times, was found on the roadside near Martin's Depot fifteen miles southeast of Laurensville. Finally, Leland said, yet another unidentified "obnoxious negro" was apparently hunted down at his home and beaten so badly that he died.

"The commonly received opinion or surmise," Leland said, was that the first three victims "were the work of one and the same party of desperadoes, who were really out in search of Crews."[30]

They did not find him.

CREWS HAD been inside Tin Pot Alley when the dispute in the square began. He left his office, examined the crowd for a moment, then "turned short around, walked rather brisker than usual down to the post office." Then the shooting started.[31]

"I comprehended the state of affairs at once," Crews wrote in a letter to the *South Carolina Republican* less than a week after the riot. "I was the one whose life was wanted in order to satisfy those blood thirst villains. I started for the woods."[32]

He hid in a hollow log. The *Camden (S.C.) Journal* reported that he "fared sumptuously" the first night, comforted by a bottle of wine and five quilts. He spent his time counting ballots in his role as election commissioner and managed to send the results to Columbia. His letter to the *Republican* followed shortly.[33]

On October 30, looking "haggard and seedy," Crews showed up at Laurensville's abandoned railroad depot where a new U.S. Army detachment was encamped. Crews demanded that Captain Estes get him out of town, Leland said. Estes, put off by Crews's trademark braggadocio, shoved him in a canvas sack and put him on a railroad hand car "disguised as a side of beef." He eventually made it to Columbia. He did not return to Laurensville.[34]

Everson arose the morning of October 21 not knowing what to expect. Copeland and the captain, his fellow Masons, would protect him as long as he stayed where he was, but Copeland's house—and probably the rest of the county—was still packed with imported gunslingers spoiling for a fight.

Downstairs, however, he was greeted by Hugh Farley, a former Confederate officer about Everson's own age, whom he had known for several years. During his Freedmen's Bureau days, Everson had helped Farley out of a mess near Charleston, and the two had a cordial relationship. Farley, probably summoned by Copeland and the captain, told Everson he had come to get him out of Laurens County.

Farley first went to Laurensville to retrieve Everson's horse. Everson approached Copeland and the captain. He knew Farley was "a perfect gentleman," but was he powerful enough to run the gantlet of armed white belligerents riding to and fro along the road between Clinton and the railroad station in Newberry? He was, they told him.

He and Farley left Copeland's at dusk. On the road they met five different squads of twenty to forty men apiece. Another group numbered maybe fifty men, Everson said. Outside of Clinton, Everson saw "as many as a hundred." At each checkpoint Farley rode ahead and talked his way through. At Martin's Depot Everson saw Wade Perrin's corpse lying by the road with his pockets turned out.

They rode into Newberry the next morning. Changing counties had not improved the ambience. The streets were filled with gunmen "with their revolvers strung," Everson said. The sheriff was a man he'd had in jail in Charleston for fourteen days for murder. He also spotted a fugitive he had chased "for thousands of miles as a bushwhacker."

Then a hoodlum he recognized from Freedmen's Bureau days called out: "There is that God damned Everson. He arrested me in 1867. I offered him $5,000 security to let me go and see my wife, and he refused, and I will never forgive him." He and his friends started moving toward Everson, who walked his horse to the front of the local coroner's office, climbed down, dawdled for a moment, gestured for his tormentor to approach, and then ran and jumped onto a passing train. Eventually he, like Crews, reached Columbia and safety. Freemasonry and Hugh Farley had saved his life. "Mr. Farley," he was convinced, "is probably the head of the Ku Klux." At least in Laurens County.[35]

IN ALL, white gunmen killed twelve men in the Laurensville riot and its aftermath: eleven blacks and Powell. The white city fathers had little sympathy for the bereaved. "Most of these were inmates of that infamous den Tin Pot," the *Laurensville Herald* reported, and attorney Simpson dismissed the dead for the most part as low-life agitators.[36]

Simpson later told congressional investigators that of course the black militiamen fled after the shooting stopped: "I think they feel conscious of deserving punishment. They know what they have done to the peace and good order and quiet of that country."[37]

But neither Simpson nor any other white Laurensville resident would put the blame for the killings on the Ku Klux Klan, an organization the town fathers categorically asserted did not exist in Laurens County. It was nevertheless clear to Governor Scott in Columbia and General Terry in Georgia that the gunmen roaming the countryside after the riot were not disorganized "rowdies," as Leland described them.[38] Scott asked for U.S. Army intervention a few days after the riot, and Terry sent two companies.[39]

Five weeks after the raid, U.S. Marshals with army help arrested eleven men for violating the victims' political rights, among them Sheriff Jones, George Copeland, and Hugh Farley. Federal charges were dismissed in Columbia—the crimes occurred after the victims had voted. The prisoners were immediately rearrested by state authorities, but Judge Vernon released them on $5,000 bond apiece, and they were never tried. The judge was impeached by the Republican-led legislature but resigned before his trial.[40]

THE LAURENS AFFAIR marked the beginning of organized white terrorism in South Carolina. The riots outraged the North and moved the upcountry into the spotlight for the Grant administration. South Carolina could be ignored no longer.

Apparently desirous of mitigating the damage, Laurensville three months later sent Simpson, Leland, and R. S. Goodgion, another town elder, to Washington to explain to President Grant and other officials what Leland described as the "rights of the oppressed" whites in Laurens County.[41] They wanted state constables gone and an end to sporadic military intervention. They were worried about the threat of black violence and the expected imposition of new federal enforcement laws.

Grant "received them courteously and listened with commendable patience" during an hour-long meeting, Leland said. He took the documents the delegates had brought and told them he would send them to congressional investigators. They never heard anything further.[42]

Somewhat disappointed, they then made the breathtakingly inept decision to visit Congressman Benjamin Butler, the House of Representatives' leading Radical. Goodgion made the approach, seeking to "appeal to his former states' rights principles," Leland said later. It did not go well.[43]

The Washington, D.C., *New National Era*, edited and published by Frederick Douglass, provided the details. "After presenting fully to Mr. Butler the deplorable condition of the whites, and the necessity for their being protected from the violence of the blacks, Mr. Butler asked him [Goodgion] to explain how it was that eleven colored men were murdered in one day just subsequent to the election and no white men were killed." And "how it happened that so many white men were in arms, at an hour's notice, the day after the election."

Butler continued in this vein for a while, the *New Era* continued, and closed with the suggestion "that there ought to be about twenty men hung in Laurens, and then the rest would cease murdering the blacks."[44]

CHAPTER SEVEN

Swimming with Sharks

On July 1, 1870, a week after his confirmation, Attorney General Amos T. Akerman's job description changed dramatically. The U.S. Department of Justice came into being, with the attorney general as its leader. Suddenly a Washington neophyte from rural Georgia was handed powers and responsibilities that none of his predecessors had ever had.

For three-quarters of a century, cabinet departments and federal agencies had run their own legal affairs, but now they were required to cede these responsibilities to the new department. Akerman took control of the payrolls and personnel records of all U.S. Attorneys and U.S. Marshals. Besides his traditional duties as the president's legal consultant and representative before the federal bar, he now ran federal law enforcement—he was the nation's top lawman.

It is unclear whether Akerman even knew that a Justice Department was imminent when Grant appointed him or simply had not thought about it. It had been extensively debated in Congress, but Akerman's personal papers, both public and private, do not mention the department's creation or the challenges it posed. The Justice Department Act was signed into law on June 22, the day before Akerman's swearing-in.[1]

Yet while he may have known nothing about how to establish a brand-new federal bureaucracy, Akerman made an immediate statement about his own intentions. He put his office in the Freedmen's Savings Bank building, closely allied with the War Department's Freedmen's Bureau. Akerman intended to focus on civil rights, and this was his opportunity to realize the goals he had outlined before Congress in 1868—the same goals enunciated by President Grant in his annual message the previous winter. Like Grant, Akerman was now in the forefront of Radical reconstruction.

He wasted no time. In late July he sent copies of the First Enforcement Act to all his U.S. Attorneys and law officers, noting that it was their "special duty to institute proceedings against all violators of the act." Under the Fourteenth Amendment and the Enforcement Act, anyone who had participated in "insurrection" against the federal government was barred from holding political office. U.S. Attorneys were told that they should "take prompt measures for the arrest and effectual prosecution of the guilty party."[2]

On paper the Enforcement Act gave the federal government the powers that Akerman needed. Besides putting U.S. Marshals in play, it also authorized U.S. Attorneys to summon state militias or the U.S. Army when extra help was needed.

In practice, however, the act fell short. Intimidation by the Ku Klux Klan and resentment among southern whites generally made it difficult for the marshals to find deputies. State militias exacerbated white animosity and even rage by their mere presence, and if, as in South Carolina, they relied on black recruits, they had little hope of competing militarily with the Ku Klux and other white vigilante groups.

As for the army, by mid-1870 five years of demobilization had shrunk the force to fewer than thirty-five thousand regulars, of whom only forty-three hundred were serving in the South outside of Texas. Units could be summoned for help, and they were effective when they arrived, but, like Colonel Smith and his Election Day contingent in Laurensville, they seldom stayed long enough to make a difference. This meant that states with serious Klan activity—the former Confederacy plus Kentucky—could only count on a few hundred men on a regular basis.[3]

The lack of credible deterrence caused U.S. Attorneys to tread carefully when pursuing Enforcement Act violators, even as it emboldened state and local officials to ignore its provisions altogether. Akerman understood these difficulties from his own experience in Georgia, but as attorney general he was palpably unsympathetic to his subordinates.

Concentrate on "the most aggravated and unequivocal cases," he admonished his U.S. Attorney in Knoxville, Tennessee, who appeared less than eager to oust former Confederates holding state jobs. "No degree of personal, social or political standing in the offender should be the slightest impediment to the prosecution."[4]

AKERMAN WAS flailing. Radicals' interest in enforcing the postwar amendments, a goal shared by Grant and Akerman, conflicted directly with one of the principal aims of the Justice Department's congressional sponsors—to save money.

Since the end of the war the federal government had been struggling to keep up with a deluge of war-related claims and litigation. Congress hoped that consolidation in a single department would streamline justice, eliminate redundant jobs, and end the practice of hiring expensive outside contract lawyers.

And by holding the attorney general to account, supporters of the new department expected to curtail the rampant patronage that for years had filled the federal justice system with political hacks and incompetents. Professionalizing the civil service was an ongoing theme among Washington reformers, and the Justice Department was, foremost, a good-government initiative.[5]

The problem for Akerman was that Congress had no interest in spending more money to hire more attorneys, whether to handle war claims, civil rights, or anything else. The idea was to economize by dumping everyone's lawyers into the Justice Department and handling everything in-house. The trouble with this strategy was that in postwar America the caseload was overwhelming.[6]

Akerman was unimpressed with the new power and influence he supposedly possessed. Even though, in theory, he could pillage other agencies for their legal staffers, he had no place to put them because he had no building of his own. He left some agency legal departments where they were and stashed the others wherever he could find space—five different locations in all. As far as its physical presence, the Justice Department effectively existed in name only.[7]

Akerman was not particularly happy with Congress either. His U.S. Attorneys received $200 per year in salary, he noted in his first annual report, far below what a similar job could earn on the outside. "I know no work for the public which is so ill paid," he wrote. And while he said he would like to curtail the department's use of outside counsel, it was hard for in-house staff to compete. "The remedy lies with Congress," he said. Pay better, if you want better lawyers.[8]

The Grant administration, for its part, all but ignored the new department, and there is no evidence that anyone there was interested in pushing Akerman to implement changes. If they had wanted a reformer, the obvious move would have been to keep Ebenezer Hoar as attorney general. Hoar had national stature and detested patronage—a perfect choice to get the Justice Department up and running.

But Grant, like the cronies in his inner circle and like much of official Washington, regarded patronage as a useful tool, as Cox's account of the Santo Domingo affair and Hoar's ouster had shown.

Grant's cabinet members as a whole were equally skeptical. Ceding legal affairs to the Justice Department would cost them personnel and authority, and no bureaucrat likes to give anything away. "It is impossible to send all papers on to the Dept. of Justice for its opinions," Secretary of State Hamilton Fish wrote in his diary. "[Doing so] would be to subjugate all other departments to that (one), and make the heads of departments responsible for opinions provided by another independent department."[9]

DESPITE THE department's inauspicious beginning, Akerman had plenty to do, both as attorney general and as the most powerful southern politician in Washington. Klan terrorism was intensifying and spreading in much of the South as the 1870 midterm elections approached.

In North Carolina the Ku Klux near Greensboro kidnapped a black town councilman in February and lynched him in the town square, thirty yards from the courthouse door. No one was prosecuted or even arrested.[10] In May the Klan ambushed and stabbed to death a white Republican state senator in a Yanceyville courthouse.[11] Republican governor William Holden proclaimed "insurrection" in the offending counties, imposed martial law, suspended habeas corpus, and sent militiamen to restore order.[12] Many of the "best" people were arrested, and by mid-July white North Carolina was in an uproar. Holden, wrote the *Semi-Weekly Raleigh Sentinel*, "without the shadow of authority," had organized what it described as "an army of *rioters*."[13] A month later Democrats won both houses of North Carolina's General Assembly and immediately moved to impeach Holden.

These exploits won the Ku Klux Klan new adherents in neighboring South Carolina. Despite relative peace during Governor Scott's reelection campaign, cross-border alliances were formed. In the aftermath of the Laurens County riot several South Carolinians had identified significant numbers of imported gunmen—from elsewhere in the state and from North Carolina.

Farther south, however, Georgia was on its best behavior, and this is where Akerman focused much of his attention during the summer months. On July 15 this last Confederate holdout was quietly readmitted to the Union. Congressman Butler had withdrawn his objections after Georgia's ratification of the Fourteenth and Fifteenth Amendments and congressional passage of the Enforcement Act.[14] Georgia was to hold statewide elections sometime in 1870, and its congressional delegation would be seated in early 1871. Then, finally, the Georgia Question would be resolved.

White Georgia was anticipating victory and itching to get after Governor Bullock, whose reputation for incompetence and corruption rivaled or even surpassed Scott's. Bullock was not up for reelection, but he wanted to keep the Republican majority in the General Assembly and planned to have his Radical adherents there vote in August to extend their mandate by two years.

Butler, in close contact with Bullock, had tried but failed to insert a similar provision into the House's Georgia Bill based on the premise that the black legislators who had been deposed in 1868 had not had the opportunity to serve out their elected terms. This maneuver was roundly denounced on the floor of Congress, not only by Democrats but also by Republicans fed up with Bullock's cronyism.[15]

Several prominent Georgia Republicans then asked Akerman for his opinion on the constitutionality of an extended mandate. This put Akerman, a known Bullock opponent, in a difficult position. Congressional Radicals—Butler prominent among them—wanted to build viable Republican parties in the former Confederacy. The 1867 Reconstruction Act and the Fourteenth Amendment had given the party a head start, helping produce Republican governments in Georgia and both Carolinas, but they had not improved Republican fortunes. By mid-1870, with election campaigns in full swing in all three states, North Carolina was plagued by Klan violence, and Georgia and South Carolina were mired in corruption and mismanagement.

The Bullock-Butler argument for prolongation described Georgia's existing government as "provisional" because the army had been put back in charge after the ouster of the black legislators in 1868. General Terry had restored them to office, but Bullock concluded that the legislature should be able to vote to extend itself for another two years to give them the time they had earned.[16]

Akerman, having endured five years of snubs, intimidation, and threats in his adopted state, was a fierce Republican partisan who, like Butler and Bullock, desperately wanted the Republicans and reconstruction to succeed in Georgia, but he did not believe flawed governments like Bullock's could accomplish either task. As a brand-new Washingtonian, however, he had to tread warily around Butler—a frequent consultant to Grant. Butler was not a good person to alienate.

Stalling was a possibility. In late July reports surfaced that both Georgia parties along with General Terry wanted Akerman's opinion on prolongation but were unsure how to ask him to give it. Readmission to the Union had ended martial law in Georgia, so Terry could no longer order up the opinion. Nevertheless, the Georgia Assembly, if it was still "provisional," had no standing to ask for an opinion. Akerman could have dawdled while the interested parties waded through the confusion.[17] But he did not.

On August 6 the Augusta, Georgia, *Chronicle*, in a dispatch probably written from a Grant administration leak—perhaps Akerman himself—reported, "Akerman is decidedly of the opinion that an attempt on the part of the legislature to postpone an election would be a flagrant and palpable violation of the constitution of the state."[18] The story was published the day after Akerman attended a cabinet meeting with Grant and just after statewide elections had laid waste to North Carolina's Republicans. Akerman clearly had Grant on his side.[19]

At a news conference a few days later, Akerman went on the record, damning the "deplorable" conditions in southern states where leaders have "become little better than lobbyists" who "sacrificed the interests of the country to jobbing and corruption." He specifically named North Carolina, South Carolina, and Georgia among the leading transgressors.[20]

Even as he spoke, he sent a letter to prominent Georgia Republicans in the Bullock administration and the General Assembly describing his views. This "Georgia letter," published in Atlanta, dismissed every element of Bullock's and Butler's "prolongation" rationale in terse, simple language. There was no mistaking his intent.

The Georgia Constitution had been state law since July 1868, the letter noted, and everyone in the state had lived under it for two years. So how was the government illegitimate, Akerman asked. "Have all the officers and people living in Georgia been laboring under a stupendous mistake?"

Akerman noted that despite federal intervention following the ouster of the elected black legislators in 1868, the constitution remained in force and mandated that elections for both houses be held in 1870. Now "some in the Assembly" claimed that they could extend their terms for two years, but no one had voted for that in 1868. Prolongation would be an "unprecedented usurpation" of the will of the people.

And if, by excluding the blacks, "the whole country [had] been offended by and perplexed by the state of things in Georgia," it was the legislature's own fault. One outrage cannot be fixed with another, he said. The black membership had been reinstated, they got their back pay, and the matter was closed, he wrote. Hold the election whenever you want, but hold it in 1870.

Finally, he said, he knew the Republicans' underlying fear was that they would lose the election, but "better (to) lose the state than keep it wrongfully." He warned Democrats, however, not to turn loose the Ku Klux Klan—authors of the "frenzy" of atrocities that had plagued the 1868 elections. Should this "serious rat" invade Georgia again, he wrote, "lawful means" to hunt it down may once again be necessary." On August 11, Georgia's Assembly defeated prolongation by a vote of 71–64.[21]

The Akerman letter received something of a mixed reception. The Washington, D.C., *Evening Star* gave Akerman full credit for the prolongation measure's defeat and noted that gallery spectators cheered the outcome when the vote was complete. The *Star* did not mention whether the enthusiasts included anyone besides white Democrats but asserted there had been "great rejoicing among the national Republicans." The national party had little enthusiasm for Governor Bullock.[22]

The *Buffalo Courier* speculated that the Republicans were regrouping after their defeat in North Carolina and that Akerman was the agent of a new Grant administration good-government strategy. "We turn with pleasure to the manly preference of Mr. Akerman for justice," the paper wrote. It was a victory over "nefarious traitors and partisans," like those in the Bullock government.[23]

In Georgia itself, the *Atlanta Constitution* grudgingly conceded Akerman's reputation as "a good lawyer" but warned of possible injustices to come. "His utterances abate not one jot or tittle from his well-earned fame as an able, cunning and unscrupulous partisan leader," the *Constitution* wrote. Be wary of "the schemes of the party Mr. Akerman plans for."[24]

AKERMAN DID NOT stop with the letter. The day after the Georgia vote, he spoke for ninety minutes before a large crowd of "prominent ladies and gentlemen" gathered at Lincoln Hall, Washington's sumptuous new downtown auditorium. The event was hosted by the Southern Republican Association, but Akerman was not interested in boosting party morale. Instead he affirmed his own and his party's commitment to civil rights and to the primacy of the federal government, then delivered a blistering rebuke to the white southerners who refused to accept the new reality.

The South had lost "on the field of war." Northern Democrats accepted the changes that the war had wrought, but the southerners had not. "[They] have declared that they will never submit to any other construction of the Constitution of the United States than that put upon it by the state rights advocates." The South needed its best people in government, he said. "[But] when Democrats are asked who should be elected governor or senator they answer . . . the very men who led them to shipwreck."

He had hoped that the war had settled the questions of "American nationality" and "equal rights for all men," but it had not. "As long as persons are organized against these doctrines and endeavor to bring contempt upon those who believe in these doctrines, we must stand up to them energetically, and never let them go."[25]

For Akerman this was a defining moment. Seven weeks after arriving in Washington as a nonentity, he had emerged as the Grant administration's voice for a radical reconstruction to be led by honest men. And he clearly had Grant's backing, otherwise Butler would have sought a private audience at the White House and slapped him down, and the rumor mongers would once again have predicted his imminent departure.

Instead, Akerman's Lincoln Hall speech was repeatedly interrupted by applause and finished to a robust ovation. Akerman, the *Buffalo Morning Express* wrote after the speech, was "rapidly making his mark at Washington and drawing national attention to himself as a man of superior ability and weight."[26]

SHORTLY AFTERWARD Akerman left the capital to spend some of the congressional recess in Georgia with Matty and his three sons, all of them under five years old. Congress was not scheduled to reconvene until December, and most of the government habitually abandoned the capital during its unbearable summers.

Georgia's Republicans invited Akerman to speak at the statehouse September 1. This was a tougher audience than Lincoln Hall. The *Constitution* condemned Akerman's performance: "[It was] one of the bitterest and most vindictive speeches we have ever heard." He denounced the sins of "the Confederacy, secession and the Democratic party" in terms harsh enough "to recall the hatreds of 1860."[27]

Two weeks later Akerman was desperately ill in Elberton. Although he may have had a recurrence of his childhood lung ailment, a chronic risk whenever he was forced indoors for long periods of time, his condition was later described as a prolonged attack of "bilious fever"—probably malaria, common in the South but also prevalent throughout much of the country in the mid-nineteenth century.[28]

Georgia's Republicans meanwhile recommended delaying November's election for a month. This would give them more time to organize and, with Congress reconvening December 5, would ensure a ready set of sympathetic Republican observers in Washington. Despite his illness—or perhaps because of it—Akerman approved what was immediately dubbed the "Akerman Election Bill." It moved the election to December 20 and gave Governor Bullock the power to appoint the managers who would referee the balloting in individual counties and, to a significant extent, control it.

The election law predictably outraged Democrats, but in Georgia in 1870 there was no way to run a nonpartisan election. The Democrats in 1868 had used Ku Klux terrorism to win the state for Seymour. The Republicans had no reason to trust them, and now, with the help of the federal government, they held the political high cards. Maybe the December balloting would be fair. Maybe not.

Akerman did not win any new friends in his home state. He had overseen "the most partisan measure" ever seen, the *Constitution* said, to buy time for Republican incumbents and allow Bullock to ensure "the people [were] to be defrauded."[29]

By the time the bill came to a vote, however, Akerman was gone. He returned to Washington September 23, still "somewhat enfeebled by his recent illness," the *New York Herald* reported. It was nonetheless a triumphant return. Georgia's Republican newspapers had put forth Akerman's name as a possible vice presidential running mate for Grant in 1872, and the *Herald* expanded on the theme, saying Akerman was "probably President Grant's choice."[30]

Akerman told the *Herald* that he did not personally draft the election bill, because he was too sick at the time, but had approved it and expected the Republicans to win in December. He told the *Herald* he "was amused at the mistaken kindness of some of his southern friends." "He has no political ambitions," the paper reported, and he intended to "return to private life" when he left office.[31]

Akerman spent the next two weeks convalescing at the Buffalo home of his friend E. Carleton Sprague. Out of the headlines and virtually incommunicado, his burst of public adulation faded quickly, to be replaced by concern about his health. By the middle of October, the *Herald*, Akerman's new northern publicist, was reporting that he would resign because of illness.[32]

THE ESTABLISHMENT once again may have been trying to write him off, but Akerman confounded this prediction, reappearing in Washington on October 11, robust and ready to work. Several important tasks awaited him, including "a great number of important cases" jostling for consideration by the Supreme Court, he told the *Herald*.[33]

His chief helper was to be the solicitor general, who would represent the executive branch in cases brought before the Court. By the time Akerman returned to Washington, both he and Grant had been lobbied hard for several weeks about the advisability of choosing Louisville attorney Benjamin H. Bristow, a Grant favorite, for the job. Grant waited to speak with Akerman and then made the appointment October 13.

Bristow, thirty-eight years old, appeared at first glance to have similar credentials in Kentucky to Akerman's in Georgia: he was a former U.S. Attorney and a leading actor in the Republican Party of a Democratic state. Beyond these basics, however, the two men had little in common. Bristow came from a prominent Kentucky family and was a partner in a leading law firm. He had served under Grant during the war and been badly wounded during the 1862 Battle of Shiloh. His close friend and law partner was Kentucky Republican Party leader John Marshall Harlan, destined to become a Supreme Court justice.

Grant had been badly beaten in Kentucky in 1868, and a different outcome in 1872 would undoubtedly require a greater Washington presence for loyal Kentuckians. Akerman—and presumably Grant—heard a lot about Kentucky's needs in the letters of endorsement that showered down from Bristow's friends and supporters. Akerman also heard a lot about how Bristow's "social position" was the equal of anyone's in the state. Kentuckians, like Georgians, apparently struggled to convince the Washington elite that their favorite sons were not bumpkins.[34]

On the surface, the Akerman-Bristow partnership seemed like an ideal pairing: Akerman was the outsider with the civil rights agenda; Bristow was the insider with impeccable political credentials. After a month on the job, however, Bristow wrote Harlan, damning his new boss with faint praise. Akerman was "a very agreeable gentleman, quite fluent of speech and without . . . loquaciousness," but his "acute mind" was not "of large caliber."[35]

THE MOST important case facing the Justice Department grew out of a demand by Treasury Secretary Boutwell that the Union Pacific Railroad pay back interest on its government bonds—$2.4 million, a huge sum in 1870. The Union Pacific, the eastern two-thirds of the transcontinental railroad, was in dire financial straits and had assumed that the interest need not be paid until the bonds reached maturity. Not so, Boutwell contended, and he threatened to withhold fees for government freight carried by the railroad and use the withheld money to pay down the bond interest. He asked Akerman's opinion on whether he could do so.

This was political quicksand, and Akerman probably did not understand how nasty it could get. Boston congressman Oakes Ames was a major stockholder in the Union Pacific's construction company—Credit Mobilier. In addition, he had induced more than a dozen of his fellow lawmakers to buy Credit Mobilier shares. His brother Oliver was the president of Union Pacific.[36]

It is also unclear why Boutwell decided to go after the railroad. Perhaps it was yet another dust-up among Bostonians, but the New York *Sun* suggested that Boutwell planned to challenge Grant for the Republican nomination in 1872 and hoped to win support by showing off his financial acumen.[37]

For Akerman, however, there was no winning strategy. Should he alienate powerful congressmen, which Boutwell was apparently ready to do, or help the railroad men and alienate Boutwell? Worse, the two Lincoln-era laws that defined the public-private partnership that built the railroad were vague on the issue of interest payments. Without an easy legal interpretation, anything Akerman did was going to be viewed as political—and probably wrong.

AT THAT MOMENT, however, Akerman did not need to worry about anything. His political star was at its apogee, and Grant sent him to New York City in late October to make sure the Tammany Democrats did not violate the Enforcement Act during elections by bribing, threatening, or otherwise manipulating voters. General Terry and Congressman Butler joined him for three days. This was illustrious company. Terry and Butler were two of Grant's most trusted civil rights advisers. Now Akerman had joined them. The elections were trouble-free.[38]

Back in Washington, Akerman received a dazzling accolade from Frederick Douglass's *New National Era* for his efforts in Georgia. It credited the "Akerman Election Bill" for uniting the state's Republicans, and it added, "Under this bill a glorious victory for the Republican cause is confidently expected in December."[39]

In early November the *New York Herald* reported that Akerman would leave the cabinet if the Republicans won in Georgia so he could become a U.S. senator.[40] In the middle of the month former secretary of war Simon Cameron, a longtime Grant insider, returned from a fact-finding mission to Georgia and predicted the Republicans would have "a fair majority" as long as the blacks voted in large numbers. He recommended, however, that a large military force be sent to oversee the balloting.[41]

Harriet Roundtree

DECEMBER 3, 1870

Harriet Roundtree didn't keep a precise count, but she saw sixty or maybe seventy men, all of them white, the ones she could see. She was asleep when they tried to sneak up on the house, but they made a lot of noise, and it was a moonlit night—about one o'clock Saturday morning. She and her husband, Tom Roundtree, farmed cotton near the town of Harmony on the northwestern edge of York County, about three miles from the North Carolina border. Tom had sold some bales in Charlotte and returned home late Friday with more than two hundred dollars. Besides Tom and herself, the only other adult at home was Bob Gist, Tom's nephew. The rest were children—ten of them.

The raiders arrived on foot, carrying pistols, long guns of various kinds, and torches made using rags soaked in turpentine. They surrounded the house and started shooting. Twenty or thirty rounds. They pounded on the front door, demanding to be let in. Harriet knew they were after Tom. He scrambled up to the loft while she went to meet her visitors. They smashed the door down before she could open it.

A dozen men swarmed into her parlor. Most wore red gowns. One had a grey overcoat turned inside out, she noticed, and a few had no disguise at all. Immediately they figured out where Tom was hiding, and he knew it. He dropped down from the loft, landed on top of a desk, and jumped out a window, sprinting hard toward the woods. He hadn't run far, maybe a hundred yards, when Harriet heard two shots. Tom fell to the ground. Several of the gunmen approached him and shot him three more times. Then another man carrying a naked Bowie knife approached him. He slit Tom's throat ear-to-ear.

"If you move, we'll blow your brains out," one of the men yelled at her as the inside men ducked out of the house to see what had happened. Gist bolted through the door. A few of the raiders shot at him but missed. He made it to the woods. Harriet's oldest daughter, Nancy, took her baby and hid in the cotton patch next to the house. Harriet stayed with the rest of the children.

A little while later, the gunmen came back. They broke open a trunk, found some silver, and took that as well as a rifle and a pistol. She recognized two of the men. One was John Hicks, a local teenager she had known for years. The other was Sam Randall, who lived about ten miles away in North Carolina. Harriet knew him from his hat and his beard. Neither wore a disguise. Randall had come around some days earlier looking for liquor. He had told Tom, "I saw the Ku Klux a few nights ago." Harriet figured he was a spy. She suspected Randall had come around to mark them.

Both Randall and Hicks were half-drunk. "Here's plenty of whiskey," Hicks said. He turned to Harriet. "How's your Ku Klux?" Harriet did not know what he meant. Nancy, hiding outside, spotted Mac Byars, another local teenager, standing by the door wearing a brown coat and blue pants—no disguise, same as Hicks and Randall.[1]

Harriet Roundtree's account, offered as testimony in district court the following month, was quite accurate. And a year later in federal court, Shaffer Bowens, a Ku Klux from North Carolina who had joined the raid, confirmed her story and added details.

THE ROUNDTREE murder took place six weeks after the Laurensville riot, and although much of the upcountry seemed to have settled down, the elections could not be undone. The Reformers had failed at the ballot box, and Governor Scott and his black and white Republicans still controlled South Carolina. A large number of York County's whites saw no point in continuing to play by the rules.

They had planned the raid about ten days in advance. Shaffer Bowens heard about it from local Klan leader Ned Turner. The Klan planned to "get" Tom Roundtree, who, Bowens said, was supposed to be a "bad negro." This could have meant a number of things: Roundtree owned a rifle, he was a successful farmer, he had money, and he voted Radical and made no secret of it. The Klan did not like blacks like Roundtree who thought for themselves, talked too much, and stirred up trouble.[2]

Bowens showed up in the early evening of Friday, December 2, at Moore's Bridge on Buffalo Creek—a well-known landmark. Some others were already there, and more kept arriving, so many in the end that they worried someone might see them. They found a thicket up the creek, lit a fire, and hunkered down.

"I asked them what they was going to do with the nigger; they said they was going to kill him," Bowens said later. "I told them I didn't think it would be well to kill him; I thought it would be best to go and talk to him or whip him, if they was determined to do something." But "they swore they was going to kill him."

Why was Roundtree targeted? He was black, Bowens testified, and "it was reported that he was a Radical." That's all he knew.

A little after midnight Saturday morning Turner mounted up, and the rest of the raiders strung out behind him. When they got close to Roundtree's farm they continued on foot, climbing a rail fence to get into the yard. Bowens said he knocked down three or four rails in hopes the clatter would send Roundtree a warning, "but he didn't take it."

The raiders surrounded the house. Suddenly someone fired a single shot. Bowens didn't know who it was, but the Ku Klux immediately let go a barrage, probing "the cracks and windows of the house." Turner eventually gave the order to cease fire, while several men used a large boulder to batter down the front door. Then they pushed inside. Bowens stood in the doorway. Roundtree opened fire from the loft, apparently shooting at the gunmen standing outside. The raiders immediately returned fire.

Suddenly Roundtree appeared at the edge of the loft. He fired once from there, apparently with a rifle, grazing Elijah Ross Sepaugh, a Ku Klux standing next to Bowens: "[He] cut him across the breast a little, and in the wrist." Then Roundtree pried up a floorboard in the loft, dropped down to the parlor and went out the window. More shots. Bowens ran into the yard and saw that Roundtree had fallen. He helped him to his feet.

Somebody shouted: "Now, damn you, go back and show us the guns!" Roundtree agreed, but after taking a dozen steps, Bowens said, he collapsed facedown right next to Sepaugh, the man he had shot. "Just as I walked up to him," Bowens said, "Henry Sepaugh, Elijah Ross Sepaugh's brother, came up, drew a long bowie-knife and walked to where I left the nigger lying struggling. Some of them had turned him over on his back." A few minutes later Bowens learned that one of the Sepaughs had slit Roundtree's throat.

The raiders found Roundtree's rifle lying in the yard but no other weapons in the house. Then they stood outside. "Somebody down in the field began hollering to 'Rally boys!' for here is them damned Ku Klux," Bowens said. He supposed it was Roundtree's black neighbors.

"Yes, God damn you," one of the men yelled back. "The Ku Klux was here."

The raiders mounted up and rode away.[3]

ON MONDAY, December 5, Harriet Roundtree, identified by her husband's slave name as Harriet Black, appeared before the York County constable and swore out a complaint against Samuel C. Randall, Malcolm B. Byars, and John F. D. Hicks for the murder of "Thomas Black," her husband. Daughter Nancy and Bob Gist accompanied her and swore out separate complaints.[4]

The constable arrested Byars the following day. He was plowing a field at his family's farm, about a half-mile from the Roundtree house. Randall and Hicks subsequently came into Yorkville to surrender. York County sheriff R. H. Glenn jailed all three.[5]

On December 12, under the headline "Inhuman Murder of a Negro," the *Charleston Daily News* reprinted an early *Yorkville Enquirer* account of the Roundtree killing. The story accurately related the facts as they were known at that moment, noting that the raiders, "estimated at sixty in number," were composed of "white men, with the exception of three, who were disguised, and whose complexion could not be distinguished."[6]

The *Enquirer*'s original story also editorialized against "these inhuman and lawless acts." Regardless of Roundtree's unnamed transgressions, "real or imaginary," the *Enquirer* said, "laws are provided to meet the exigencies of the case, without a necessity of resorting to mob violence; and the sooner the strong arm of the civil law arrests and brings to punishment the perpetrators of such outrages the better it will be for all."[7]

At the preliminary hearing a month later, Hicks, who was only sixteen years old, was released on a $1,000 bond, and Byars, who was eighteen, on a $1,500 bond. Randall, older and out-of-state, was discharged for $3,000. The same group of local leaders stood bail for all three, who pleaded not guilty. Trial was set for January 16.[8]

These events were noteworthy at that moment, perhaps even remarkable. Despite the brutalization they had been subjected to, Harriet Roundtree and two co-plaintiffs, all three of them black, on the first working day following the murder, had unhesitatingly sought justice from county officials—all of them white—and had sworn out complaints against three white attackers. None of the three was accused of being the actual murderer, but all were arrested—two of them teenaged boys—and indicted as accessories, thrown in jail, and kept there for a month. The local newspaper correctly described the crime as a white-on-black murder.

Harriet's trust in the system probably arose from her own and York County's limited experience—up to that time—with Ku Klux terrorism. She undoubtedly had seen her share of racial animosity but nothing like this. Klan country was in North Carolina—something to be whispered about with her neighbors over the border. Until now.

County institutions, unmolested and largely unintimidated up to that time, reacted to the Roundtree killing as they would have reacted when faced with any grotesque crime. Sheriff Glenn, warmly regarded by the black community, immediately acted on Harriet Roundtree's complaint and did his duty. The accused surrendered, and the *Enquirer* was indignant. York County appeared to have taken a stand.

THEN CAME the trial. Harriet Roundtree and Nancy Black, the daughter who had fled to the cottonfield, appeared as witnesses before district Judge William M. Thomas. Nancy was "a half-grown girl, quite ignorant and very much embarrassed in the investigation," according to I. D. Witherspoon, a prominent York County attorney who attended the trial as an observer. Harriet, however, "was very composed." She related how she heard Hicks or Byars tell "this fellow Randall to come out of a trunk that he was pillaging," and she described Byars and Hicks as "neighbor boys." She said she knew them the moment she saw them. Daughter Nancy also said she recognized Byars and remembered Randall ransacking the trunk.[9]

The defense, however, brought "twenty or thirty witnesses," Witherspoon said. He couldn't remember the exact number, but they provided alibis as "clear and satisfactory . . . as I have ever known established." These included William C. Black, an elderly former member of the state legislature who had once owned Tom Roundtree and Nancy, and Samuel Hunter, "an intelligent freedman," who had known Randall from childhood "as a harmless, inoffensive man."[10]

These two, and other "disinterested persons . . . parties not connected to the case," testified that none of the three defendants was anywhere near the scene of the crime, Witherspoon continued. Hicks was sick in bed that night, "quite an invalid—a boy that looked like it would be almost dangerous for him to be away from home," Witherspoon said. He even appeared to be sick during the trial.[11]

Lucky for Hicks, two of the "disinterested" defense witnesses were his parents. Young John was sick when he came home from school Friday afternoon, his mother said. Nevertheless, he stayed up late mending shoes, and went to bed about 10:00 p.m. When the dogs started barking about 2:00 a.m. Saturday, his father continued, he went to investigate and saw John in bed on his way out the door. At 4:00 a.m. he woke John, told him to make a fire, and then sent him "out." When John returned, he had found out from someone he had seen that Tom Roundtree had been killed. The prosecution made no move to cross-examine.[12]

As for Mac Byars, a half-dozen witnesses testified he had spent the night of the murder at his grandmother Artemisia's house. "Mother" needed someone to cut wood for her because "her colored man" had gone to Charlotte, the court record said. Young Mac lived anywhere from six to twelve miles from Artemisia. He had no way to reach grandma's house, cut wood, and walk home in time to help kill Tom Roundtree.[13]

Randall's alibi was established by two friends who swore they spent Friday evening drinking whiskey with him at his house in Cleveland County, North

Carolina. When Albert Frances left "after midnight," Randall was sound asleep. Martin S. Brown confirmed the story, adding that "Randall was a little tight that night." The court record noted that Randall only lived about six miles from the Roundtree cabin, but, besides having apparently passed out, he did not own a horse.[14]

Having finished with the alibis, the defense next called several witnesses to demolish Harriet Roundtree's credibility. The county constable said she had been induced by politically motivated white Radicals to denounce the accused. Besides, argued William C. Black, Harriet's former owner, Harriet's character was "rather bad," and he "would not believe her on oath."[15]

Freedman Samuel Hunter, a Baptist lay preacher, described his friend Randall as "one of the best-natured men in the world," while Harriet was "weak-minded."[16] Three more witnesses followed, testifying that they, like Black, wouldn't believe Harriet. They described her as a "very bad, spiteful, malicious woman," Witherspoon said.[17] County Commissioner Hugh Roberts denied he had suggested to Harriet that she name Hicks, Byars, and Randall in her complaint, as the constable had testified, and said he did not know anything about Harriet's character.[18]

The defense rested. No defense witness was cross-examined, nor was any attempt made by Judge Thomas or anyone else to find out who else was involved in the killing or, if Harriet was lying, what reason she might have had to select two teenagers and a drunkard—noncombatants—for prosecution from among some five dozen men implicated in the murder of her husband. There was no need for further testimony, Witherspoon said, because "the alibi was proved by so many witnesses that in some cases the state made no effort."[19] All three defendants were acquitted on January 20, 1871.[20]

SO MUCH for the integrity of York County. The defense had used several Ku Klux stratagems to tear apart the plaintiffs' case. The defendants were, it was sworn, nowhere near the scene of the crime. One woman accuser was said to be too ignorant to have known what was happening, the other to be evil, subversive, and easily led by dishonorable white men. The prosecutors took the word of the defense witnesses and did not bother to question them or rebut their version of events.

In case York County's black citizens missed the point, the same jury—on the same day—convicted freedman William Wright of perjury for falsely accusing his white neighbor Abraham Sepaugh (presumably a relative of the Roundtree Sepaughs), as one of a dozen Klan attackers who gave him a whipping in October 1869.

Sepaugh had been tried and acquitted nine months earlier and immediately accused Wright of making up his story of the beating. At Wright's trial Sepaugh testified that he was in bed at the time the beating allegedly occurred. Other witnesses testified that Sepaugh was at home. No one testified on Wright's behalf, including Wright himself, who, Witherspoon said, was "too ignorant" to understand what was happening. Not that ignorant. Shortly after the guilty verdict was read, Wright "ran off," Witherspoon said, and was never seen again.[21]

In the ensuing days and weeks, a number of questionable stories arose among York County whites to explain the Roundtree affair. He was certainly dead, but why had he been killed? Was it money? The two or three hundred dollars Roundtree had earned from selling cotton Friday was gone Saturday after the raid—no surprise there. One story held that a gang of blacks who knew Roundtree had ambushed him on his return and had stolen the money. Unfortunately for the purveyors of this yarn, the *Enquirer* was on the record saying the attackers were white.[22]

The "bad negro" version probably arose somewhat later, and was presented several times in different forms to fit other York County acts of terrorism committed by the Klan. Roundtree planned to use his cotton money to buy guns and murder "all the whites in the neighborhood," Yorkville tanner Joseph Herndon later told congressional investigators. He was killed to keep him from buying the guns.[23] In other words, his death was his own fault.

These sophistries spoke to southern whites' fear of the race war. What if their former slaves had guns? What if they had money? What if they were not ignorant? Tom Roundtree probably could not read or write, but that didn't mean anything. A lot of upcountry whites were in the same fix. Hicks and Randall both signed their names when they were bonded, but Byars made "his mark," just as Harriet Roundtree had made "her mark" on the original complaint. Black equality—in earnings, education, voting, gun ownership, or practically any other endeavor—made white people nervous.[24]

AS FAR AS can be ascertained, Harriet Roundtree was the last black plaintiff in York County who bothered to seek justice in a South Carolina state court in 1871 and quite likely for a considerable time after that. Her husband had been killed and her money stolen, and then, for trusting the system, her character had been besmirched and her own life threatened. Eventually she was driven from her home and forced to seek shelter at the Yorkville army garrison.[25]

On January 23, three days after the Roundtree verdict, white cotton farmer Dennis Crosby's gin house went up in flames. He lost not only the building but also his cotton gin, six hundred pounds of cotton, and fourteen hundred bushels of cottonseed. Just after midnight on January 25, as many as five fires burned simultaneously at white-owned plantations, and the flames could be seen from downtown Yorkville. H. C. Thomasson, three miles north of town, lost a barn, four thousand bundles of forage, and a wheat thresher but managed to save his horses. Less than a mile away R. W. Shaw saw his straw house and fodder go up in flames.

Six miles southeast of Yorkville, arsonists burned S. N. Miller's gin house, gin, wheat thresher, cottonseed, and four bales of cotton. Some of his livestock were killed. A half-mile away, Hugh Warren lost his gin house and gin, his cotton press, and six bales of cotton. On January 27, fire at Jane Thomasson's plantation, five miles north of Yorkville, destroyed her gin house and gin, three hundred bushels of cottonseed, and a wheat thresher.[26]

The *Yorkville Enquirer* continued to report in measured fashion about these events but noted in its February 2 edition, "It is but proper to state . . . that the persons who have suffered by these fires are of the highest respectability." And: "It is noteworthy that they have taken little or no part in political matters." They were victims, "the last persons to suspect of being engaged in 'Ku Klux' operations." The *Enquirer* was starting to show the strain, however, as it moved to reassure white readers that there was "little doubt" that blacks set the fires. Still, it was not their fault: "Of course they are prompted to do so by base white men [who incite the] deluded negroes [to] acts of violence."

The Klan did not believe in guiltless blacks. The fires continued, and on Saturday, February 25, as many as a dozen masked and hooded gunmen rousted black farmer Anderson Brown and his family from their home about four miles north of Yorkville. They asked Brown his name and then marched him away from the house. His family heard gunshots. One son counted twelve. The next morning Brown's body was found about two hundred yards from the house. He was gut-shot and wounded in the shoulder and arm. And he had a bullet hole in his forehead. Making sure.[27]

On March 10, the Columbia *Daily Phoenix* published a letter to the editor, signed by "Observer," who said, "[Brown] had not figured prominently as a politician, but enjoyed the reputation of having burned one gin house and one barn, the property of inoffensive citizens, the week previous [to his death]."[28] In York County a war had begun.

CHAPTER NINE

False Hopes

Attorney General Amos T. Akerman left Washington for Georgia in mid-December 1870, ostensibly to spend the holiday season with his family. He told President Grant that his health and "personal motivation" prompted the trip, along with a desire to get "at least twenty miles from a telegraph office."[1]

That may have been a fond hope, but it was unrealistic. Akerman might make it to Elberton for Christmas dinner, but the main purpose of his trip, as he well knew, was to monitor elections for half of Georgia's state legislature and seven seats in the U.S. House of Representatives. Akerman had managed to alienate both Republicans and Democrats during the fall campaign, first by overriding Republican governor Bullock's efforts to delay the elections for two years, then by endorsing an election law that put the entire voting apparatus in Bullock's hands. The election itself—spread over three days just before Christmas—was Akerman's event.

The mystery in all this was the unbridled optimism shared by both the national Republicans and the state party. As far as the *Buffalo Commercial* was concerned, victory was a foregone conclusion. It was understood, the paper said, that Georgia's new Republican General Assembly would make Akerman a U.S. Senator. Georgia's Republicans predicted he would become President Grant's 1872 vice presidential running mate.[2]

None of this made any sense. Unlike South Carolina, Georgia had a majority white population. Even with U.S. Army detachments helping black voters get to the polls, Republicans still needed significant white help to win a fair fight, and they had no possibility of getting it. Democrats had disdained the elections in 1868 and had boycotted the polls in large numbers, but that would not happen again. Worse, the idea that white Georgia would look kindly on Akerman—once a respected Republican attorney, now a firebrand Radical reformer—was a pipe dream.

Any lingering doubts were dashed December 17 when the *Atlanta Constitution* published an "Election Address" written by establishment stalwarts and former Akerman associates Robert Toombs (his wartime patron) and Linton Stephens, the brother of erstwhile Confederate vice president Alexander Stephens.

The letter embarked on a tortured and specious legal argument contending that both the Akerman-blessed election law and the Fifteenth Amendment were unconstitutional and "marked by futility and nullity." By giving blacks the right to vote, the letter said, the election law and the Fifteenth Amendment had bypassed the Georgia Constitution and were thus unlawful.

What the letter did not mention was that while the U.S. Constitution did indeed give states the right to conduct elections, it also said that "Congress may, at any time by Law, make or alter such regulations." The Fifteenth Amendment was such an alteration.

Then, in a nakedly racist effort to suppress the black vote, the letter deliberately confused the U.S. and Georgia constitutions, claiming falsely that voters "shall have paid all taxes" before being allowed to cast ballots. By voiding the poll tax of 1869, the Georgia election law had devised an "unconstitutional" (only in Georgia) "contrivance" to "allow the poor, defaulting negro to cast his vote although he should afterwards be persecuted and sent to the penitentiary under the laws against illegal voting."[3]

Akerman could not let this pass. No sooner had Toombs and Stephens published their screed than Akerman published one of his own. In a letter addressed to the Republican state committee, he condemned Georgia's Democratic Party, "a morose, resentful, fault-finding organization" prone to "foolish undertakings." "[It] grumbles at many things which it pronounces wrong without offering to establish in their stead anything better."

The letter was reminiscent of Akerman's 1868 House testimony, but its tone was considerably harsher and more partisan. He blamed the Democrats directly for Georgia's backwardness, then all but accused them of treason. "[The Democratic Party] looks upon the growth of the nation without any pride; it looks upon a firm, prudent and just administration of affairs with no satisfaction," he wrote. "It is offended at the presence of the nation's soldiers, whose business it is to repress the foreign enemy and aid in enforcing the law against domestic criminals."[4]

Akerman's patience in two years had faded dramatically, as had any optimism he may have had that southern whites could be cajoled into abandoning their intransigence. "I doubt whether from the beginning of the world until now," he wrote later in a letter to General Terry, a kindred spirit, "[that] a community, nominally civilized, has been so fully under the domination of systematic and organized depravity."[5]

His convictions remained as unflinching as ever, but they were now buttressed by a stubborn ruthlessness that he did not have in 1868. He had told Congress then that the application of federal law would restore order in the

South and make unnecessary continued military occupation. Now, however, he had come to regard U.S. Army intervention almost as a necessity. This new-found belligerence, coupled with his growing contempt for the rejectionist South and its Ku Klux foot soldiers, had fueled his intransigence. He had grown tired of negotiating.

General Terry, now stationed in Louisville, sent troops to Georgia for election security. The December 16 *Daily Columbus Enquirer* reported the arrival of four companies of soldiers from South Carolina—about four hundred men—to be distributed in and around Macon. This was the garrison that had been sent to Laurens County after the October Klan riot.[6] Troops in the hundreds were about all Terry could manage at this point. He moved his small forces around like chess pieces to counter each emerging threat.

Election results began trickling in after Christmas, and it soon became clear that Republicans' optimism was hopelessly misplaced. The Democrats swept to power in a repudiation of the Bullock administration. In a reactionary declaration of states' rights and white supremacy, Democrats won seventy-one out of the eighty-six contested General Assembly house seats and nineteen out of twenty-two seats in the state senate. Four out of seven U.S. House members-elect were Democrats.[7]

Akerman's national standing predictably plunged. Two months earlier he had been the darling of official Washington; by Christmas Day he had become the architect of disaster. The naysayers wasted no time consigning him to oblivion.

The Georgia results were sufficient "to preclude the possibility, if it ever existed, of Attorney General Akerman's election to the U.S. Senate," the *New-York Tribune* wrote on December 26.[8] As 1871 dawned, national pundits sealed Akerman's fate: "All persons wishing to compete for the attorney generalship of the United States will forthwith submit sealed bids," the *World* (New York City) wrote. "The Georgia election having gone Democratic, Mr. Amos T. Akerman will soon be out of place."[9]

The *New York Herald* had George Williams, "a sop for the Pacific Slopers," standing in the wings, with Akerman gone in a few weeks, voluntarily retiring "for the purpose of devoting himself to the more congenial pursuit of the practice of his profession in Georgia."[10]

Speculation continued through January and most of February. Williams was the name most frequently heard, but the *Cincinnati Enquirer* also spread the first of many rumors to come that Solicitor General Benjamin Bristow, Akerman's new deputy, was the chosen successor.[11] Akerman offered no public reaction to the Georgia debacle, nor did President Grant.

And nothing happened.

Akerman neither quit nor was fired. Grant, at least publicly, expressed neither dismay nor anger. Akerman almost certainly had relayed his pre-election misgivings to Grant, and must have cleared the "Akerman letter" with him before sending it, so the loss could hardly have been a shock.

But it had consequences. It doomed whatever hopes Grant may have had for carrying Georgia in 1872 and signaled the national Republicans' abandonment of the Bullock government. Akerman hoped for a brighter future for Republicans, but, given white opposition, chances for a resurgence were slim.

Akerman's biggest mistake, however, was that he had not done enough to quash Republicans' pre-election euphoria and prepare them for the worst. As a result, he was left with no political cover and ended up having to shoulder all the blame for a defeat that was all but preordained.

He had a heavy price to pay for this oversight. The Georgia result gave anyone who had a pending dispute with Akerman an open opportunity to question his competence. Congress and the Union Pacific Railroad were the first to take advantage.

On December 15, just before leaving for Georgia, Akerman had released his opinion in the Union Pacific dispute, agreeing with Treasury Secretary George S. Boutwell that the government could call for immediate payment of $2.5 million in interest owed by the company on federal railroad bonds. For Akerman, required to provide an opinion on the matter, anything he did would make an enemy. He chose to alienate the railroads.

Under laws passed by Congress in 1862 and 1864, the government issued $16,000 in bonds to Union Pacific for each mile of completed road. The government also paid 6 percent annual interest on the bonds. The government essentially financed construction.[12]

Bonds were to be redeemed after thirty years. In the meantime, one-half of the fees charged to the federal government for its use of the line—for telegraph services and transport of goods, troops, munitions, mail—were withheld and put toward Union Pacific's debt principal. The government also received 5 percent of Union Pacific's annual earnings for the same purpose.[13]

The unusual dispute between the Republican administration (Boutwell) and the Republican Congress arose over the ambiguity of the two laws in determining when Union Pacific had to repay the bond interest. Both Akerman and Congress agreed the language was opaque.

Akerman's finding not only endorsed Boutwell's demand for interest payments now. He also described the bond agreement as an "act of bounty"—a gift to Union Pacific that could never be fully repaid to both its investors and the government. In such a relationship, he concluded, common law gave the "donor"—in this case the government—the right to interpret the agreement.[14]

Union Pacific in late 1870 was an easy target. Its finances were in disarray, and accusations of mismanagement, cronyism, and outright corruption had swirled around the company for years. Despite all this, Union Pacific stock in mid-November was trading at $24 per share. By early December, however, uneasiness over Boutwell's demands had dropped the price to $18, and rumblings of discontent grew in Congress, where numerous members were holding Union Pacific paper.

This was undoubtedly the crux of the dispute, and it was no accident. Republican congressman Oakes Ames of Massachusetts, Union Pacific's chief financier, in 1868 had arranged to sell shares in Credit Mobilier, Union Pacific's construction company, to members of Congress. That is where the shares would do the most good," he wrote to an investor. "[Anyone who might have a complaint] cannot help being convinced that we should not be interfered with."[15]

By late 1870 Credit Mobilier stockholders included, among others, Vice President Schuyler Colfax, Massachusetts senator Henry Wilson, and representatives James A. Garfield and John Bingham of Ohio. On December 9, an outraged Senate opened a Judiciary Committee investigation into the legitimacy of Boutwell's demands. When Akerman's finding was released, the stock plunged to $9 per share.[16]

By the time Akerman returned to Washington with the arrival of the new year, the Union Pacific affair had escalated into a full-scale intra-party mess, and by February both the railroad and the Judiciary Committee began to leak details of their deliberations. Boutwell came in for his share of unflattering scrutiny, but he was an ex-congressman of considerable stature. Akerman, the outsider who had botched the Georgia elections, was a much easier target.

On February 5 the *Nashville Union and American* predicted bad times for Akerman. The paper based its story entirely on unnamed sources, mostly, it seemed, from the railroad: "Mr. Akerman's days are probably few," the *Union and American* wrote. "The Pacific Railroad magnates are after him . . . and call him all sorts of names."[17]

This initial approach did little harm, and it may even have enhanced Akerman's reputation, for the railroad and its leadership cabal did not command much public sympathy. A few days later, the *New York Herald* felt safe in casting Akerman as a gallant knight doomed to be muscled aside so the all-powerful "Pacific Railroad ring" could put "a more pliable man in his place."[18]

A week after that, however, the *Herald*'s tone changed markedly, its views undoubtedly influenced by an irritated Congress. The House had decided Akerman's finding was not "sound law," and the Senate Judiciary Committee—composed entirely of lawyers, the paper pointed out—had agreed. Committee members spoke of Akerman in "terms far from complimentary as to his legal abilities."[19]

The *New York Evening Post* took this criticism to a higher level, reporting that Grant intended to get rid of Akerman, not because of the Georgia results but rather because "several of the justices of the Supreme Court" had "advised the president . . . that Mr. Akerman had not thus far displayed even ordinary legal attainments" in his appearances before the court.[20]

And on February 23, with the Senate's report finished and ready for publication, the *Atchison Daily Patriot*, serving the Kansas hub of another powerful railroad, piled on. Under the headline "Akerman's Blunder," the *Patriot* damned Akerman's opinion for failing to recognize "the plainest provisions of the law on the subject," dismissed Akerman as incompetent, and blamed him for putting Boutwell "in an ugly position, the result of basing an important action on the opinion of a lawyer of Mr. Akerman's modest attainments."[21]

The committee report, released the following day, agreed with Union Pacific's view that if Congress had intended for the railroad to pay interest on demand, the legislation would have said so.[22] Rather than dispute the "act of bounty," the committee embraced it. Congress regarded the transcontinental railroad as a national treasure and from its conception had determined to give Union Pacific whatever it needed to build it, virtually without obligation. "The company was not expected to pay the interest as it should become due," the report said. "It was, indeed, more than hinted that the company never pay anything."[23]

Given such a "work of national importance," the report continued, Akerman had behaved badly by relying upon a "technical rule of judicial construction"—the "act of bounty"—as an excuse to defy "congressional wishes."[24]

On March 3, the last day of the Forty-First Congress, lawmakers passed an amended appropriations bill restoring fee payments to Union Pacific that had been withheld by Boutwell. The bill left open the question of interest payment, but the ultimate outcome was regarded as a total victory for the railroad. The stock price recovered immediately.[25]

Akerman's—and Boutwell's—biggest mistake was obvious. They had let Congress define the debate. The Akerman opinion earned little more than a mention upon its release and quickly vanished into obscurity. Publicity came only through unflattering leaks by the opposition, who dismissed Akerman's arguments as incompetent and even unpatriotic—easy insults in the wake of the Georgia results.

This characterization was absurd. The Senate's position had nothing to do with the law but was simply a political statement: Union Pacific did not have to pay the interest or even, perhaps, the principal—because Congress said so.

What lingered for Akerman, however, was the damage done to his reputation as an attorney. He received high marks from the *Buffalo Weekly Courier*, for an "unsuccessful wrestle with laws which had been framed, beyond the possibility of misconstruction, in the interest of a great swindle." Nonetheless, the report concluded, Akerman's performance "was more creditable to him as a patriot than as a lawyer."[26]

THE ONLY indication of discontent that Akerman offered in rebuttal came in his annual message to Congress, and this had nothing to do with Georgia or Union Pacific. He had no building, scattered office space, and no money to pay his staff, let alone expand it. He wanted to more than double the annual salaries of U.S. Attorneys to $500 in smaller districts and quintuple them to $1,000 in larger districts. And he wanted per diem doubled across the board.[27]

Akerman's level of frustration was almost tangible. His chief interests—civil rights enforcement under the Fourteenth Amendment and the Enforcement Act—posed complexities that left his overworked, underpaid, and frequently underqualified subalterns at an almost hopeless disadvantage. In October he gently reminded his U.S. Attorney in Baltimore that while black voters "should have applied" to him for help in challenging a restrictive voter registration law, the issues in the case were complicated. The prosecutor should budget his time and concentrate, at least temporarily, on cases "where the law is clear."[28]

Worst of all, the admittedly "meager" statistics Akerman had been able to gather from the South showed not a single prosecution under the Enforcement Act.[29] He had too many emergencies—in Georgia, the Carolinas, and elsewhere—and too few lawmen.

He certainly knew about the Laurens County riot and, by year's end, probably the Roundtree murder, but just as the South Carolina upcountry was becoming a central focus of Ku Klux terrorism, General Terry was forced to scavenge his Laurensville infantry for Christmas holiday duty policing Georgia.

Grant shared Akerman's views, and in his own annual message to Congress, delivered December 5, 1870, he shared his misgivings and set the stage for what became the last gasp of Radical reconstruction. He alluded only once to the growing Klan terrorism in the South but did so in his first paragraph. "It is to be regretted," he said, "that a free exercise of the elective franchise has by violence and intimidation been denied to citizens in exceptional cases in several of the States lately in rebellion."[30]

At that point, North Carolina, savaged by Klan violence throughout most of the year, remained Congress's main preoccupation, but by the time of Grant's message the Democrats were back in power, Governor Holden had been impeached, white hegemony had been reinstalled, and Klan violence had abated, in part because there was no need.

South Carolina was a different story. Laurensville had caught national attention, but the pivotal event came on New Year's Eve, when black militiamen accosted one-armed white bootlegger Mat Stevens in Union County—York County's neighbor—and killed him when he refused to hand over his whiskey.

White citizens were in an uproar, and the following day gunmen invaded the county seat of Unionville, about thirty miles southwest of Yorkville, and shot up the town. One black militiaman and the white deputy sent to arrest the militiamen were killed.

Local lawmen quickly arrested twelve black suspects and put them in the Union County jail. On January 4 several dozen Klan members broke into the jail, kidnapped five black prisoners, took them into the forest, and shot them, killing two and badly wounding the other three, who were rearrested.

Governor Scott took a conciliatory tone, declining to ask for federal intervention or impose martial law. But on February 12, an estimated five hundred Ku Klux invaded Unionville for the third time, apparently provoked by the possibility that the three prisoners wounded the previous month would be moved to a safer location.

The Klan this time grabbed ten black prisoners from the jail while holding the county sheriff and his wife at gunpoint. They then assembled in military formation and marched out of town. Two prisoners were hanged, six more were shot by firing squad, and two escaped, only to be recaptured later and executed for the Stevens murder.[31]

These events horrified South Carolinians. Stevens's death spoke to whites' fear of a Haiti-style, vengeance-driven race war and gave them incontrovertible proof of the folly of arming blacks and letting them roam the countryside. At the same time, however, the murder's aftermath dismissed whatever remained of the fairy tale that the Ku Klux Klan was little more than a figment of overactive Radical imaginations. It also brought considerable shame and outrage for white South Carolinians who understood that this grotesque episode reinforced northern prejudices against them as unlettered cutthroats and murderers. For blacks, once again ignored as nonentities in the public soul-searching that followed the Union County murders, the bloody aftermath had demonstrated, as Harriet Roundtree could have told them, that justice was not for them—only terror and lynching.

CHAPTER TEN

Bar Fight

FEBRUARY 26, 1871

Rose's Hotel, on downtown Congress Street, with its wide verandas and upper balconies, was a Yorkville landmark. William E. Rose, the owner, was a railroad man and a renowned South Carolina innkeeper who had built the hotel before the war as an elegant, upcountry stopover. After the surrender he moved to Columbia to tend his other properties. He became a Republican state senator in 1868 and closed the hotel but kept it in good condition and leased parts of it to favored clients—among them the York County militia.[1]

By late 1870, half the building was given over to D. S. Russell & Co.'s Bar Room, a popular gathering place and repository for local gossip.[2] Dave Russell, the thirty-six-year-old proprietor, lived in the hotel, knew pretty much everybody in town, and, like many in his profession, was a good listener, a cautious speaker, and a reliable keeper of confidences. Russell was a Republican. That was no secret, but nobody held it against him. Everybody told him things.

The other half of the building was leased to York County. Like Russell, County Treasurer Edward M. "Ned" Rose, son of William E., lived and worked in the hotel. He collected taxes and held the county money in his office safe. Besides the militia, other county offices were lodged in the hotel along with their records.

Ned too was a Republican, but, unlike Russell, Yorkville's nearly fifteen hundred white inhabitants did not like him. Ned was the local rich boy whose daddy had gotten him an easy, well-paying job during hard times, along with a nice place to live. He was regarded as untrustworthy—not the person to hold your money, let alone the county's—and, to make things worse, he got on well with the county's blacks, which made him "not liked in the county at all," as Russell described him later.[3]

The new year found Yorkville in an uneasy state. The Roundtree murder was less than a month old, and pretrial hearings had begun. Spartanburg County, sixty miles west of Yorkville, was having an upsurge in Ku Klux beatings and murders. Then came the bootlegger shooting in Unionville and the subsequent murders of the imprisoned black militiamen.

York County's white residents—almost exactly half the county's population—were increasingly apprehensive. Armed black militiamen resumed marching in Yorkville's streets as they had during the election campaign, and nervous white townspeople—many of them Klan members—countered by sending out five- and six-man armed security patrols after nightfall.[4]

On January 16, 1871, Governor Scott responded to demands by the General Assembly that he increase the militia presence in Laurens, Union and Spartanburg counties to minimize the threat of violence. With the Laurensville companies still in Georgia, the U.S. Army presence in the state was minimal. Scott issued a "general message" denying that any of his counties were, as the assembly put it, "riotous and refractory."

He admitted that his black militiamen could not compete with the Klan, and even if he had more men, he had "no means" to pay them. No money. No troops.

Then came wishful thinking: "The civil law of the state ought to be sufficient . . . to protect the person and property of every and any citizen of the State, however humble, friendless or obnoxious." Sending extra troops during what he called a "time of profound peace," would be a remedy "as bad as the disease," because it would suggest "that we are living in a condition of social anarchy."[5]

These platitudes failed to soothe York County. Four days after Scott's pronouncement, the Roundtree defendants were acquitted and set free, and soon after that the gin houses of white landowners started to go up in flames.

Next, copies of a "resolution" from "Headquarters K.K.K." appeared in prominent public places about Yorkville. This communiqué threatened to kill ten "leading colored people" and two of their white sympathizers every time arsonists torched a white-owned property. Also, should "armed bands of colored people"—the militia—be found patrolling county roads, their officers were to be executed.[6]

The authenticity of this missive was immediately called into question by the *Yorkville Enquirer*, whose editors claimed never to have seen it. Although it was dated January 22, it was only printed in Columbia's *Daily Phoenix* February 1, apparently after a Republican state senator received a copy in the mail and passed it on to the *Phoenix* editors. By that time, however, events in York County were starting to prove the sincerity of the resolution—never mind its origin.[7]

TROUBLE BEGAN at Rose's Hotel late on the night of January 24 or early in the morning of January 25. Nobody was really sure. But sometime around midnight Ned Rose went upstairs to his bedroom, poked a "sixteen-shooter" Henry rifle out a window, and opened fire until he ran out of bullets. Then he reloaded and fired again.[8]

Startled citizens awakened and went into the street where Ned could easily be seen blasting away. More startling were the half-dozen fires lighting up the night sky at farms off in the distance. Tom Roundtree's avengers were at large in the countryside.

Very shortly the story spread that Ned's barrage had been a signal for blacks to light their fires, although no evidence emerged that this had actually been the case. Dave Russell doubted the story. Ned had spent the evening drinking in the saloon until friends cut him off and took him upstairs. Apparently uninterested in bedtime, he decided instead to spray the neighborhood with gunfire. Ned was already unpopular, but after this episode, Russell recalled later, "everybody was down on him." He advised Ned to leave town and stay with his father in Columbia. Ned ignored him.[9]

At this point York County's unrest had begun to catch the attention of Columbia. Ku Klux activity in the county was "rife," a special dispatch from the capital reported in the *Charleston Daily News*. Ten buildings had been torched the previous week, undoubtedly in response to the Roundtree murder. The Klan had promised retribution, and forty black men had suffered serious beatings. Whites continued night patrols in Yorkville's streets amid "great excitement" countywide.[10]

Governor Scott sent state militia commander Major General C. L. Anderson to Yorkville January 30 to meet with a select group of "leading citizens," predictably all white, and with a larger group the following day, the *Yorkville Enquirer* reported. Anderson learned that the county's difficulties had "arisen principally from the ill-advised policy of organizing and arming" black militia companies and the "reckless, dangerous and indisciplined [*sic*] use" of their weapons. Anderson should disarm the militia, the citizens told him, and the Yorkville militia company's white officers agreed.[11]

Anderson immediately ordered the militiamen to turn over arms, ammunition, and military accoutrements to Sheriff R. H. Glenn, "to be deposited by him in a place of security," the *Enquirer* continued. "The citizens assure Anderson that this would prevent a collision."[12]

Neither Anderson nor Yorkville's city fathers bothered to include York County's black citizens in these consultations. Apparently Anderson, like most of York County's whites, had either failed to connect the fires to the Klan's "indisciplined" use of force in murdering Tom Roundtree or had chosen to ignore the obvious linkage. And apparently no one mentioned that York County's white militia officers faced Ku Klux threats if they did their jobs. The *Enquirer* dismissed as "untrue" the reports of Klan beatings of black men.[13]

With 1871 barely underway, it was apparent that whatever meager attempts had been undertaken to promote racial cooperation in York County had been abandoned. For many of the whites, the New Year's Eve murder of Union County's Mat Stevens undoubtedly served as a first warning that the blacks were readying for the dreaded race war. The post-Roundtree arsons in York County were the next step.

For York County's black citizens, disarming the militia took away the only protection—however limited—they had against white oppression. The local courts had resoundingly failed to bring justice in the Roundtree lynching, and angry blacks—there is no record whether they were militia members or simply furious citizens—took revenge by burning down farm buildings. This availed them nothing. The state, like the local courts, betrayed them by taking their weapons. Now they were defenseless.

And the widespread beatings, far from "untrue," were common knowledge among both blacks and whites. Interviewed by congressional investigators in mid-1871, U.S. Army major Lewis Merrill estimated that York County's white raiders had beaten between three hundred and four hundred blacks since the October elections, and those figures ignored "numerous minor cases of threats, intimidation, abuse and small personal violence, as knocking down with a pistol or gun."[14]

DISARMING YORK County's militia offered immediate new opportunities for the Ku Klux Klan. On February 11 between forty and fifty armed horsemen visited white militia captain John Faris's home about 2:00 a.m., rousted him out of bed, and took anywhere between seven and twenty-seven repeating rifles he had confiscated from his black soldiers.

The raid was Saturday. On Monday morning Faris came to Yorkville, spoke to no one, got aboard the first train to Columbia, and never returned. Other Klan forays ensued until the marauders had accumulated an estimated two hundred rifles.[15]

Despite these intimidations, York County's Ku Klux had not yet become a particularly sophisticated enterprise. Four days after the Faris raid, Klansman Ed McCaffrey gathered a half-dozen comrades to break into the office of Yorkville's probate judge and steal the ammunition for the militiamen's confiscated Remingtons. After a few drinks, the conspirators set to work. McCaffrey, a silversmith, had a duplicate key, but it broke off in the lock. Then they tried a wire jimmy, but that didn't work either, so they forced the door.

They found a box of cartridges, picked it up, left the office, and walked away. They stopped when they reached McCaffrey's house.

"What are you going to do with them?" someone asked.

McCaffrey didn't know. They talked it over and then dumped the cartridges in McCaffrey's well and went home. The next day townspeople found the empty box on the front porch of the Presbyterian Church. Sheriff Glenn then gathered up whatever guns and ammunition remained in town and shipped it all off to Columbia.[16]

The main culprit in this messy affair, it turned out, was S. B. Hall, the probate judge. By his own admission, Hall, a Union League member and nominal Republican, had joined the party simply to partake of the spoils of public office. He had given the office key to Sheriff Glenn, who passed it to his clerk F. C. Harris, who gave it to McCaffrey.[17]

Then on Monday night, February 20, a week after Faris's departure, between 260 and 275 armed North Carolinians rode into Yorkville. Barman Dave Russell recognized several of them and apparently counted them himself, but, ever cautious, he told investigators later he could not remember any names.

Russell said the new arrivals were worried that trouble was brewing in neighboring Chester County, thirty miles to the south, and might spill over into York. Russell—again cautiously—supposed the riders had come to Yorkville "expecting a fuss between whites and blacks." There was a lot of anxiety in town, even though the militiamen were disarmed.[18]

The visitors bivouacked in J. William Avery's apparel and dry goods store. Avery, a former major in the Confederate army and a transplanted North Carolinian, was probably Yorkville's richest man. He was also the chieftain of the York County Ku Klux Klan—something else Russell neglected to mention later (he may not have known).[19]

With no armed black militia members to molest, the North Carolinians departed the following day. On their way out of town, they surrounded Russell as he walked along the street. "We are your Ku Klux!" they chortled, and then they gave three cheers and rode off. It was all in fun.[20]

And then it wasn't. Sometime after the North Carolinians left, Russell heard that the Ku Klux were after Ned Rose and planned to attack him. Here Russell was quite specific in his testimony. He had been in a "roomful" of people—probably the saloon—and heard Avery and McCaffrey talking about it. Another bar patron asked Russell specific questions: Would Ned shoot back if he was attacked? How much ammunition did Ned have? Did Ned live in the hotel? Was Ned's family in town? Russell, in typical barkeep fashion, was quite likely noncommittal.[21]

The talk among the drinkers that day was that Klan members were going to attack the York County courthouse Saturday night, February 25.[22]

Sometime during the day on February 25, Springs Withers, an acquaintance of both Russell and Ned, came into the bar. Withers acknowledged that he was a Ku Klux but also said he was a Republican. Russell didn't believe that, but he believed it when Withers said "they" were coming for Ned that night. Russell would later testify: "[Withers told me that] his life depended on me if I divulged his secret, but he did it to save me and Ned Rose."[23]

Nothing happened Saturday, but Russell had heard enough. He told Ned Sunday morning to take the cash out of the treasury safe and put it in a bank. Ned demurred, but Russell insisted: at least give it to a trustworthy citizen. Russell knew Ned was holding $20,000 of York County's tax money.

Late Sunday Russell went to church, ate dinner, and returned to the bar. It was raining and a crowd was milling around outside with umbrellas, talking about how Rose for certain was going to be attacked that night. Inside the saloon Withers was back and had been drinking all day. There were also two women in the bar along with James Porter, the bartender.

Russell told Porter to untap his liquor barrels and "peg them up." "We'll stay awake tonight," he said. "When they come, unlock the door and let them right in, and we will both meet them at the door."

At that point Ned had finally become a believer. He was terrified. He wanted to stay the night with Russell.

No, Russell said: "Clear away; you had better not stay here."

"Do not worry." Ned slapped his chest: "The money is all right here."

But Russell was worried. He had nearly two thousand dollars invested in his saloon, he told Ned. "If they raid in here after you, they may destroy everything I have."

Late Sunday night between forty and fifty Klan members began gathering in a clearing about a mile outside of Yorkville. They were all disguised, wearing hoods, masks, and other paraphernalia. Most were from "the country," Klansman Bill Owens, a Yorkville carriage-maker, said later. Everybody was armed—with Henrys, stolen militia Remingtons, or their personal weapons. Owens had a shotgun. The leader that night was probably townsman John Tomlinson, a Yorkville pharmacist. Owens knew him by his Klan number and recognized his disguise: "In red flannel, with white stripes all over him."[24]

Most of the Klansman were "minors" like Owens and had no idea what was planned for the evening. The "aristocrats" soon told them. They were going to raid the county treasury and kill Ned Rose, "put him out of the way." There were objections. "[But] I could not say anything," Owens recalled. His loyalties to the Klan were already suspect, and if he had spoken up, he "would have been swung."[25]

The invaders moved into town about 12:30 a.m. Monday, stopped at the courthouse, regrouped briefly, and walked quietly toward Rose's Hotel.[26]

RUSSELL WAS asleep when Ned came into his bedroom and awakened him. A large band of armed men wearing hoods was approaching. Anticipating trouble, Russell already had boots on. As he lit a candle, he heard pounding on the saloon door.

"God damn you, give me that Rose!" someone yelled.

Russell hurried downstairs and saw Porter, alert and carrying a pistol. "Put it away," Russell said. Russell checked that his money drawer was locked, then went to the back door and opened it. Three men wearing disguises grabbed him and pulled him outside into the back lot. One of them stuck a pistol in his face. "Shut the door," the man said.

"Shut it yourself," Russell replied.

"That's Russell," another man said. "Damn you, go away. We don't want you."[27]

OUT ON THE front porch Bill Owens loitered with the rest of the Klan members waiting to get into the building. Beating on the door got no reaction. "Unlock the door!" someone yelled. Springs Withers, very drunk, yelled back from inside that he didn't have a key. Someone found a timber nearby, and the raiders used it as a battering ram, bursting into the saloon where Withers, Porter, and the two women awaited them.

The raiders surrounded Withers, demanding to know what he was doing there, even though the answer should have been obvious. "Let him go," interceded Owens, who knew Withers. "He's all right." Withers staggered out the door.[28]

They turned next to Porter. He was twenty-seven, a mechanic by trade, and bartending to help out Russell, a relative. "Where's Ned Rose?" they demanded. Porter didn't know. "You're a liar," they told him.

They set out to search the hotel with Porter in tow, pummeling him with fists and rifle butts and demanding that he tell them where Ned was hiding. They "broke in everywhere as they went along—all the doors," Porter said later. In the treasurer's office they upended shelves, "strewed about the papers and books and pulled out all the drawers." They helped themselves to some loose rifle ammunition and other "little articles," Porter later told congressional investigators. Then they went into the neighboring "cash room," found a "hammer or ax," and tried to get into the safe.

"Don't do that, it's not right," one man cautioned. The would-be safecracker ignored him, but the others stopped him and left the office to continue their search, though not before they broke into the "money drawer," where Ned apparently kept ready cash. Porter did not know whether any money was taken, but a two-dollar bill was later found lying on the floor.

Ned Rose appeared to have vanished, and Porter's captors eventually decided to leave. They walked him out the front door and pushed him along, firing their guns, cursing him, threatening to kill him, and repeatedly demanding that he give up Ned.[29] They turned up the main street until they reached the home of black preacher Tom Wright, suspected of having something to do with the arson attacks.[30] Wright was not at home, but they broke down the door and "proceeded to ransack the house from top to bottom," Porter said.

Then they moved on until they reached Hobbs & King's Carriage Factory. They took Porter around the back.

"We must give him a few, anyway," one of his captors said.

Nobody had a hickory switch, Porter said, apparently York County's weapon of choice. "So they went and got an old buggy and jerked a piece out of that about the dash, and struck me three or four licks with that by turns, until it broke all to pieces." Searching further, they found a caper bush, cut some switches from it, and beat him some more until those broke. Then they freed him. Go home, they said, never return to the saloon, and never have anything to do with Ned Rose.[31]

WHILE MUCH of this was happening, Russell waited in the backyard of his saloon. The Ku Klux sentries there ordered him three times to leave, threatening to shoot him if he didn't. Finally he wandered out of sight and waited until the last of the raiders departed around daybreak. He lost $1,100 worth of whiskey, wine, and cigars, along with blankets, a buggy harness, and other personal items.[32]

There was no sign of Ned on Monday, but on Tuesday he appeared on the street and in a newspaper interview recounted how he had heard noises outside the hotel after midnight Monday morning. It was only with "the greatest difficulty" that he escaped.[33] That he was bold enough to emerge from hiding only a day after the attack can probably be attributed to the arrival of a company of U.S. infantrymen only hours after the Klan raiders left the hotel. The raid had been scheduled for Saturday night, as Withers had reported, but the Ku Klux plotters delayed a day after they learned that the army company was supposed to arrive by train from Chester. The Klan sent railroad workers to pry two rails from the roadbed about two miles south of Yorkville, standing one of them in plain sight so the engineers on the troop train would see the "casualty" in time to stop before derailment. The soldiers spent Sunday in Chester and arrived in Yorkville Monday. It took about twenty minutes to repair the track.[34]

Later Tuesday Ned wrote a letter to his father in Columbia, saying, "The K.K.K. made a raid on me Saturday night, but I got out of the way." Besides getting the date wrong, Ned claimed the raiders had emptied his safe of $1,000 ("it may be less, I cannot tell yet") and "fired about 150 shots" at him as he was running. Ned lingered as a ward of Yorkville's new army garrison until soldiers eventually escorted him to Chester. There he caught a train to Columbia and was never seen again. York County's $20,000 disappeared along with him.[35]

The Rose's Hotel affair and the events that preceded it suggested that York County's Ku Klux Klan was at that point neither a serious nor a particularly competent organization, although it already knew how to murder blacks without mercy.

Despite the comic opera overtones, however, the raid's organizers—the Klan "aristocrats" of York County—quite likely gained many valuable insights from these events. They managed to muster dozens of unknowing foot soldiers for the purpose of committing illegal acts—even murder—and were able to carry out their missions without defections. The townspeople may not have abetted the Ku Klux, but they certainly condoned their activities and at least in part even regarded them as entertainment, as they stood in the rain in hopes of catching a glimpse of Ned Rose and his pursuers.

And the sloppiness of these endeavors undoubtedly encouraged York County's "responsible" white citizens to ignore the Klan or dismiss it as what attorney I. D. Witherspoon called "a set of irresponsible men." For Witherspoon, the Ku Klux "disorders" were the "result more of personal prejudice to the individual that has been punished or disturbed than from any regular organization."

Certainly a key factor in turning the Rose's Hotel attack into something of a mischievous lark was the fact that the target and collateral victims were white. But when the targets were black, participation was not a casual adventure undertaken after drinks at the local bar. Harriet Roundtree could attest to this, as could the family of purported arsonist Anderson Brown, murdered only a day before the Rose's Hotel raid.

CHAPTER ELEVEN

Running Out of Patience

In a special message on January 13, 1871, President Grant sent Congress an exhaustive set of reports on white terrorism compiled by U.S Army officers in the field. This was Grant's response to the Senate's request nearly a month earlier for information on Ku Klux Klan "outrages" in North Carolina.

Grant was interested in more than North Carolina, and his first batch of reports included dispatches, letters, and memoranda from all over the former Confederacy. He had accumulated or reviewed these over five years—as commanding general of the army, then secretary of war and finally as president. He submitted some complete reports—mostly summaries compiled by army field commanders and letters from political leaders—but the mass of information was "too voluminous" to send in its entirety, he wrote. Lawmakers were free to review the complete archive at the White House whenever they wished, and he offered to provide copies of individual documents when requested.[1]

Four days later Grant sent a second cache dealing exclusively with North Carolina. And two days after that, in the waning days of the Forty-First Congress, the Senate created a Select Committee to investigate the Ku Klux Klan. Republican senator John Scott of Pennsylvania (no relation to the South Carolina governor) was named chairman.

The committee's initial brief was to focus on North Carolina, but Grant's priorities had had an effect, and when the new Congress convened in early March, its scope was expanded to include the rest of the former "Insurrectionary" states, and it was made a joint committee with the House. What eventually resulted was a thirteen-volume report comprising thousands of pages of testimony collected from hundreds of witnesses, ranging from high-ranking Klan leaders and their foot soldiers to the Klan's victims, black and white, who had witnessed the murders of friends and family and who themselves had suffered beatings, torture, assaults, and robberies.

Grant's release of the reports marked an important moment, both for the president and for the Republican Congress. Once again there was no mistaking Grant's message. His cover communiqué, with its accompanying dispatches, described near anarchy throughout the South.

The unvarnished field officers' reports documented five years of outrage and condemned the inability—and the unwillingness—of local authorities to arrest or try the perpetrators. In letter after letter, Republican political leaders and terrified citizens—both black and white—pleaded for military intervention. South Carolina governor Scott as early as 1868 had asked the army to control upcountry counties "overrun with lawless mobs." Local law enforcement in York and Chester counties no longer existed, he said. In 1869 General Alfred Terry, then the military commander in Georgia, reported that many parts of that state had "no government."[2]

To suggest, as Secretary of State Fish and others did in early 1871, that army comrades and congressional Radicals were pushing a reluctant but malleable Grant toward an unnecessary confrontation with his former enemies was a serious misreading of the president.[3]

Nobody needed to push Grant. The reports contained no material from federal law enforcement—the attorney general, the U.S. Marshals, or the federal courts. Instead they constituted a conversation among General Grant, his army commanders, local officials, and citizens with direct, personal experience of both the war and its bloody terrorist aftermath. Butler, in Congress, and Terry, in the field, first in Georgia and now in Louisville, were uncompromising hardliners. And now Grant also had Akerman in the cabinet. But Grant, far from being their unwitting tool, predated all of them. He had fought the war and had been reading the dispatches for years. He knew what was happening, and he wanted Congress to do something about it.

IT IS NOT entirely clear why Grant chose this moment to step forward so personally and so sharply, but the failures of the First Enforcement Act and of his annual message to stop Klan terrorism or halt voter intimidation at southern ballot boxes undoubtedly stoked his displeasure. And only a week before submitting the first set of dispatches, the Klan had broken into the Union County jail for the second time to kidnap five black prisoners and murder two. This was probably Grant's tipping point.

The field reports—in their brutal detail and their categorical condemnation of southern law enforcement—made the case for stronger federal intervention. And at this juncture in postwar America, they also showed that the U.S. Army was the Ku Klux Klan's most implacable adversary, even though their numbers had dwindled after six years of mustering-out and deliberate shrinkage. Those who remained, however, and those who had since enlisted, were mostly committed professionals.[4]

The Klan knew this. J. W. Avery in Yorkville had no qualms about murdering black militiamen and running their white officers out of town, but he wanted nothing to do with the U.S. Army company poised to arrive from Chester the night the Klan went hunting for Ned Rose. So he stopped their train.

Democrats, both inside and outside Washington, scrambled for political purchase. Unable to deny the appalling events in Unionville or refute the evidence of hundreds, if not thousands, of similar crimes in Grant's stark reports, they initially tried to deflect it by accusing the Radicals of unfairly singling out the South.

Scott's "Outrage Committee" failed to realize "that a screw or two were loose in Northern Society which called for investigation," the *Petersburg (Va.) Courier* wrote. "We will venture to say that for one murder, robbery, seduction, burglary, arson, wife beating and wife desertion at the South, there are at least two fully as atrocious [in the North]."[5]

This was nonetheless a weak riposte. By releasing the army dispatches, Grant had once again tried to make his point. He was stubborn, and he was relentless. Sugarcoated excuses and what-abouts were not going to satisfy him.

CONGRESS'S FIRST response, its Joint Select Committee to Inquire into the Condition of Affairs in the Late Insurrectionary States, was not enough, and Akerman, Terry, Butler, and quite likely Grant himself were doing their best to gather more resources to suppress the Klan. Besides Butler and other well-credentialed Radicals, a key congressional figure was North Carolina senator John Pool, a close associate of select committee chairman Scott.

Pool was focused primarily on his home state, whose 1870 troubles were still fresh in the minds of his congressional associates, and he prevailed on the Scott committee to study North Carolina first. Akerman, Terry, Butler and increasingly Grant, however, were looking across the border. South Carolina was the new hot spot.[6]

At Pool's urging, California's Cornelius Cole, a leading Senate appropriator, contacted Akerman and offered him $50,000 to hire Secret Service agents to infiltrate the Klan and report back to federal authorities—spies. Akerman eagerly accepted. In a January 23 letter to Cole he lamented that Klan victims were "for the most part poor and ignorant men" with no knowledge of how to use the law to their advantage and no desire to step forward because of "well-grounded apprehension of danger to themselves." Independent eyes and ears could help gather the evidence to overcome these shortcomings.[7]

Akerman, hard-pressed to finance his ballooning Justice Department, welcomed any infusion of new money, but lack of usable intelligence, in his view, was not the crux of the Ku Klux dilemma. Evidence of the Klan's predations was readily available everywhere, not just in South Carolina. And in too many cases, like the Roundtree lynching, the evidence was blatant.

Using the evidence was another matter. "Whether it is possible, under our form of government, to redress such wrongs, when a large part of the resident population wink at them, I do not know," he wrote in a February 11 letter to one of his U.S. Attorneys. The federal government was not equipped to handle common crimes, he said. "[The Fourteenth Amendment has] great powers," he concluded, "[but] our present legislation is hardly sufficient."[8]

Akerman's tolerance for the intransigent South, as he had shown in Georgia a few months earlier, had all but disappeared, yet he had never wavered in his conviction that federal law—specifically the Fourteenth Amendment—was the tool that could eliminate the Klan. Greeted by congressional incredulity, if not derision, the first time he spoke of this in 1868, Akerman's views by early 1871 had become the benchmark for whatever initiative Reconstruction Republicans might choose. If the federal government wanted to stop terrorism in individual states, the Fourteenth Amendment and, in matters of voting rights, the Fifteenth Amendment were the only tools at hand.

The dilemma confronting Akerman and like-minded colleagues in Congress was how to give the amendments enough force to destroy the Klan and discourage its enablers among the antebellum elite and the southern populace as a whole. It was not enough to have civil rights on the books; the law needed to be effectively applied.

On paper, the First Enforcement Act was a formidable piece of legislation that gave the federal government the authority to prosecute and try violations of civil rights, but it was focused on elections and voting.

Crimes against women and children—attacked, beaten, raped, and traumatized during targeted raids against husbands, fathers, sons and brothers could not be prosecuted because women and children could not vote. Also, crimes like the murder of Tom Roundtree had no apparent motive related to elections beyond the fact that the victim was a black man who had voted Radical. The Enforcement Act, as written, apparently did not cover that.

Akerman believed that the Fourteenth Amendment, properly applied, could trump local law in any case involving not only a voter's civil rights but also the constitutional rights of any citizen—man, woman, or child. He had said this in so many words in 1868, and nothing had changed. The 1870 Enforcement Act, as he told his U.S. Attorney, was not doing the job. Something more powerful was needed.[9]

ON JANUARY 9, New York congressman John C. Churchill introduced legislation to amend—and strengthen—the Enforcement Act. It did not fix the most profound civil rights problem—the lack of any legal protections for blacks, but it did intend to improve their access to the polls by putting the administration of U.S. congressional and presidential elections directly under the supervision of the federal government. On its face the new legislation marked a dramatic subjugation of an individual state's right to oversee its own balloting. It was also a tacit assertion that traditional locally run elections were plagued by incompetence, corruption, and outright malice toward black citizens.

The act put federal elections under the watchful eye of independent "supervisors" who would police every aspect of the process from registration to recounts and report transgressions to local U.S. Attorneys. Violations would trigger intervention by the U.S. Marshals Service, or, in the case of serious unrest, by the U.S. Army.[10]

With overwhelming Republican majorities in both houses of Congress, passage of the new enforcement act was a foregone conclusion. Had there been any doubt about its need, the Ku Klux dispelled it February 12 by invading Unionville for the third time, kidnapping ten more black prisoners and murdering eight of them. Three days later the House opened floor debate on Churchill's bill.[11]

It was a perfect opportunity for Radicals to make an emphatic statement about civil rights and the need for the federal justice system to shield the nation's new black citizens from harm. On the House floor Churchill, an upstate New York Republican, began in this vein by noting in his introductory statement that "for some years past grave doubts have prevailed in different portions of this country as to whether the declared results of elections have truly expressed the will of the people."[12]

But immediately the debate veered off in a different direction. Democrat Fernando Wood, a fellow New Yorker, interceded to inquire if "doubt" had arisen about the "integrity and honesty" of elections in New York. This was a contrived question, a well-worn congressional ploy designed to elicit an "I'm so glad you asked" response.[13] Wood, a former New York City mayor and renowned Tammany chieftain, had broken ranks with the current Tammany leader, the notorious Boss Tweed. The prearranged question gave Churchill the opportunity to ignore Klan terrorism in favor of denouncing Tammany corruption, apparently his real purpose. Wood, his downstate accomplice, undoubtedly enjoyed Churchill's ensuing rant, not only because Churchill was smearing his rival but also because Wood could keep his own hands clean by keeping his mouth shut.

A couple of Republicans attempted to steer the debate toward the predations of the Klan but were unsuccessful. There may have been white terrorism in the South, but Republicans, at least according to Churchill, were equally distressed about irregularities—Democratic irregularities—in Manhattan and the Bronx.[14]

There appeared to be few Republicans on the floor, but the Democrats showed up in force to decry what Wisconsin's Charles A. Eldredge succinctly described as a "hideous" bill designed solely to usurp states' rights: "It will bind the several states hand-and-foot and deliver them over to the federal government, subjugated and helpless, the mere tools and slaves of Congress."[15]

This was a predictable argument, but Democrats took it further, charging that the new act's real intention was to give the federal government and its Republican majority license to interfere in elections anywhere it wished. Indiana's Michael Kerr condemned the new law as "shamelessly partisan, defiantly neglectful of the rights and liberties of the people, made to elect Republicans and to defeat the election of Democrats."[16]

This was not an empty criticism. The Republicans were intent on preserving and expanding their congressional majorities. The new act had the potential to send thousands of federal agents and soldiers to "monitor" ballot boxes. Churchill's comments had come only a few months after Akerman, Terry, and Butler had observed elections in New York—with armed soldiers standing in the wings. Democrats suggested—forcefully—that the new law would give Republicans the option to send their own thugs—masquerading as "supervisors"—to any precinct that needed a helping hand. Ultimately, however, the bill, as predicted, passed the House easily by a vote of 144–64.[17]

The Senate debate took place in a marathon session that finished near midnight on February 25. The formidable Roscoe Conkling, another New Yorker and one of the state's most powerful politicians, shepherded the legislation safely through a mind-numbing series of Democratic amendments, each of which was soundly defeated. Although twenty-five senators—twenty-two of them Republican—did not bother to show up, the bill passed, 39–10.[18]

The Second Enforcement Act, at least in theory, had strengthened the ability of the federal government to interpose itself between black voters and southern whites intent on denying them access to the polls, either through intimidation or outright terrorism. But House debate on the measure had unfolded as an exercise in local New York politics, and Senate Republicans greeted the bill's arrival with a collective yawn.

The obvious conclusion to be drawn was that the passage of time had dimmed national outrage over the treatment of southern blacks and weakened civil rights as a political weapon for Republicans. Elections in North Carolina and Georgia the previous year signaled that the presence of black voters could not sway the southern electorate to any significant degree.

Also, the new Georgia delegation was seated in the waning days of the Forty-First Congress, making the country whole again for the first time in a decade, soothing another lingering focus of national turmoil.

Finally, outrages like the Unionville lynchings no longer appeared to stoke the passions of northern voters. Blacks were losing whatever constituency they had. Little wonder that the white South did not take the new law seriously.

THE KU KLUX KLAN, however, had not been forgotten as the Forty-First Congress drew to a close. On February 13, two days before Churchill's bill went to the floor, Congressman Clinton L. Cobb, a Republican back-bencher, introduced legislation somewhat ambiguously entitled "A Bill to Protect Loyal and Peaceable Citizens of the United States in the Full Enjoyment of Their Rights, Persons, Liberty, and Property," aimed at enabling citizens to make claims against those who had wronged them.[19]

The bill's language and intent, however, were anything but ambiguous. "Large numbers of lawless and evil-disposed persons, especially in the States lately in rebellion . . . have formed secret organizations," the preamble said, "some of which are commonly known as the Ku-Klux Klan, having for their main object to defeat certain classes of citizens of the United States in the liberty, rights, and equal protection of the laws guaranteed by the Constitution."

These groups, the preamble continued, "by the use of disguises . . . by perjury, violence, threats, overawing the local authorities, and otherwise," were able to ignore state law enforcement. "It has been thus rendered imperative on Congress to enforce all constitutional guarantees."[20]

Cobb's bill named the eleven states of the Confederacy and Kentucky as the biggest offenders. It envisioned a new federal infrastructure of "commissioners," not unlike Churchill's supervisors but with one crucial difference. Instead of policing elections, the commissioners were tasked with policing "any outrage" done to any "person or citizen" within their jurisdiction and arresting the offender or offenders. The bill defined "outrage" as any act "with intent to hinder, impair or deprive such citizen of "any right guaranteed under the Constitution of the United States."

The commissioners could release suspects on their own recognizance or on bond or hold them under a concept known by the Latin term "mittimus" until the arrival of a federal circuit or district judge to hear the case.

The rest of the proposal attempted to address every reported abuse of local law enforcement in the Klan-infested states. Witnesses who failed to appear in court would be fined. Marshals or deputies who did not enforce the law or who allowed prisoners to escape would be fined. Commissioners could deputize a posse or call on local militias or detachments of U.S. Army if they needed help.

Anyone found in disguise on a public highway would be charged with a misdemeanor during the day or a felony at night—all accomplices equally guilty. Everyone involved in a break-in, a shooting, or an assault would be guilty of a felony. Taking weapons out of someone's house was a felony. Joining a secret organization and taking an oath was a felony. Anyone who concealed an offender or otherwise hindered law enforcement would be guilty of the same crime as the offender. Arson, mayhem, and murder were capital crimes—anyone involved would be jailed without bail.

Victims of these outrages could sue for damages in federal court against a single offender or against all "the inhabitants" of their city or county. If the single offender could not pay damages, he could petition the rest of the community to share the burden. If the federal courts decided that local courts had not dealt properly with this provision, damages would be doubled.

Misdemeanor convictions carried fines of $500 to $1,000 and prison terms of six months to one year. Felonies carried fines of $5,000 to $10,000 and prison terms of five to twenty years at hard labor. An offender convicted of a capital crime would be "hanged by the neck until . . . dead." Last, federal courts and commissioners would have final jurisdiction over everything the proposed law had described.[21]

Cobb's bill had everything the Second Enforcement Act lacked. It lumped violations of constitutional rights together with violations of civil rights and punished perpetrators with draconian penalties. It was deliberately aimed at the South, deliberately aimed at the Klan, and deliberately intended to implicate and punish anyone who abetted or looked the other way when an offense was committed.

THE BILL was no spur-of-the-moment exercise, even though Cobb, with no legislative credentials to speak of, may have seemed an odd vehicle to advance it. This fooled no one. Cobb was from North Carolina, undoubtedly acting as a surrogate for Senator Pool. And for Ben Butler. Although the bill may have borne Cobb's name, the ruthlessness of its language suggested that Butler, champion of the Radicals and scourge of the Democrats, was its principle author. Democrats treated it as such and immediately tried to have the bill killed when it arrived on the House floor. They only got fifty-six votes. Then they tried to amend the bill and send it to the Judiciary Committee instead of the Reconstruction Committee, as Cobb had requested.

That was when Butler stood up: "I hope that amendment will not be agreed to," he said simply. It was not, winning fifty-six votes just like the earlier proposal. Butler was chairman of the Reconstruction Committee.[22]

The third shadow figure involved in the Cobb bill was almost certainly Amos T. Akerman. The Cobb proposal allowed federal authorities to prosecute any offender accused of depriving "any person or citizen" of any constitutional right. This implied that the Fourteenth Amendment applied not only to political rights but also to the Bill of Rights, one of Akerman's key beliefs.

The Cobb proposal specifically cited violations of the Second Amendment (the right to bear arms) and the Fourth Amendment (unlawful search and seizure) as actionable by federal officers. Crimes that accompanied those violations—assaults, shootings, arson, murder—were also actionable. Night riders would no longer get away with beating up mothers and children.[23]

The new proposal embodied virtually everything Akerman had espoused for years. Pass the right law, he had said in 1868, and the federal government would have "power over the legislation of any state." The Cobb bill was that law.

Its future was uncertain. With less than three weeks left in the Forty-First Congress, Butler had to get the bill out of committee, bring it to the floor, insert it into the Speaker's "regular order," have it debated, and have it voted on. And for a good part of the time it would be competing for attention with Churchill's Second Enforcement Act—introduced in early January.

On February 16, the day after House passage of the Churchill bill, and again on February 20, Butler returned to the House floor to describe the Reconstruction Committee's progress. His belligerence was untempered. He reminded his colleagues of the Union County massacres, dismissed complaints about using the federal government to override state law enforcement, and told those who complained that the bill ignored civil rights violations in the North that they were welcome to extend its reach throughout the country—if they could find actionable cases. He did not care.[24]

With only two weeks left in the Forty-First Congress, Butler had no chance to get the bill to the House floor, but he was too skilled a legislator to spend his days wasting time. By submitting the Reconstruction Committee report only days after passage of Churchill's legislation, he signaled that he and his fellow Radicals regarded the Second Enforcement Act with little enthusiasm. And by describing, yet again, the pervasive terrorism that plagued the South, he was asking his colleagues how they expected the Second Enforcement Act to cope with it.

Butler also quite likely had decided that he needed to speak to the not-quite-converted in his own party. Moderate Republicans had misgivings about federal interference in state affairs and did not want to punish the South endlessly. Butler undoubtedly wanted to know: would the Cobb bill have the votes?

On February 28, Butler brought the bill—at this point dubbed the "Butler Bill"—to the House floor for the fourth and last time. He submitted a resolution calling on his colleagues to "suspend the rules" of regular order and vote on the bill without debate.

Passing legislation in the House "under suspension" required two-thirds of those present to approve the resolution. Ordinarily members used this procedure as a convenient way to bring nonpartisan and mostly noncontroversial legislation to the floor and pass it quickly. The Cobb bill had neither of these traits, but Republicans had a big enough majority to potentially pass Butler's resolution without a single Democratic vote. Butler just missed: the vote was 128 to 66, with 46 members not voting, two votes short of two-thirds.[25]

In the crush of legislation before Congress adjourned, a failed resolution earned little more than a passing glance. The Memphis *Public Ledger*, however, noted the "infamous character of Butler" and heralded the "defeat in his attempt to pass the bill to establish a criminal code for, and organize a reign of terror in the South." His Radical associates, the *Ledger* continued, "at last" were "alarmed."[26]

The *Ledger* should have been more cautious, for Butler's resolution was not necessarily a last-ditch effort to trump the Second Enforcement Act. Butler had said nothing against the Churchill bill and had voted for it. Instead his last-minute effort could be seen as a clever maneuver to take the temperature of his caucus.

He may have lost the vote, but he could read the tally in the *Congressional Globe* and now knew by name who among his Republican colleagues had opposed him and who among them had not voted at all. He knew how many he needed to convince and who they were, and the Forty-Second Congress was about to begin. As the *Alexandria* (Va.) *Gazette* said bluntly on March 2: "General Butler will make another effort."[27]

AT THE WHITE HOUSE, President Grant indirectly weighed in on these events at a cabinet meeting February 24, the day before passage of the Second Enforcement Act. The new legislation was not the congressional commitment he wanted, and he was not happy. He read a report from South Carolina chief constable John Hubbard describing assaults, whippings, and killings across the state, including the murders of trial judges in Union, Spartanburg, and Laurens

Counties. “He expressed a determination to bring a regiment of cavalry and perhaps one of infantry from Texas,” Secretary of State Hamilton Fish wrote in his diary.

The Texas troops, Fish said, paraphrasing or quoting Grant, were currently protecting from Indians a white population “who annually murder more Union men, merely because they are Union men, than the 602 Indians could kill of them.”[28]

Grant was running out of patience.

AMOS T. AKERMAN.
Attorney general of the United States, 1870–1872. Akerman was the first federal lawman to use federal courts and the Fourteenth Amendment to protect the civil rights of black citizens and destroy the Ku Klux Klan. Library of Congress.

AMOS T. AKERMAN AND
MARTHA ("MATTY") REBECCA GALLOWAY.
Photographs probably taken shortly after their marriage in 1864. Image courtesy Mark Akerman.

ULYSSES S. GRANT.

President of the United States in 1869–77. Grant was a strong supporter of reconstruction and enemy of the Ku Klux Klan during his first term. Library of Congress.

ROSE'S HOTEL, CONGRESS STREET, YORKVILLE.
Headquarters of the York County militia, county offices, and Major Merrill's U.S. Army detachment during Reconstruction. Image courtesy of Culture & Heritage Museums, York County, South Carolina.

INDEPENDENCE DAY, YORKVILLE, 1867.
Blacks and whites gather in Congress Street, the year before ratification of the Fourteenth Amendment, the election of Ulysses S. Grant, and the appearance of the Ku Klux Klan in York County. Image courtesy of Culture & Heritage Museums, York County, South Carolina.

NATHAN BEDFORD FORREST.
A onetime slave trader, Forrest was a Confederate cavalry leader who became the first and only "Grand Wizard" of the Ku Klux Klan. Library of Congress.

ANNOUNCEMENT.
The first meeting of the York County Ku Klux Klan, *Yorkville* (S.C.) *Enquirer*, April 2, 1868. Newspapers.com.

ALL persons having claims against the estate of JAMES H. DAVIS, deceased, are hereby notified to present them, properly attested, within the time prescribed by law. Those indebted to the estate will please make immediate payment to the undersigned.

W. B. HILL, Administrator.

April 2 14 3t*

K. K. K.

DEAD-MAN'S HOLLOW, SOUTHERN DIV.
Midnight, March 30.

General Order, No. 1.

REMEMBER the hour appointed by our Most Excellent Grand Captain-General. The dismal hour draws nigh for the meeting of our mystic Circle. The Shrouded-Knight will come with pick and spade; the Grand Chaplain will come with the ritual of the dead. The grave yawneth, the lightnings flash athwart the heavens, the thunders roll, but the Past Grand Knight of the Sepulcher will recoil not.

By order of the Great Grand Centaur.

SULEYMAN, *G. G. S.*

April 2 14 1t*

PLANTERS! PLEASE NOTICE

THAT I am sole Agent for the Districts of Chester and Union, and am authorized to sell in York District, the following Implements and Agricultural Machinery. D. Greisers'

J. RUFUS BRATTON.

Ku Klux Klan leader, York County, S.C. Bratton led the raid that ended in the lynching of black militiaman Jim Williams in March 1871, then fled to Canada to avoid federal prosecution. Image courtesy of Culture & Heritage Museums, York County, South Carolina.

CONGRESSMAN BENJAMIN BUTLER. Radical Republican leader, 1867–1875, and confidant of President Grant, Butler was a key figure in passing the Ku Klux Klan Act of 1871, the tool used by U.S. Marshals and the army to arrest and imprison Ku Klux Klansmen throughout the South. Library of Congress.

JOSEPH HAYNE RAINEY. The first black member of the House of Representatives, born into slavery in Charleston, South Carolina. His father purchased his own and his family's freedom in the 1840s. His eloquence on the floor of the House marked a key moment in the debate and eventual passage of the 1871 Ku Klux Klan Act. Library of Congress.

GENERAL ALFRED TERRY.
U.S. Army district commander, 1869–1872. An uncompromising advocate of reconstruction, Terry was a close collaborator in taking down the Ku Klux Klan in South Carolina. Library of Congress.

DAVID T. CORBIN.
U.S. Attorney for South Carolina and chief prosecutor during the Ku Klux Klan trials in Columbia, 1871–73. Library of Congress.

U.S. ARMY MAJOR LEWIS MERRILL.
York County, S.C., 1871–1873. An officer of dragoons with extensive experience in guerrilla warfare, Merrill worked closely with Attorney General Akerman to arrest and bring to trial members of the Ku Klux Klan. Library of Congress.

"THE UNION AS IT WAS," BY THOMAS NAST.

From the antebellum "White Man's Government" to the postwar "Lost Cause" to "Worse than Slavery," cartoonist Nast shows how black citizens by the 1870s had fallen prey to the Ku Klux Klan. Library of Congress.

CHAPTER TWELVE

Lynching

MARCH 5, 1871

York County storekeeper Elias Ramsay had no disguise and no idea what was supposed to happen. He had no love for the Ku Klux, but the Broad Rivers Klan had forced him to join the previous week after giving him a beating for selling liquor to the blacks. Broad Rivers leader Chambers Brown had simply told him to show up at the Pinckney Crossing below Yorkville at 9:00 p.m. Dr. Bratton and the night riders from Yorkville would meet him there.[1]

Ramsay complied. He was a minor, not an aristocrat, like Brown or Dr. Bratton, so he did what he was told.[2] Ramsay had ridden overland, riding east with the four Shearer brothers and a few other friends. He was a Confederate veteran like many of the horsemen. None of his immediate companions knew any more than he did about why they were there.

When they reached Pinckney Crossing, they stopped to wait. They had acquired more riders along the way, most of them hooded and gowned, and at the crossing Ramsay could count perhaps twenty men.

An hour later they spotted Bratton's people approaching. It was about nine o'clock. Right on time.

"Who goes there?" shouted Hugh Kell.

"Friends," came the reply.

"Friends to whom?" Kell asked.

"To our country!"

The combined riders now numbered well over sixty. Their immediate task was to initiate the Shearers into the Klan.

Harvey Gunning read the oath, calling on the Shearers to swear upon "the Holy Evangelists of Almighty God . . . on the side of justice, humanity and constitutional liberty as bequeathed to us in the purity by our forefathers." It rejected the principles of the "Radical party" and stipulated that members of the Klan had to be at least eighteen years old (many were not) and white: "No person of color shall be admitted to this order."

Much of the rest of it was solemn mumbo jumbo, quickly forgotten. The only part that lingered in the minds of every Ku Klux was the last sentence of

Article 3: "Any member divulging, or causing to be divulged, any of the foregoing obligation, shall meet the fearful penalty and traitor's doom, which is Death! Death! Death!"[3]

The combined force remounted and headed south about four miles, stopping once to water the horses, then stopping again a few hundred yards farther on to consult with two men who rode out to meet them. The riders asked who had "the guns." It was a "black militia man," one of the men said. Ramsay now thought he knew the plan—disarm the blacks who still had their militia rifles.[4]

The column reached Joe Moore's mill around midnight. Ramsay, waiting with the others, saw a big black man being led out of a small house—a prisoner. Some of the riders beat on him a bit, then talked to him about how he was supposed to take them somewhere. One of the questioners was probably Dr. Bratton. Then they blindfolded the prisoner and forced him to climb up behind one of the riders.

The column headed southeast in single file, and turned toward a schoolhouse after sixty yards or so. The horse carrying the blindfolded man was falling behind. "This goddamn nigger is too heavy!" the blindfolded man's rider shouted.

"Put him down," Number Six hollered back. The rider stopped next to a fence. Gadsden Steel, the blindfolded man, took off his mask and stepped down.

"You go home and go to bed," the rider said. "And if you are not there when we come along, we will kill you the next time we call on you. Run, god damn you, run."[5]

Ramsay saw all this and had no idea what it meant. The big black fellow was sitting behind someone, then he wasn't. If he was supposed to be the guide to wherever they were going, why was he blindfolded? And if he was a prisoner, why was he set free?

They rode on, and soon the column of horsemen stretched for one hundred yards. The riders were losing contact with one another as they moved slowly along a potholed road muddied by late-winter rains. Ramsay heard people talking four or five horses ahead of him.

"We're going to hang Jim Williams," someone said.

Ramsay didn't recognize the voice. And who was Jim Williams?[6]

UP AHEAD, a detail led by Milus Smith Carroll, one of Bratton's trusted subordinates, was sent ahead to search for guns in Brattonsville and its surroundings. The core of Brattonsville, in southern York County about four miles east of McConnellsville, was the cotton plantation of John S. Bratton Jr., a brother of

J. Rufus and resident custodian of the vast family property. Brattonsville had been settled by William Bratton, a Scots-Irish immigrant, a century earlier. Since then it had grown into a massive enterprise—six thousand acres of land and almost 140 slaves during its antebellum heyday. It was smaller now and less profitable but still the biggest employer in the area. Jim Williams was a sharecropper on the Bratton plantation, and a great number of other militiamen lived there, either farming shares or working as day laborers.[7]

Carroll and his men rousted Andy Tims, one of Williams's lieutenants, but there were no other militiamen around. "They all had business away from home that night," Carroll wrote later. This was either a deliberately misleading statement or surprisingly naïve. Pretty much every able-bodied black man in southern York County had been routinely laying out at night precisely so they could avoid the Ku Klux. When Carroll knocked on Henry Haynes's door, his wife cracked it open and handed him a rifle and a bayonet: "Here, take it for Gawd's sake." Tims had already roused Haynes, and both men were on their way to warn Williams that the Klan was coming.[8]

BACK ON the potholed road, Ramsay and the rest of the riders turned into the woods and traveled "some distance," maybe as much as three miles. They stopped in a piney thicket on the side of a hill. Ramsay didn't hear any orders, so he dismounted and sat down.

Hugh Kell told Ramsay to watch his mule. Then Kell and several others—ten or twelve in all—moved off into the forest on foot. The Shearer brothers and Robert Hayes Mitchell stayed with Ramsay to handle the mounts and mind the extra equipment, probably because none of them had disguises. John Caldwell was also left behind—he said he was sick. Ramsay knew the Shearers from his own neighborhood and knew Mitchell from Confederate army days. Ramsay knew nothing about Caldwell, except that he lived in Yorkville.[9]

JIM WILLIAMS and his wife Rose heard the Klan coming through the woods around 2:00 a.m. Williams had enough time to dash outside and duck beneath the house. Rose was waiting for the gunmen when they came through the front door. She thought there were maybe nine or ten men, but she wasn't sure. "I was scared because I thought they was going to kill me, too," she said later.

The invaders called out for Jim Williams. Rose Williams couldn't recognize any of them because of the disguises, and she didn't know any of their voices. Her husband wasn't home, she said. Dr. Bratton, leading the group, "reflected for a moment," recalled Carroll, one of the assault group, then told his men to tear up the plank floorboards. They found Williams easily.[10]

The Klan told Williams to hand over the militia rifles he was supposed to have—ten or fifteen, they thought. "He gave them the guns, there were but two in the house, and then they asked him for the others, and cussed," Rose Williams said. Jim Williams said he never had any of the militia's guns. They pushed him out the door, Rose continued, "then they came in the house after me, and said there were some guns hid. I told them there was not."

They took her word for it, but after they left she heard her husband making "a fuss," Rose Williams said. She ran to the door "to go down and beg them not to hurt him." The raiders stopped her. "[They] told me not to go out there." She cracked open the door to peek out and saw Williams and his captors walking into the trees.[11]

"We hauled him out and placed a rope around his neck, and started back toward our horses," Carroll recalled. "We had got back about halfway . . . when someone spied a large tree with limbs running out, ten or twelve feet from the ground, and suggested that that was the place to finish the job."

Bob Caldwell stepped forward, grabbed the rope end, and climbed up the tree. The rest of the group forced Williams to follow him. Caldwell tied the rope to the limb, then told Williams to jump off. He refused, so Caldwell pushed him. Dangling by his neck, Williams grabbed the branch with his hands and held on. Caldwell pulled a knife and hacked at Williams's fingers, finally forcing him to let go.

"He died cursing, pleading and praying, all in one breath," Carroll said.[12]

RAMSAY AND his companions heard nothing for maybe twenty or thirty minutes. Then a single sob "like a woman in distress." Then nothing again. Ten minutes later the raiders returned. No one spoke. They reclaimed their horses and rode in silence out of the woods and into an open field, where they paused. Ramsay went up to James Neil and asked him what had happened.

"Some men are powerful hard-hearted," Neil said. Then he turned away.[13]

John Caldwell wasn't satisfied with silence. Unlike the other horse handlers—country people only recently initiated into the Klan—he was a townsman who had been a Ku Klux since 1868, his membership sponsored by York County chieftain J. W. Avery himself. Caldwell rode up to Bratton and asked him if he had found Jim Williams. Yes, Bratton said, he had.

"Where is he?" Caldwell asked.

"He is in Hell, I expect."

"You didn't kill him?"

"We hung him," Bratton said.

"Doctor Bratton, you ought not to have done that."[14]

Bratton pulled out his watch: "We have no time to spare," he said. "We have to call on one or two more."

The riders emerged from the fields surrounding the Williams house about 3:00 a.m. They were on the main road leading from Yorkville south to McConnellsville and Chester. They stopped at a black man's house—Elias Ramsay couldn't recall whose it was—to search for guns, then the column divided. One group turned right, the other turned left.

Ramsay went left. His column made more stops, collecting guns. Eventually he noticed they were approaching the Bratton plantation. They stopped in a field above the big white house known as the Homestead. Somebody was handing out cheese and crackers, ham and whiskey. Ramsay didn't see the ham or the cheese, but he got some crackers and whiskey. Then someone else called out for people to raise their guns. It looked like they had collected a dozen or maybe more.

But it wasn't over. Will Johnson called for a squad to walk down to the Homestead. Ramsay was tapped. They stood outside and hollered for John S. Bratton, who appeared in his underwear. Why were all the men—black men—working on his place carrying guns, someone asked.

He "could not help it," Bratton replied. His farmhands were militia, and "the state armed them," he said. He was not a Radical, he added. He had nothing to do with it.

It was another strange moment. The Klan knew enough to hunt down and murder the leader of the McConnellsville militia, but they apparently had no idea that so many of the black laborers and sharecroppers on Bratton's property might be Williams's fellow soldiers. Ramsay may also have wondered why Bratton bothered to explain himself. If you were J. Rufus Bratton's brother, you were nigh untouchable in York County.

Ramsay mounted up with the other squad members and headed north toward Yorkville until they met up with the rest of the column. They made six more stops that Ramsay counted, always looking for guns. It was after daylight when he left the column at Philadelphia Church and went home.[15]

ANDY TIMS, Henry Haynes, and Andrew Bratton (no relation to the white Brattons) knew they were too late. When they reached the Williams cabin, they found Rose sitting in the front doorway. Jim wasn't there, and Rose didn't know where he was or what had happened to him.

Tims and his two companions searched around but found nothing. They needed to alert the rest of the militia. They started back, heading west toward Bratton's plantation on foot. The Klan had already left when they arrived, probably a good thing for all concerned. Now that it was daylight the Brattonsville militiamen were back at the plantation. They were not happy that their captain was missing.

Tims and his comrades—around seventy men in all—set out to track the Ku Klux. It was not hard. The riders had left countless horse tracks and had dropped bayonets, bandoliers, and other assorted paraphernalia along the way. Tims marked the militia's progress by the white mens' houses they passed: "Robert Lindsay's . . . Ed Crawford's . . . Mr. Mendenhall's." They checked Mendenhall, thinking the column might have stopped there, but the stables were locked. They continued until they reached "Mr. Garwin's." There they found a mule, "muddy and sweating" and wearing a saddle.

"We then went into the Blackjacks," Tims said later, a stretch of muddy wetlands, meadows, and upland rough country about thirteen miles southeast of Yorkville. They started toward Williams's house, but before long they saw horse tracks in the meadow where the Klan had regrouped hours earlier.

About one hundred yards farther along, they found where the raiders had left their horses. "We saw Williams hanging on a tree—he was dead," Tims said. The Klan had hung a sign around the dead man's shoulders before they left: "Jim Williams on his big muster."

"His toes just touching the pine leaves," Tims recalled.

It was a bit after nine o'clock on Monday morning, March 6.[16]

JIM WILLIAMS was left hanging in the tree all day, with seventy armed and enraged militiamen surrounding him. Tims left for Yorkville to find the county coroner, who did not arrive until the next morning. The militiamen were still there, and they were still enraged.

The coroner eventually got them to disperse, then had Williams cut down and taken to Brattonsville for inquest. They placed the body in the general store run by Napoleon Bratton, another of J. Rufus's brothers—just down the road from the Homestead.

What happened over the next two days was hard to ascertain. March 7, the day after the lynching, apparently elapsed without disturbance, with Williams's body remaining in the general store. Rumors, however, abounded among the whites.

On March 8 "the negroes threatened to kill that neighborhood out that night," local merchant Thomas M. Graham said later, although he had no first-hand knowledge of such threats having been made. But the whites of Brattonsville certainly believed they were in danger, for that afternoon they sent a letter to Yorkville asking Major Avery for help. "They were fearful they were going to be killed that night; and that all the women and children had gathered in one house that night and were very much alarmed," Graham said. He described Avery as a "merchant." Avery, with more than a dozen armed men, arrived in Brattonsville that evening to find everything quiet.[17]

Reports that an angry crowd had at one point gathered across the road from the general store could not be confirmed, but tensions remained. Later in the evening Andy Tims, apparently fearing a confrontation, approached Avery and told him where to find some militia guns. Avery and his men returned these to Yorkville March 9. The *Charleston Daily News*, drawing liberally from a report in the Columbia *Daily Phoenix*, on March 15 wrote that Jim Williams had been killed by "parties unknown."[18]

THE KU KLUX had won a decisive battle in York County. Jim Williams, captain of the McConnellsville militia and a respected leader of York's black citizens, had been lynched, and Ku Klux Klan members were not held accountable or even named. Most of Williams's militiamen were finally disarmed, and the county was now at the mercy of the night riders.

But it was not over. The Williams murder occurred in the middle of five days of chaotic racial violence in neighboring Chester County. This benefited Bratton and his Klansmen at first, overshadowing the Williams raid. But the Chester riots also focused federal attention on the upcountry Klan—and on York County—as never before.

First, Klan terrorism had engulfed York's neighbor counties in North Carolina. Then came prolonged violence in Spartanburg to the west and the New Year's outrages in Union County to the southwest. And now Chester, due south. York, terribly violent in its own right, was ready to become the next focus of the Ku Klux upheaval.

THERE WAS no dispute about the basic events in Chester County. The shooting began Saturday night March 4 when white gunmen opened fire on black militiamen near the home of white militia Captain Jim Wilkes at Carmel Hill, a rough-and-tumble area in cotton country west of Chester, the county seat. One horse—ridden by a white man—was killed.[19]

A second attack on the same house Sunday night was also driven off. On Monday, the same day Jim Williams was lynched, Wilkes marched his men into Chester and made camp on the edge of town. The militiamen told town officials they wanted protection from Klan attacks. Benjamin Gore, a black sergeant in the Wilkes company, later told congressional investigators that the Klan wanted to murder Wilkes. Town officials asked the militiamen to withdraw, disperse, and go home. Some did, but a large number went into the nearby woods and, unseen by the Chester townspeople, made a new encampment.[20]

Late Monday night as many as two dozen white gunmen—imports from other counties who had responded to a call for help from local Chester officials—arrived at the Chester train station, perched on a rise about four hundred yards from town.[21]

A few hours later new arrivals from Rock Hill, in York County, and a detachment of Chester's own militia company got into an argument, which quickly escalated into a two-hour gun battle. No one was killed, but the Nicholson Hotel next to the railroad depot, where most of the imports were staying, took a beating, rudely awakening owner John Nicholson and his wife, their bedroom showered with fallen plaster.[22]

Tuesday morning, while Jim Williams's body lay in Brattonsville's general store, Wilkes and the Carmel Hill militia returned to Chester. Part of the company bivouacked near the train station where the Chester company had camped. The rest of Wilkes's men gathered in the yard of Major John C. Reister, the regimental militia commander based in town. Reister—white—was widely distrusted and disliked by Chester's white establishment.[23]

At that point, large numbers of whites from all over the upcountry were gathering in Chester. A pitched battle seemed inevitable, but the county sheriff and militia leaders negotiated a truce. The Wilkes militiamen were to march five miles out of town uncontested, disband, and go home. The militiamen agreed, but, once clear, most decided to stay together during the night to protect themselves and then return to Carmel Hill the next day.[24]

Wednesday morning another shootout between the retreating militiamen and white gunmen began at New Hope Church, on the road from Chester to Carmel Hill. The militiamen were forted up in the church, but the whites circled the building and drove them out, then chased them throughout the day as they dispersed in all directions. Eighteen militiamen made it to York County and were taken into protective custody.[25]

ONLY MUCH later did two of the participants in the Chester events—Gore, the militia sergeant, and Alexander Wylie, the white physician who had inadvertently set off the rock-throwing melee at the Chester political rally the previous summer—describe in detail what had occurred over the five days.

Gore said the Saturday and Sunday attacks were carried out by costumed Ku Klux. The dead horse had been ridden by one of the attackers. The Wilkes company went to Chester, Gore said, to get protection for Wilkes and to talk with Reister. The depot shootout Tuesday, he said, was instigated by late-arriving gunmen from York County challenging the Chester militiamen. Gore said the militia refused to disband, on either Monday or Tuesday, because they were scared that if they split up they would be pursued and massacred by the hundreds of Klansmen that they saw streaming into Chester undisguised.

That was what happened at New Hope Church, Gore said. When the Wilkes company began its trek home Wednesday morning, the militiamen spotted white gunmen coming "wholesale from every direction." Wilkes ordered his men to take cover behind rocks "by the roadside." The whites opened fire "right away," Gore added. The militiamen returned fire but, badly outnumbered, had to abandon the church after eight to ten minutes. Gore did not know how many men were killed in all that day but named five, including two men "tied together and run pretty near to death until their tongues hung out," who then were "shot on Turkey Creek Bridge."[26]

WYLIE, WHO described himself as a "unionist" and an occasional Republican voter, recounted the white version of events. The weekend shootouts began when the Wilkes militiamen shot the horse from ambush. And while the Wilkes militiamen claimed that they came to Chester only for protection, they spent a lot of their time patrolling the roads going in and out of town and threatening passersby.

The depot fight began when a new arrival from York County asked a Chester militiaman "to see his gun," Wylie said. The militiaman backed away, causing his rifle accidently to discharge, and both sides immediately opened fire.

The white townspeople saw the militia's two refusals to disband as betrayals of trust. They were convinced that the only reason the blacks had come to Chester was to threaten and maybe burn the town—and because they needed more ammunition.

Wylie said the Wednesday confrontation began when Wilkes's militiamen, hiding behind large boulders in the New Hope churchyard, ambushed a group of white horsemen as they passed by. One white man was badly wounded in the leg, but the riders quickly regrouped and surrounded the church. The militiamen briefly withstood the assault, retreated in good order to a nearby hill for a couple of volleys, then broke and dispersed.

Wylie described the pursuit as "self-defense." He said he thought "three or four" people were killed in the shootout. He and Gore agreed there might have been more killed than the five named by Gore, and both agreed that one of the dead was a noncombatant—a young teenager. All of the dead were black.[27]

Reporting on the events in Chester was as muddled as the events themselves. Both the Columbia *Daily Phoenix* and the *Charleston Daily News* carried short dispatches March 7, describing the weekend confrontations in Carmel Hill. These appeared to be based on a telegraphed message or letter received in Columbia by Lucius Wimbush, the black state senator from Chester who Wylie had tried to restrain at the August political rally.[28]

On March 10 several papers across the country ran a New York–datelined story based on a dispatch from Columbia. Almost everything in it was wrong. It cited the lynching of Jim Williams "at Carmel Hill" and the subsequent beatings "of a number of his men" as the events that precipitated the Chester violence. Williams's men "retaliated," and since then the fighting had been "continuous." Williams, the story continued, "was defeated Monday night, and his people fled to the army camp at Yorkville."[29]

THESE EARLY reports contributed little to the printed record, but they underscored the sense of dread and near panic among both blacks and whites in South Carolina's upcountry. Each side was terrified of the other.

For the blacks, the Ku Klux Klan had become a constant menace. They could hide in the woods or under the house, but they could be hung from an oak tree if the Ku Klux found them. If they refused to give up their weapons, like Jim Williams or the Wilkes company, the Klan and their white allies would kill them or pursue them without cease.

Whites were unable or unwilling to see the effect a Jim Williams lynching could have on their black neighbors, but five days of uninterrupted confrontation and frequent violence got their attention, tapping into their fears of a race war.

Wilkes's militia came into Chester not "for protection," white townspeople thought, but instead to get ammunition. Much later investigators asked Wylie, an apparently measured, careful man, what he thought Wilkes was planning when he moved his men into the woods outside of town.

"My opinion was that Jim Wilkes's intention was to make an assault, and take the provisions in the town, and massacre the whites and commence massacring from the cradle up."[30]

ON MARCH 9 Governor Scott sent a telegram to Washington asking President Grant to send more troops to South Carolina. "An actual state of war exists in York and Chester counties . . . fighting for four days by Ku Klux from North Carolina and this state . . . I will be compelled to declare martial law."[31]

And in a statewide proclamation issued the same day, Scott lamented the "serious disturbances" and blamed the violence on "armed and disguised men . . . arrayed in open opposition to the civil authorities" and who attacked "unoffending citizens" who had "been taken from their dwellings and deliberately murdered in cold blood."

He called on the county sheriffs to restore order and authorized them to deputize as many men as they needed and to call for help from the army if necessary. He concluded, "[If this fails,] I shall feel it my imperative duty to suspend immediately the writ of *habeas corpus* and proclaim martial law [in Chester and York]."[32]

The York County Ku Klux did not hesitate to take advantage of these events. A Klan "Extract of Minutes," published in the March 9 edition of the *Yorkville Enquirer*, denounced "bogus organizations" that were making threats and maligning them and their "august name." "*Stop it!*" they demanded. "Honest, decent, well-behaved" people, "whether white or black," would be protected by the organization, the manifesto continued mildly. "But we intend that the intelligent, honest *white* people (the tax payers) of this county *shall rule it!* We can no longer put up with negro rule, black bayonets, and a miserably degraded and thievish set of law-makers . . . the scum of the earth, the scrapings of creation. We are pledged to stop it; we are determined to end it, even if we are 'forced by force, to use force.'"[33]

Whites at this juncture apparently had little doubt who was in charge in York County. On page three of the same edition of the *Enquirer*, about a half dozen "Special Notices" appeared, all of them intended to mollify the Klan. "I believe that our government should be a white man's government, and I am no longer a radical. J. W. A. Harkness." This was followed by "A Card. This is to notify my friends and the public that I renounce my allegiance to the Radical party and to the Loyal League, from this time forward and forever. H. J. Hullender."[34]

The Ku Klux had taken control of York County.

CHAPTER THIRTEEN

"Unlawful Combinations"

President Grant called the Forty-Second U.S. Congress into session Saturday, March 4, 1871, the day after the Forty-First Congress adjourned. Senate Republicans had four fewer seats than they had had the previous day but still enjoyed a massive 55–16 majority. In the House, however, the Republicans' hundred-seat majority had been cut by half. They were still comfortably in control with 144 seats to the Democrats' 93, but the days when the Radicals could effortlessly roll the opposition were over.

This became apparent almost immediately. Speculation about the early session and its agenda focused on whether Grant would make a new effort to annex the Dominican Republic and what the new Congress intended to do about the Ku Klux Klan.

The Dominican question was a Senate matter. Two-thirds of the upper house had to ratify the annexation treaty, and, to have any chance, Grant needed to marginalize Senator Charles Sumner, the incumbent Foreign Relations Committee chairman and annexation's most outspoken opponent. That he would try to do so had been known for "some days," the *New York Evening Post* reported March 7. If that did not work, the *Post* continued, "other committee members" would be swapped out, "so the Administration would have a majority" for the treaty—at least in committee.[1]

The Ku Klux Klan offered a much different set of difficulties. The Senate could be relied on to endorse whatever the administration wanted, but the House was a mystery. Insiders in Washington assumed that the "Butler bill"—giving the federal government jurisdiction over virtually all crimes that violated any citizen's civil or constitutional rights—was Grant's legislative vehicle of choice.

But the landscape was different now. Congressman Butler may have had enough votes in the previous Congress, but moderate Republicans were growing tired of supporting hardline measures that failed to produce the desired results. "[Republicans] seem to be fearfully demoralized at the sight of so many Democrats," the *New York Herald* wrote on March 8. "They have no hope that a Ku Klux bill can be passed." "Bold Ben Butler" was ready to give it a try, though, the paper said.[2]

The underlying theme in both of these endeavors was the growing dissonance within the Republican Party. Sumner had served for years as Senate Foreign Relations Committee chairman and had impeccable credentials as a front-line advocate for black rights. Whether this legacy would be enough to offset his opposition to Grant's Dominican ambitions and keep his gavel was unclear, but it was an intramural dispute.

The same was true in the House. Democrats' augmented presence gave them a somewhat louder voice in the Klan debate, but the success of whatever legislation or other strategy Butler and his allies pushed forward would ultimately depend on bringing Republicans into line and holding them there. Butler was a canny legislator, and he had a staunch ally in the cabinet in Attorney General Akerman, but, as in the Dominican question, Grant's strength—or lack of strength—would likely be the decider.

GRANT MADE no public statement about his intentions regarding Santo Domingo, but, in welcoming the new congressional leadership at the White House on March 6, he mentioned his concerns about the Klan.[3] Three days later, in a private letter to House Speaker James G. Blaine, he spelled out exactly what he wanted.

Many senators and House members had asked him what legislation interested him in the new Congress, Grant wrote, and he wanted to make sure that he was not "wrongly interpreted." There was "a deplorable state of affairs" in parts of the South that "demanded the immediate attention of Congress," he continued.

He would support specific legislation to protect "life and property" in the former Confederacy when local authorities failed to enforce the law, he told Blaine. "But if committees are to be appointed and general legislation entered upon, then I fear the object . . . will be lost." Although Grant insisted he was not writing to Blaine "to dictate what Congress should do," that was exactly what he was doing. He did not want Congress to study the problem and issue reports, and he was not interested in another vague, glancing blow like the Second Enforcement Act. He wanted a law with teeth.[4]

His other priority appeared to be resolved a day later when, after six hours of hand-wringing debate, the Senate ousted Sumner from the Foreign Relations Committee by a vote of thirty-three to nine. Twenty-five senators, however, were either "absent" or otherwise indisposed and did not vote.[5]

As far as annexing the Dominican Republic, however, Grant had lost interest. The day after Sumner's ouster he wrote to former New Jersey senator Alexander Cattell, a well-connected Washingtonian, to tell him that rumors of a Dominican revival were "profoundly untrue." Cattell could be counted on to spread this news quickly and widely.[6]

Grant had made his point. He had induced the Senate to shove Sumner aside, mostly out of personal spite but also simply to demonstrate that he could do it. A majority of senators may have wanted Sumner to stay in his old job, but ducking the vote was as far as they were willing to go. Now Grant was ready for the Ku Klux Klan.

THE KLAN was as active as ever, and the federal government did not seem able to do anything about it. In Kentucky the state post office superintendent shut down mail service along the Louisville–Frankfort–Lexington corridor because of continued threats made against the black postman, attacked and beaten on the mail train in February. Tampering with the mails was a federal crime.[7]

On March 10 Senator Scott released a damning report from the "Outrage Committee" detailing North Carolina's Klan atrocities. At the Justice Department, Attorney General Akerman planned to use the report as evidence in putting the North Carolina Klan on trial in federal court.[8]

The *Richmond* (Va.) *Dispatch* made clear that, as far as the South was concerned, the Scott investigation had settled nothing. It gave the committee's majority findings two succinct—and accurate—sentences: "The Ku Klux does exist, is composed of members of the Democratic or Conservative Party, has a political purpose, and has sought to carry it out by murders, whippings, intimidation and violence against its opponents. It binds its members to carry out decrees of crime and protects them from conviction."

The minority report, however, enjoyed several hundred words of analysis, describing the committee's "grossly and wildly exaggerated" allegations and blaming North Carolina's festering discontent on the "despotic powers of the Congress of the United States."[9]

NORTH CAROLINA at this point, however, was becoming a side show. The main event had moved to the South Carolina upcountry, and both Grant and Akerman were paying increasing attention. The same day that Grant wrote to Blaine, he received South Carolina governor Scott's telegram warning him of an "actual state of war" and importuning him to send more troops. First reports of the Chester riots were arriving, and General Terry in Louisville, eager to help but short of manpower, had undoubtedly briefed the War Department—and therefore Grant—on the plight of the fleeing Chester militiamen in York County.

Grant had ordered several companies of cavalry sent to South Carolina, and on March 11 Akerman wrote Governor Scott to tell him help was on the way. Scott, however, needed to make a formal request, Akerman told him, to indicate that the Klan disturbances were so serious that the legislature could not be convened.[10] This stipulation—enshrined under the Insurrection Act of 1807—would enable Grant to deploy the U.S. Army within the United States. Akerman, ever the legalist, was waiting for new legislation that would extend the Insurrection Act mandate to include civil rights violations, but until such a law was passed—if it was passed—the Insurrection Act was all he had.

Five days later, South Carolina attorney general Daniel H. Chamberlain sent a brief reply by mail to Akerman on behalf of Scott notifying him that the governor had received Akerman's admonition. Scott's formal request soon arrived and appeared to satisfy Akerman.[11]

FOR REPUBLICANS grappling for a strategy to use against the Ku Klux, these events could serve as fuel for either side in the debate. Radicals contended that unabated white terrorism, with its newest upsurge in South Carolina, meant that a stronger federal hand was needed. Moderates could point to the turmoil as proof that the stronger hand—military occupation and the two existing Enforcement Acts—had not worked, and that it was time for reconciliation.

Blacks only figured peripherally, if at all, in these arguments. Radicals wanted to punish white intransigence. Moderates wanted everyone to accept that white intransigence could not be quelled and move on to other business.

The constituency for black civil rights was dwindling. Lincoln, Thaddeus Stevens, and other lions of abolition had died, and much of the blacks' remaining support six years after the surrender came from army officers—Grant, Butler, and Terry among them—whose soldiers had shed blood to end slavery, and from radicalized civilians like Akerman, whose efforts to support black rights had been met with denunciation and threats.

The task for the House Radicals was to figure out what Klan legislation, if any, the rest of their party was willing to support amid this confusion, and to overcome the obstacles that were sure to appear.

The central House figure in the new Congress, as in the previous one, was Butler. He was the new chairman of the Judiciary Committee, his bill had all the publicity, and he was the House member who had the ear of President Grant.

There was, however, a new voice. Ohio's Samuel A. Shellabarger, a key House Radical immediately after the war, had been newly reelected after a two-year absence, and on March 7 introduced a bare-bones Klan bill authorizing the president to call out federal troops to suppress "combinations" too powerful for local authorities to control, and to step in when local authorities failed or refused to enforce the law. The president did not need a state's permission to act. Shellabarger's bill was a marker—simple yet draconian—a signal that he had entered the debate.[12]

If the debate were to take place. With no legislation having yet reached the floor, the House spent most of March 7 fending off attempts—mostly by Democrats—simply to adjourn until December: doom the possibility of new Ku Klux legislation by having no Congress available to write it.

Butler rose to make sure that members understood: "There is a state of things in the Southern part of this country which calls for legislation." But Speaker Blaine cut him off as he started to read a letter from Governor Scott. The topic of the day was procedural matters, Blaine explained, and Butler was not allowed to talk about something else.[13]

On the evening of March 14, at a meeting of the Republican caucus, however, Butler won its endorsement for Klan legislation, apparently a combination of his Forty-First Congress bill with inserts from Shellabarger.

The next day Butler began the debate by giving notice that he intended to introduce the new bill, but objections showered down from members contending that nobody was available to study the proposal since standing committee members had not been named, and complaining that the bill could not be printed until the following day. Butler once again stood down.[14]

Then John A. Peters of Maine offered a resolution to appoint a select committee of thirteen members to investigate "the late insurrectionary states" and report their findings to the House in December. This was the proposal to expand the Ku Klux investigation beyond North Carolina.[15]

How, Butler demanded in reply, could this measure be brought forward while his own had to "lay over" for a day? The Speaker ruled that since the Peters resolution was neither a bill nor a joint Senate-House resolution, it could be debated.

Members were not fooled by the parliamentary fog. The resolution could be an escape hatch for moderates who did not want new Klan legislation. Form a committee, write a report, and maybe everybody forgets the whole mess—exactly what Grant had warned against in his letter to Blaine. But Blaine apparently had his own ideas. Members had little doubt that Peters—from the same state as Blaine—was doing the Speaker's bidding. Was Blaine trying to make his own preference known or simply offering members an alternative to the Butler juggernaut?

Butler had no doubt. "I am opposed to this resolution, and I trust all who attended the caucus last night will oppose it, as they are honor bound to do."[16] The caucus had committed itself to Klan legislation, the chair had shunted him aside a second time for trying to talk about it, and then the Speaker had put his stamp of approval on a measure that would give members an excuse to do nothing.

Butler got nowhere, Blaine called the vote, and the resolution won overwhelmingly, 126 to 64. Butler rose to make sure that everyone understood him: "Under no circumstances do I desire to be placed on that committee."[17]

Blaine ignored that too. After disposing of some procedural matters, he announced the select committee members. He named Butler first and Shellabarger second.[18]

It was a significant setback for Butler, but the battle was nowhere near over. On March 16, the following day, Butler rose again. He had examined the resolution vote, he said, and complained of a "trick that was played" on Republicans who voted for the bill because they thought it was the only legislative action they were going to get.[19]

Colleagues were not pleased. What exactly did he mean by "trick"? The word festered nastily on the House floor.

Butler did not back off. The resolution had been "sprung upon" the House. Many Republicans decided to join Democrats in a "seeming majority to a measure illusory in its character and useless in action," he said.[20]

Then Peters stepped forward. He acknowledged that Blaine ("my friend") had written the resolution. Peters had shopped it to colleagues, including Butler. There was "no trick; no concealment," he said.[21]

At that point an incensed Blaine handed the gavel to a colleague and arose. Did Butler deny him "the right to have drawn that resolution?"

"I have made no assertion on that subject one way or the other," Butler replied.

"Did I not take it to the gentleman and read it to him?" Blaine asked.

"Yes, sir."

"Did I not show him the manuscript?"

"Yes, sir."

Butler, rare for him, appeared momentarily speechless. Blaine was taking the House bully to the woodshed, and the House bully was flustered.

And Blaine was not finished. He noted that this was the first time in two Congresses that he had given up the gavel. He believed in the tradition that the Speaker, as "Speaker of the whole House," remain silent except on matters of procedure. "But I denounce and despise the insolence of the gentleman from Massachusetts."[22]

This remark won an ovation.

Butler, however, had had time to regroup. He rose as a "humble member." He did not "seek a quarrel or unfriendliness" with the Speaker of the House, and he acknowledged that Blaine had asked him to chair the select committee.

But, he recalled, quoting himself in his conversation with Blaine: "I'll be damned if I will. I will have nothing to do with it."[23] This riposte was greeted with considerable laughter, and the tension began to dissipate.

It was time to hear from other members—Republican members. One can only wonder at Democrats' amusement as they watched the majority publicly display its intraparty rancor.

Shellabarger had no quarrel with the investigation and had voted for it, but Republicans ought to understand that the select committee's efforts ranked second to legislation, he said. "In a time of what is called, with a strange charity, 'profound peace,'" he said, "[murder] stalks, almost unchallenged, through half of the republic."[24]

Henry L. Dawes, chair of the tax-writing Ways and Means Committee, was not interested in more laws. "Abundant legislation" already passed had left the South "in this hour worse than ever." Would it not be better, to "try some other mode," he asked, "even if it be but an experiment?"[25]

Michigan's Austin Blair described how the Butler bill, with Shellabarger's views added to it, had become too unwieldy. He did not think proper legislation could be put together in a short session. What was needed in the South, he said, was "not law, but the execution of the law," he said. The existing proposals were sloppy and not good enough.[26]

Finally, Ohio's Job Stevenson, named to the select committee, arose. He opposed the committee but wanted to serve on it because he saw "little apparent hope" of "more vigorous action" in a Congress "enervated and disorganized" as "the Republican part of this House" was by "faction and quarrel, jealousy, spite and hate."[27]

It is difficult to ascertain how much of this exchange was real and how much was political theater, ginned up by Butler and his allies—if they were allies—to bring Klan legislation to the front of the House agenda.

There can be little doubt that Blaine had been truly enraged, but this may have been caused more by his surprise at Butler's remarkable tactlessness than by any deep policy disagreement. It is hard to believe that Blaine wrote the committee resolution in deliberate opposition to Grant's wishes without an ulterior motive.

That motive might well have been to give the House Radicals the ammunition to bring forward a Ku Klux bill by putting it in opposition to the committee resolution. Butler, either with or without Blaine's encouragement, seized the opportunity by creating a false choice—either the select committee or legislation. As Shellabarger had noted, there was no obvious reason why members could not have both.

This certainly would have been Akerman's choice in the Justice Department. Legislation was his priority, but he was pleased to have the North Carolina report for the cases he hoped to bring in that state, and now Senator Scott and his colleagues, with House participation, wanted to expand their investigation to the rest of the former Confederacy. All to the good.

The only reason there could not be a committee *and* legislation was because Butler had said so. But by setting up his false choice he was able not only to warn against a whitewash but also to bring Klan legislation to the front of the agenda.

EVEN AS these skirmishes ignited in the House, Senators Henry Wilson of Massachusetts and Frederick T. Frelinghuysen of New Jersey weighed in with their own Klan legislation. These two Senate bills, like Shellabarger's, were markers, but they showed that the Senate was ready to push anything the House might pass. Without referring to the Ku Klux Klan by name, both senators emphasized the need to prosecute Klan outrages as constitutional rights violations in federal court, and both gave the president authority to use federal troops to suppress Klan activities.

Wilson's bill "for the protection of persons resident within the United States against unlawful combinations and conspiracies," emphasized that common crimes committed in conjunction with rights violations would be treated as felonies.[28] Frelinghuysen titled his legislation "A Bill Intended More Fully to Enforce the Fourteenth Amendment to the Constitution of the United States." His approach was weakened, however, by a lingering focus on the rights of the accused—as if he doubted the courts' ability to hold sway.[29]

Several days later, Kansas senator Samuel Pomeroy introduced a third bill giving the president the authority to reimpose military rule over unruly southern states. This proposal had no chance but included one eye-catching feature: it authorized the president "at his discretion, to suspend the writ of *habeas corpus*," giving federal authorities the ability to hold prisoners indefinitely without charging them.[30]

ON MARCH 20, Butler introduced the "Butler bill"—virtually the same legislation he had tried to pass in the previous Congress. At twenty pages, it was at least four times the size of any of the other bills then under consideration. Even this early in the debate, it looked awkward and unwieldy.[31]

Also on March 20, Shellabarger presented a new bill. It was only two pages long and just as sketchy as his first effort. He focused on "conspiracy" to commit "any act against the person, property or rights of another [person]" as the key factor in determining which offenses would be targeted by federal authorities. Then he tied himself in rhetorical knots trying to bring common crimes into the federal orbit.[32]

Both of these measures were badly flawed. The Butler legislation was a fully formed last gasp for an expiring Congress. Carving up a now outdated, twenty-page document was not a convenient starting point. The Shellabarger bill was a skeleton. It wanted to put Ku Klux crimes in federal court but seemed to have no idea how to do so except by congressional fiat.

Still, Shellabarger's slapdash opener seemed to be a better fit for the new Congress. It could be easily mulled over, amended, and filled in. It could be fixed. Butler's proposal was too bulky.

AKERMAN MUST have had a mixed reaction to these first steps. The emphasis on federal prosecution was encouraging and consistent with his own view that court proceedings were preferable to martial law. It was also apparent that Congress now wished to use the Fourteenth Amendment not only to bring civil rights conspiracies into federal court but also to prosecute the common crimes associated with them.

Not so encouraging, however, was the new laws' reliance on elaborate descriptions of the offenses that could be tried as rights violations. Shellabarger, in particular, had neither mentioned the Fourteenth Amendment nor acknowledged that the prosecution of Klan crimes had a constitutional rationale.

Akerman, by contrast, believed the Fourteenth Amendment spoke for itself and had said so before Congress in 1868. Under the Fourteenth Amendment, Ku Klux raids and any offenses that accompanied them were federal civil and constitutional rights violations, almost by definition. No more needed to be said.

Congress now needed a push, and on March 23 Grant sent both houses a special message to make his position known and to signal the direction he wanted Congress to take. He warned: "A condition of affairs now exists in some states of the Union rendering life and property insecure."

He cited Kentucky's mail delivery attacks and the Senate's North Carolina report. "That the power to correct these evils is beyond the control of state authorities I do not doubt," he continued. "That the power of the Executive of the United States acting within the limits of existing laws, is sufficient for present emergencies is not clear. Therefore, I urgently recommend such legislation as in the judgment of Congress shall effectually secure life, liberty and property, and the enforcement of law in all parts of the United States."

The legislation would expire at the end of Congress's next session, June 1, 1872, he continued. "There is no other subject upon which I would recommend legislation during the present Congress."[33]

This was the Blaine letter rewritten—almost certainly with Akerman's help—for congressional consumption. The timing was elegant, the goal unequivocal, and the effect immediate. No sooner had the clerk finished reading the message on the House floor than Shellabarger proposed the creation of a special committee to decide what the House should do about it. Before the end of the day Blaine had appointed a nine-man panel with Shellabarger as chairman and Butler as vice chair.[34] The committee was the mechanism tasked with writing a new enforcement act.

Grant had more to say. Akerman drafted a presidential proclamation released March 24. It condemned violence by "combinations of armed men, unauthorized by law," for disrupting "the peace and safety of the citizens of the State of South Carolina." So intense were these disturbances that local authorities were "unequal to the task of protecting life and property and securing public order."

"I Ulysses S. Grant, President of the United States, do hereby command the persons composing the unlawful combinations aforesaid to disperse and retire peaceably to their respective abodes within twenty days from this date."[35]

This was Grant now ready to invoke the Insurrection Act. Troops were on their way to South Carolina, he had received Governor Scott's formal request for help, and, with Akerman's encouragement, he had met with a three-member South Carolina delegation led by Attorney General Chamberlain.[36]

The proclamation was yet another escalation in Grant's prolonged campaign to get the South to heed his warnings. But it was also intended to prod Congress into action. Without the requisite legal authority, his deadlines could mean nothing.

The proclamation got the intended publicity, but reactions were dramatically different, depending on geography—and politics.

There were two versions of Ulysses S. Grant, the *New York Times* wrote. "Every man in the country knows that when President GRANT commands an insurgent and unlawful combination of men to disperse, it is equivalent to the command of Gen. GRANT." It was time to capture "a couple dozen of these white cotton cowards," the *Times* continued, put them on trial in federal court, and get convictions.[37]

In Yorkville, the *Enquirer* dismissed the need for intervention: "No sane person in South Carolina is ready to believe [that] there is any reason or just cause [for it]." Instead, the *Enquirer* wrote, Grant intended to use the Ku Klux Klan as an excuse to reimpose "military rule" in southern states so the Republicans could stay in power.[38]

The *Enquirer* had missed the point. It did not matter why Grant threatened to intervene. His proclamation in effect told South Carolina that he wanted the Ku Klux Klan to be gone, and he gave the state twenty days to make it happen. The crippled Confederate states could complain all they wanted, but there was nothing they could do about it.

CHAPTER FOURTEEN

Bratton's "Peace"

MARCH 26, 1871

York County's white establishment was worried. Upcountry South Carolina had become an object of national disgust, and the Jim Williams lynching was the latest in a seemingly endless chain of Ku Klux outrages. York County now found itself in the center of this maelstrom.

Terrorism was bad for business, and the county fathers needed to control the damage. They sought a measured approach, but this effort foundered initially when an anonymous Yorkville "Observer" in a March 12 letter to the *Daily Phoenix* in Columbia attempted to explain how the county had come to such a pass.

Anderson Brown, killed by the Ku Klux, was an arsonist who burned the "property of inoffensive citizens," Observer wrote. There was "well-defined suspicion" that Ned Rose was "the head of the incendiaries" who set the fires. Jim Williams, hung by "persons in disguise," was "one of those armed with *breech-loading guns, bayonets and ball cartridges* in a time of profound peace." Williams "is also reported as the head of a company of *colored Ku Klux*—at least, he had made such admissions."[1]

York County needed a calming presence, and it was J. Rufus Bratton who stepped forward. On March 13 a "meeting of the citizens" took place at the York County courthouse, and Dr. Bratton was "called to the chair," the *Yorkville Enquirer* reported. It was well known, Bratton told the gathering, that the peace of the community was "seriously disturbed by repeated acts of lawlessness and violence." These needed to stop. Bratton had an assistant read a series of resolutions, including a pledge "to use every exertion to insure the protection of life, liberty and property, and to restore law and order."

Bratton asked all the townships in the county to hold meetings—of both black and white citizens—to talk about peace and report their findings to the *Enquirer*. Each town should appoint delegates to a subsequent "general meeting" to be held in Yorkville. The resolutions were unanimously adopted.[2]

Bratton's fellow Klan members must have marveled at their leader's brass. Less than a week after lynching Jim Williams, he had effortlessly reassumed his role as one of York County's "best people." There is no record of why he decided to intervene, but it probably had much to do with the expected arrival of the U.S. Army. As a self-appointed community leader, Bratton might have a chance to ingratiate himself with these new residents and take their measure. As a Klan chieftain he would have no chance at all.

Nonetheless, York had a steep climb if it wanted to recover its respectability. The South Carolina upcountry had become the latest symbol of everything that was wrong in the postwar South: the intolerance, the ignorance, the lawlessness, and the murderous terrorism. On March 8, only two days after the Jim Williams murder, a short news item reprinted all over the country recounted how Republican legislators in Columbia had ordered armed pickets to guard the highway "because of well-grounded fears of a Ku Klux raid upon their body."[3]

The same day, the *South Kansas Tribune* reported Governor Scott's intention to send a delegation to Washington to ask Grant to put a stop to Klan outrages: "These infamous whelps have become so bold and defiant in their deviltry, that order-loving men of any party are not safe to remain."[4] The next day Scott wired Grant about "an actual state of war" in the upcountry, and two days after that Grant ordered U.S. cavalry companies to be sent to York, Union, and Spartanburg Counties.

"There is no sufficiently armed and equipped militia to give the needed protection [against] trained soldiers who held the United States at bay for four years," the *New-York Tribune* reported. Scott had told Grant that the Ku Klux Klan, "formerly thought to be a mere political ghoul," was a "thoroughly equipped" and well-armed organization—a "terrible fact."[5]

And Ku Klux arrogance only grew. In Unionville a communiqué dated March 9 from "K.K.K. headquarters, Ninth Division," was posted around town. "Ignorance is the curse of God," the Klan wrote, beginning with a quote from Shakespeare's *Henry VI, Part 2*. "For this reason, we are determined that the members of the legislature, the school commissioner and the county commissioners of Union shall no longer officiate." These officials had fifteen days to resign. "[Otherwise] retributive justice will as surely be used as night follows day."[6] A little over a week later, The *Charleston Daily News* reported that the county sheriff and school commissioner were already gone.[7]

Lacking the careful cunning of Dr. Bratton in York, white resentment elsewhere chose defiance over conciliation, winning support not only at home but also in parts of the Democratic North, eager to cast aspersions on Republican failures in the outcast states. Columbia's *Daily Phoenix* gleefully reprinted a story from the New York *Sun*, laying the blame for the violence on the corruption and incompetence of the Scott government. The South Carolina Klan was "an undeniable fact," the *Sun* correspondent wrote. "There are indications he [the Klansman] intends throwing off the mask which has hitherto hidden his identity, and coming out boldly to throw over the present regime, and endeavor to save his state from the talons of the vultures that are sucking her life's blood."[8]

LESS THAN two weeks after the Jim Williams murder, South Carolina attorney general Daniel Chamberlain arrived in Washington to plead Scott's case, telling reporters that in some parts of South Carolina "civil authorities are unable, by reason of the Ku Klux organization, to enforce the laws."[9]

On March 21 Chamberlain met with Grant and spoke of the need for troops. Grant assured him that besides the cavalry, there were an additional twelve companies of infantry on the way—a total of around fourteen hundred men.[10]

The president told Chamberlain that he thought there was now more disorder in South Carolina than in any other southern state. "If two regiments will not do it, ten shall be sent there, and kept there, if necessary, as long as this administration is in power," Grant said.[11]

The *New-York Tribune*, reporting on the meeting, cited "prominent South Carolina Republicans"—undoubtedly the Chamberlain delegation—suggesting that the new troop presence would either cause a "collision" with the Klan or cause "the outrages [to] cease." The *Tribune*'s sources predicted peace, because the Klan had never confronted the army. "But if the Ku Klux have become so strong and bold as to plunge the state into civil war," the *Tribune* continued, "the quicker it comes, they say, the better it will be for the people."[12]

Shortly after the meeting Attorney General Akerman drafted Grant's March 24 proclamation condemning "unlawful combinations" in South Carolina and giving them twenty days to disperse. Denunciations echoed across the state. On March 24, a "Columbia Letter" appeared in the New York *Sun* denying that Chamberlain during his Washington visit had said "that it was impossible to execute a civil process in South Carolina" or that only the "strong arm" of the federal government "could prevent the murdering of negroes." Instead, the letter said, Chamberlain told Grant that troops were needed to "preserve the peace and prevent the depredations of the negroes, as well as the atrocities of the Ku Klux." Chamberlain, who had returned to Columbia the previous day, had apparently discerned that South Carolina's white establishment was displeased.[13]

Bratton, for one, took Chamberlain—and Grant—seriously. On Saturday, March 25, delegates chosen during meetings in the various York County townships gathered at the county courthouse in Yorkville for their peace meetings. Blacks in one room, whites in another.

According to the *Enquirer*, almost no one showed up for either session. The whites convened, then adjourned, deciding to meet again the following week.

They appointed a committee to prepare an agenda. Bratton was one of the committee members.

The *Enquirer* found the blacks' meeting somewhat more consequential. Chairman Charles Bessier, a county constable, reportedly "confessed that he, as well as many others, had been deceived by the Radical Party; that whereas he was once blind, he can now see his error, and was willing to use all his efforts to secure the object of the meeting." Peace, one supposes.

Then they too adjourned until the following week. In a particularly cynical move, Bratton served as secretary for the blacks' meeting, since few freedpeople could write. The meetings had accomplished nothing, but Bratton had established his bona fides as a peace-seeking mediator.[14]

The next day the army arrived.

MAJOR LEWIS MERRILL led three companies of the U.S. Seventh Cavalry into South Carolina's upcountry. One went to Spartanburg County, one went to Union, and the third came to Yorkville, along with Merrill, who set up his headquarters in Rose's Hotel. Each company had about ninety men.

Merrill was an 1855 West Point graduate and an experienced professional. He was thirty-six, a tall, well set-up man who had spent his entire career as a commander of dragoons—light cavalry armed with infantry rifles as well as swords. He wore wire-rimmed glasses that, according to one reporter, "gave him the head, face and spectacles of a German professor, [despite] the frame of an athlete."

He seemed an apt challenger for the Ku Klux Klan. He had chased guerrillas in "Bleeding Kansas" before the war, been wounded in Arkansas in 1863, hunted outlaw irregulars in Missouri as the war wound down, and for most of the postwar period had fought Indians on the western plains, based in Fort Laramie under the command of General George Armstrong Custer.[15]

He came from a family of lawyers and had served on several courts martial, earning a reputation not only for his abilities as an evidence-gatherer and for his expertise in military justice, but also for his familiarity with civilian law. These traits may have made him attractive to General Terry, his new boss and a lawyer himself by profession. But maybe not, for Merrill carried some unpleasant baggage.

In 1869 he had prosecuted a quartermaster accused of fraud who was eventually acquitted. During the trial, it came to light that Merrill and the defendant had spent time gambling outside the courtroom—probably not the wisest thing Merrill had ever done. A year later Merrill wrote the quartermaster demanding $200 that he said he was owed. The quartermaster claimed he had already paid the debt, which he said was illegitimate in the first place. He demanded that Merrill pay back the $200, accusing him of messing up the prosecution during the trial in return for a bribe. Merrill in turn demanded a court martial to clear his name, but none was held because no offense had been formally alleged.

Unfortunately for Merrill, Custer found out about the dispute and had the quartermaster write up his side of the story, then asked Merrill to respond. Merrill, in Yorkville by that time, wrote a nasty letter chastising Custer for failing to support his demand for a court martial. Custer sent the case history to Terry, who passed it to the War Department where the whole matter was dropped. Whether some of this happened before Merrill left Fort Laramie is not known, but it is certainly possible that Merrill's new posting may have had nothing to do with his equestrian skills or his keen legal mind. Custer may simply have wanted to get rid of him.[16]

Merrill was in Kansas when he got his orders. On his way to South Carolina he stopped at Terry's headquarters in Louisville to get briefed on his new job. At that point he knew nothing about the Ku Klux Klan except what he had read in newspapers. "I fully believed [these] were enormous exaggerations," he said later.

"To satisfy my curiosity on that point more than anything else, in the course of my official conversation with General Terry, I asked him how much truth there was in the newspaper stories."

"When you get to South Carolina you will find that the half has not been told you," Terry replied.

Merrill decided to keep an open mind. He arrived with the belief that the Klan outrages were "sporadic instances of mob violence." He was "fully impressed with the idea that they were a few occasional cases that might be regarded rather as vigilance committee matters than anything else."[17]

After Merrill had been in Yorkville for a few days, he approached attorney I. D. Witherspoon and asked to meet with some of the town's notables. "I am satisfied that some means could be devised by which these disturbances would cease, and the necessity of military intervention or interference would be entirely avoided," he told Witherspoon, who agreed to arrange the gathering.

Attendees at the meeting, the first of several to be called or attended by Merrill in Yorkville, included, among others—as Witherspoon described them—"merchant" J. W. Avery and J. Rufus Bratton, "one of our leading citizens."[18]

The conference apparently served its purpose. Merrill would later testify before the joint congressional committee: "[I] was impressed, for a number of days . . . from my conversation with the principal people here, and from the appearance of things, that there was every probability, and I so reported, of a speedy termination of these acts."[19]

Merrill, however, was no fool, nor was he lazy. His brief was to maintain public order, but he was not allowed to intervene in local criminal investigations unless local authorities—all white—asked for help, which was never likely to happen.

Instead of doing nothing, he decided to use his time asking questions and collecting evidence of crimes committed in the county since the October elections. By all accounts, these efforts went largely unnoticed by the ubiquitous Witherspoon and other stalwarts of Yorkville's white power structure.

And the information that surfaced later—in congressional inquiries and court testimony—suggested that he must have begun gathering intelligence almost immediately after his arrival. He read court records and coroners' reports, and he chatted with well-connected whites and developed confidential informants among white tradesmen, artisans, and farmers.

And he also talked to the black population—farmers, former militia members, women, and community leaders. One key informant was lay preacher Elias Hill, crippled by childhood disease but a keen observer of Klan activities in Clay Hill, a Ku Klux hotbed. Another informant, almost certainly, was Andy Tims, Jim Williams's trusted lieutenant.

Nobody until Merrill had ever asked the blacks about the Ku Klux Klan and the crimes it had committed. Merrill sought them out, and they also stepped forward. Available evidence suggests that this was a dialogue so foreign to the whites of York County that even had they known it was taking place, they would have had no idea what it portended.[20]

YORKVILLE GREETED Merrill and his dragoons with only a brief announcement in the *Enquirer* and without any accompanying embellishment.[21] But with Merrill's cavalry in place and York County's affairs at least visibly stabilized, Dr. Bratton and his friends moved ahead with their peace mission.

The black "peace meeting" met Saturday, April 1, again with Bratton as secretary. A committee of three, which included Tims, presented a resolution, affirming a desire for "the restoration of peace and harmony" and the "perpetuation of kind feelings and true friendship among all classes—both white and black." But then, completely out of context, the resolution asked the York County members of the state legislature—"our immediate representatives"—as well as the probate judge and the school commissioners to resign, "believing that such action, and such only, on their part, will secure and place the object of our desires on a lasting basis."

After this extraordinary development, former county auditor Nelson Davis, identified only as "colored," stood up to speak. The *Enquirer*, to its credit, published his remarks, the first time a black Radical had been quoted in the paper in recent memory. The meeting was not about resolutions, Davis said. The delegates were there "to put down the Ku Klux." Yes, the legislature was passing corrupt laws, spending money it did not have, and unjustly taxing citizens, but, the *Enquirer* wrote, Davis "appeared to have an idea" that resignations "could not, in any way, assist to purge out and purify" the government. He urged every black man in the room to vote no.

No other black delegate wanted to speak. Then Chairman Bessier invited former Confederate general E. M. Law, apparently an observer at the meeting, to give an opinion. He endorsed the resolution, noting that it was "folly to talk about peace, harmony and true friendship among all classes," as long as "virtuous, intelligent white men" were represented in Columbia by "vice and ignorance." The resolution passed.[22]

The white delegates met two days later and delivered a report. It too was a remarkable document: "Without intending to justify the acts of violence which have been committed in this county," the report opened, "it is proper to set forth the fact that the negro Radical government of this State is responsible for all the evils that are upon us."

The Reform Party had offered to share state and county legislative seats and administer South Carolina "for the benefit of all," the report continued. Instead, "the antagonism of races was preferred; the black vote was massed against the white man." As a result: "The whole power of the state [is] committed to the hands of carpet-baggers and negroes."

The report denounced the Republicans, "[whose] party . . . with Federal bayonets, forced such a government upon such a people—upon men of their own race and country. . . . [The] native [white] South Carolinian [is] as powerless in [his] halls of legislation as a marble statue!"

The report continued with the list of white grievances: Whites paid all the taxes. Blacks were setting fires. "Thirty thousand black bayonets have been distributed, while white men are not considered fit to be trusted with arms."

No surprise, then, that "such outrages" met resistance, the report said, in a barely veiled excuse for Ku Klux behavior. "Those who sow to the wind, let them take care lest they reap the whirlwind!"

The whites were pleased that Scott disarmed the militia. Nevertheless, the report finished, the white delegates resolved: "That the existing negro government of South Carolina is a reproach to the civilization of the age; a stain upon the manhood of an intelligent and gallant people, who have so long and so patiently endured and submitted to be ruled by their former slaves. We are tired of it and will exert every legitimate and constitutional means to effect a change."[23]

With these "peace gatherings" Bratton and his white associates may have thought they had won a key victory. They had effectively damned the Scott government as a band of ignorant blacks and venal whites, and the black delegates had agreed with them, despite anything Nelson Davis may have said. The only possible explanation for this charade was a realization by the black delegates that their community was helpless. Their leaders were being murdered, their weapons confiscated, their homes raided, their women raped, and their valuables stolen. Their only recourse was surrender.

Bratton, asked later to describe the results of these two encounters, all but agreed with the evaluation. He understood that the black delegates had agreed at their meeting to renounce politics in return for the white delegates' guarantee of order and quiet. "They would be protected in all their rights," Bratton said. "The whites had no objection to it . . . they meet the blacks on halfway ground. They are perfectly willing to enter into any measures that will restore peace and harmony." Reduced to its essentials, Bratton's evaluation, undergirded with its threat of renewed violence, was easily understood: once the blacks gave away their political rights, the whites would order the Klan to stand down.[24]

The entire affair played out to considerable fanfare. The same *Enquirer* edition that reported on the "peace meetings" carried a paid advertisement by Major Avery on page three entitled "Governor Scott's militia."

Pleased that the militia had been disarmed and that objectionable local officials had been fired, Avery urged "every white man in the county" to preserve the peace. "[Thus] every man, woman and child may come, in safety [to] see my large and elegant stock of Goods, just purchased in Northern markets." At his department store, he planned to sell at "low rates, for the money and money only." There would be "absolutely no credit," he emphasized.[25]

The same edition of the *Enquirer* also carried an ad for Southern Life Insurance, Bedford Forrest's erstwhile employer. General John B. Gordon, Georgia's Ku Klux chieftain, was still the president. "References" in York County now included I. D. Witherspoon and "Dr. J. R. Bratton."[26]

CHAPTER FIFTEEN

Enforcement

Following publication of President Grant's March 24 proclamation, events in Congress began to move rapidly. Grant had given the Ku Klux Klan a deadline of twenty days, but his words carried no weight without the necessary legislation. The *Yorkville Enquirer*, for one, was not impressed, sneering at the ultimatum as an empty threat—Grant's attempt to "wage war by proclamation."[1]

The *Enquirer* had spoken too soon. On March 28, 1871, Congressman Samuel Shellabarger, chairman of the Select Committee on the President's Message, introduced "House of Representatives Bill (H.R.) 320, to enforce the provisions of the fourteenth amendment to the Constitution of the United States."

This baseline bill was five pages long. It attempted to marry the two proposals championed by Shellabarger and Vice Chairman Benjamin Butler at the end of the previous Congress. But bolstered by their House colleagues' growing resolve and Senate support, they had closely focused the new measure on implementing the Fourteenth Amendment to protect citizens' civil and constitutional rights.

The bill had four sections. The first gave unequivocal jurisdiction to federal law enforcement and federal courts to arrest, prosecute, and sentence offenders. The second section described how to apply the law in order to get cases into federal court.

The third section made it "lawful for the President" and "his duty" to intervene, including with military force, if a state could not or would not protect the rights of citizens under the Fourteenth Amendment. The fourth section authorized the president, in extreme circumstances, to declare "unlawful combinations" in "rebellion," to suspend habeas corpus, and to impose martial law, as long as the "combinations" were warned in advance.

The second section was the weakest, seeking a legal rationale for sending common crimes to federal court, something virtually unheard of up to that time. Attorney General Akerman's approach was simply to enable the Fourteenth Amendment to trump state law whenever the federal government decided that an individual state violated a citizen's constitutional or civil rights.

Shellabarger and Butler, however, were not ready to invoke the amendment by fiat. They wanted a framework for its application. The new bill retained Shellabarger's original focus on conspiracy as the key factor in determining which offenses would be targeted by federal authorities—aiming the legislation directly at the Ku Klux Klan and similar organizations.

But it also retained, from the previous Congress, Shellabarger's hackneyed definition of these offenses as crimes that normally "would not be punishable" under federal law but under this bill would be treated as if they had been committed "under the sole and exclusive jurisdiction" of the United States—as in territories or other federal entities. This section also retained Butler's exhaustive list of actionable crimes.[2]

Despite the awkwardness, the bill was a strong framework, and whatever misgivings Speaker Blaine might have previously had about new Klan legislation—if he indeed had had such misgivings—suddenly disappeared. When Shellabarger inquired about scheduling debate on the bill, Blaine dismissed his concerns: "The position of the bill is that it must occupy the whole time of the House."[3]

And with the exception of occasional procedural matters, that is what happened.

ON MARCH 31, Congressman Charles W. Willard of Vermont introduced a second version of H.R. 320, described as "an Amendment in the Nature of a Substitute" to the initial bill. Barely four pages long, it dramatically streamlined Shellabarger's original offering. It put civil rights violations in federal courts and made federal laws apply. But it dropped Butler's long list of offenses and simplified Shellabarger's confusing case instructions. The Willard substitute simply treated violations as if they had been committed on federal soil—territories, public lands, and Washington, D.C.

It added a new section requiring prospective federal jurors to take an oath that they had never participated in, aided, or abetted "the combination or conspiracy," a version of the so-called "Ironclad Oath," used in the past to prevent former Confederate officeholders, soldiers, and their supporters from serving in postwar positions of authority. As in the baseline version, the president was authorized to summon troops, proclaim rebellion, and suspend habeas corpus. There was, however, no mention of martial law.[4]

The legislation was a welcome crystallization of the ideas envisioned in both the Senate and House, but it was never debated, per se, nor did it come to a vote. It was ordered printed and sent to Shellabarger's committee.

But it was not forgotten. The Willard substitute in most respects was the embodiment of Akerman's core belief in the overarching power of the Fourteenth

Amendment. He may even have written it, although there is no evidence that he did so. But, if not, why would a little-known congressman from Vermont decide to submit a detailed rewrite of perhaps the most important law of the Forty-Second U.S. Congress?

There appears to be no record that Akerman and Willard knew each other or discussed the bill. There was, however, a connection. Both were Dartmouth graduates—Akerman in 1842 and Willard in 1851. Akerman was an active and very well-known—Dartmouth alumnus. Willard was a Montpelier lawyer and newspaper editor.[5]

The Willard substitute was built on the fundamental Akerman concept that the Fourteenth Amendment protected constitutional rights—all constitutional rights—and that constitutional and civil rights violations by states were federal crimes. There was no need to list specific offenses.

And in reviving the Ironclad Oath, the substitute extended the reach of a measure detested by Confederate soldiers and officeholders who had been barred from holding public office after the war unless Congress removed their "disabilities." Akerman himself, a former Confederate officer, needed a dispensation in 1869 to become U.S. Attorney for Georgia. Using the oath in the Willard substitute would enable the court to disqualify and prosecute for perjury any juror in a federal trial who lied about participation, however peripheral, in any Klan-related scheme. Juries in Klan trials conducted under this stipulation would be filled with Union loyalists—whites and blacks. Akerman had toiled on blacks' behalf for years before juries stacked with unrepentant whites; the substitute bill would give the Klan a taste of its own medicine.

Finally, by endorsing suspension of habeas corpus but eschewing martial law, the substitute adhered to Akerman's belief that federal law, applied as powerfully as possible, was the key to destroying the Ku Klux Klan. Imposing martial law did little besides feed southern resentments.

ON APRIL 6, Shellabarger brought his final version of H.R. 320 to the floor, and it incorporated most of Willard's ideas. The bill was now closely and consistently focused on the Fourteenth Amendment. Its reach had been expanded to include protection against intimidation—of jurors, witnesses, law enforcement, federal employees, and voters. The president could suspend habeas corpus but could not declare martial law. The Ironclad Oath, however, was no longer in the bill.[6]

Shellabarger's presentation came after nine days of bitter but frequently eloquent debate. Republicans focused on terrorist atrocities, southern intransigence, and the linkages between the Ku Klux Klan and the Democratic Party, all but accusing the Democrats of treason.

Democrats insisted the violence in the South was no worse than in the North. The federal government, they said, was trampling on states' rights, and the current crisis was a myth concocted by the Republicans so they could use the army to keep them in power.

As the debate progressed, however, the Democrats moved beyond these traditional protests to focus on suspension of habeas corpus, described by Kentucky's James Beck as a license for the president "to declare war on any State or people" and to send troops wherever he wished. Both he and other Democrats called on Republicans to vote against this "military despotism." This approach appeared to have some resonance.[7]

Wavering Republicans, however, may have drawn inspiration from two black South Carolina congressmen, Robert Brown Elliott and Joseph Hayne Rainey. Both men stood in the front lines of racial upheaval and had no use for Democrats' contention that reports of white terrorism were overblown. They made no effort to hide their anger.

Both spoke late Saturday, April 1. Elliott, a British-born and -educated lawyer who emigrated to the United States after the war, chronicled the published threats of South Carolina whites over the previous three years, including an 1870 *Charleston News* dispatch describing the "solid black vote" for Republican candidates as "a declaration of war by the negro race against the white race."

He noted that South Carolina's blacks, during the war, farmed the land of the whites and protected their wives and families. But after the surrender, whites repaid them with the "shame of your boasted chivalry," sent them into "exile" with "the pitiless lash," or condemned them to "swift murder."

The whites sought their revenge "by moving at midnight along the path of the assassin!" he continued. "Who is the barbarian here, the murderer or the victim?"[8]

Rainey spoke during the evening. He was the first-ever black member of the House of Representatives, born into slavery in Charleston and drafted during the war to serve as a steward aboard Confederate blockade runners. He jumped ship in Bermuda and worked there as a barber until the war ended.

Like Elliott, Rainey recounted the "murderous deeds" of white terrorism and put the blame on Democrats: "The stain is there to prove your criminality before God and the world in the day of retribution which will surely come."

He scoffed at local law enforcement: "[It is] secretly in sympathy with the very evil against which we are striving." Victims' only recourse, he said, was the federal government: "Tell me nothing of a Constitution which fails to shelter beneath its rightful power the people of a country!"

Rainey closed with a warning: "When myself and colleagues shall leave these Halls and turn our footsteps toward our southern homes, we know not but that the assassin may await our coming, as marked for his vengeance. Should this befall, we would bid Congress and our country to remember [that] 'bloody treason flourish'd over us.'"[9]

Speaking in Congress late on a Saturday was not an easy path to serious press coverage, but both men—always identified by journalists as "(black)" or "(colored)" when they were first mentioned—got handsome publicity in Republican circles.

The *Harrisburg* (Pa.) *Telegraph* described Elliott's speech as "the sensation of the House," and a few days later the *Pittsburgh Commercial* used Rainey's "modesty and dignity" as the occasion for a full-scale denunciation of the Democratic Party.

Under the headline "Give Them a Chance," the *Commercial* wondered why Democrats greeted with "sardonic derision" and "unconquerable prejudice" every attempt by blacks to improve their lot. "We demand for the black man, as for the white, a fair field and no favor."[10]

AS MARCH gave way to April it became apparent that Butler and Shellabarger had done their work well. Butler, who relished playing the villain, had earned widespread enmity from both sides of the aisle—including from the Speaker of the House—but in doing so had ensured that Ku Klux legislation became a priority for the new Congress. Shellabarger, a principled hardliner but relatively soft-spoken, brought a bill to the floor that incorporated many of his colleagues' ideas.

As different amendments appeared and members took the floor, an increasing number of Republicans acquired a stake in the bill's success, and it showed. On April 7, two weeks after Grant's proclamation, the House comfortably passed H.R. 320 on a straight party-line vote, 118–91.[11]

A week later the Senate passed the bill, with amendments, by a vote of 45–19.[12] A conference committee met to resolve remaining differences. On April 19, the *Urbana* (Ohio) *Union* described the Senate bill as "far more stringent" than the House version. Part of the reason was because Attorney General Akerman, with President Grant's support, had pressed the Senate to restore the Ironclad Oath, the *Union* reported. Akerman also had the Senate insert a new measure allowing victims of the Klan to sue for damages not only from their attackers but also from the offending town or district as a whole.[13]

The Third Enforcement Act, more familiarly known as the "Ku Klux Klan Act," was passed by both houses of Congress and signed into law by President Grant

April 20, 1871. The Ironclad Oath remained, as did suspension of habeas corpus. Victims' right to sue communities was gone, and so was martial law.[14]

The implications of the new law were only dimly perceived in South Carolina. In Columbia, the *Daily Phoenix* in mid-March had branded it as the Radicals' "last desperate hope" to provoke a "Ku Klux war" that would "inaugurate civil strife and bloodshed in the South and revive the war spirit in the North."[15]

And as late as March 29, the *Sumter* (S.C.) *Watchman* was confidently predicting the bill was further from passage "than ever," still harping on the "bitter pill" that Butler had been forced to swallow at the end of the previous Congress during the vote approving the joint congressional Klan investigation.[16]

That dustup was long forgotten. On April 17, even as the Ku Klux Klan Act awaited passage, Senator Scott's Klan investigation was reauthorized—reconstituted, to no one's surprise, as the Joint Select Committee to Inquire into the Condition of Affairs in the Late Insurrectionary States. It had seven senators and fourteen House members. Butler, per his wishes, was not named. The committee's brief was to investigate the Ku Klux Klan throughout the South. Its first concern was South Carolina. As Shellabarger had noted a month earlier, there was no reason why there could not be both legislation and investigation.

None of this boded well for white South Carolina, and on April 20 the *Yorkville Enquirer* took a thoughtful and somewhat somber tone, noting that the debate was "attracting more attention from all sections of the Union, than any measure . . . before Congress for many months."

The Senate's hardline response was "surprising," the *Enquirer* said, "even to the most ardent supporters of the measure." The paper highlighted the habeas corpus provision and mentioned the Ironclad Oath and the right to sue counties for personal damages, provisions "that Attorney General Akerman, with the approval of the President," had suggested.

The *Enquirer* summarized the law as nothing less than Grant's tool to suppress "alleged disorders in the South . . . whenever he judged it necessary."[17]

At a May 2 cabinet meeting, Akerman read a draft proclamation announcing Grant's intention to enforce the Ku Klux Klan Act. The president signed the draft, and the proclamation was issued the following day. It described the new law as one "of extraordinary public importance." While it applied to all sections of the country, the proclamation said, it focused on "certain localities" in the former Confederacy.

"Reluctant to call into exercise any of the extraordinary powers thereby conferred upon me except in cases of imperative necessity," the proclamation said, "I . . . nevertheless . . . will not hesitate to exhaust the powers thus vested in the Executive whenever and wherever it shall become necessary to do so."

Should local law enforcement fail to protect its citizens, the proclamation concluded, the federal government would summon "all its energies for the protection of its citizens of every race and color and for the restoration of peace and order throughout the entire country." This was Grant's latest—and perhaps last—warning.[18]

FOR AKERMAN, the Ku Klux Klan Act marked the successful culmination of a three-year battle to put the defense of civil rights under the purview of the federal government and to do so without resort—at least nominally—to martial law. Now he had to plan his next steps.

In the following weeks he met with Secretary of War William Belknap to discuss cooperation and coordination between his U.S. Marshals and Belknap's soldiers—the forces controlled by General Terry in Louisville.[19]

Akerman also needed more and better information about what he was up against. Bedford Forrest's 1868 newspaper interview was then the only "semi-official" account of the Klan's reach and resources. Akerman's $50,000 intelligence stipend—proposed at the behest of North Carolina's Senator Pool—was approved in an appropriations bill that Grant signed March 3. A bit less than a month later Pool asked Akerman to send a detective to North Carolina.[20]

Unfortunately, Akerman replied, "the insuperable obstacle . . . is in the want of money." Only on July 1, the beginning of the coming fiscal year, would the $50,000 become available. Pool went back to the Senate, and the money was advanced.[21]

Early in June, Senator Scott's committee, undoubtedly with Akerman's knowledge and approval, sent Joseph Hester, a well-spoken deputy marshal from North Carolina, to deliver a letter informing President Grant of plans to use the new money to hire undercover agents—making sure the boss knew what was happening.

The letter, an elegant circumlocution asking permission for what was in effect a fait accompli, was introduced and signed in Scott's decorative cursive, but the body of the letter was written in Pool's unmistakable scrawl. The letter writers, "fully satisfied of the character and competency of Mr. Hester," asked the president to let Akerman know of Hester's qualifications so Akerman would "feel authorized to proceed in the matter, at once." Akerman was hesitating "for want of instructions." Congress, the letter continued, had appropriated $50,000 "to be put into operation without delay in order to insure success."[22]

The committee need not have worried. Hester, one of Akerman's prospective undercover men, caught up to Grant in West Point, New York, where he was on vacation. Grant endorsed the letter June 10, handed it back to Hester, and told him to deliver it to Akerman—who, of course, already knew it was coming.[23] On June 10, Acting Attorney General Benjamin Bristow (Akerman was at home in Georgia during the summer recess) confirmed Grant's directive and appointed Hester as a Justice Department "detective" to investigate and prosecute "crimes against the United States" in North Carolina "and the country contiguous thereto."[24]

The key phrase was "contiguous thereto." Pool was interested in North Carolina, but Grant clearly was more interested in the South Carolina upcountry, much of it, including York County, "contiguous" to its northern neighbor. Grant's directive—probably approved and perhaps even written by Akerman in Georgia—had the dual benefit of getting the president what he wanted without alienating Pool.

In South Carolina Akerman enjoyed an initial stroke of good fortune. His recently reappointed U.S. Attorney for the state, David T. Corbin, was, like his superior, a dedicated believer in the power of the Fourteenth Amendment. By the spring of 1871 he had a record of able service and had also distinguished himself as one of the few U.S. Attorneys who had not incurred Akerman's wrath for ignoring Ku Klux atrocities, inadequately policing violations of the Ironclad Oath, or complaining about the inadequacy of his staff.

Corbin had had little help advancing his career. He was thirty-seven in early 1871, a Vermonter born to poverty, and, like Akerman and Congressman Willard, a Dartmouth alumnus. Corbin graduated in 1857, passed the Vermont bar in 1859, and briefly entered private practice before volunteering for the Union army at the outbreak of the war. At Dartmouth "he was sound but not brilliant," recalled former Vermont governor Samuel Pingree much later, damning his classmate with faint praise.

Beginning with Pingree, authors of Corbin's sparse biography appeared uniformly unimpressed by a man offhandedly described in a Dartmouth memorial as a "quiet, unassuming, courteous gentleman." Yet as a captain of volunteers, he fought under General George McClellan through the entire 1862 Peninsular Campaign and was decorated for bravery after being badly wounded at Savage's Station, the last battle of this Union debacle.

He spent several months in a prison hospital before being exchanged and was mustered out of the army because of his wounds. He was subsequently reappointed to Lincoln's "Invalid Corps," where he served until the surrender, mostly as a judge advocate. In the fall of 1865 he joined the Freedmen's Bureau and moved to Charleston.[25]

He resigned from the bureau in 1867 but had clearly impressed someone important, for he was immediately hired as U.S. Attorney even as he prepared to leave the state. By the time Akerman reappointed him four years later, he was serving as a South Carolina state senator, most of the time as Senate president and chairman of the Judiciary Committee. He had a thriving law practice in Charleston and was married to a cousin of the poet Bayard Taylor. His wife had come to South Carolina from Chester, Pennsylvania, as a schoolteacher with her sister, who had married Corbin's law partner.[26]

Akerman may not have known about Corbin, but, besides Dartmouth, they shared modest beginnings in New England, tepid endorsements from many of their peers, and a commitment to reconstruction and the rule of law. When the Ku Klux Klan Act went into force, Akerman had a valuable subordinate already in place.

IN WASHINGTON, however, Akerman was struggling. As he reached the end of his first year in office his early flirtation with stardom had summarily collapsed with his failure to produce a Republican election victory in Georgia.

His bureaucratic skills were also found wanting. He had little aptitude or inclination for organizing the fledgling Justice Department and got no support from Grant or his fellow cabinet members, none of whom were interested in streamlining government or giving up their legal fiefdoms.

Logistics continued to be chaotic. Akerman was still in the Freedmen's Bank Building, but Bristow and his assistants were on F Street, some blocks away. In October 1870 Akerman was forced to ask the Treasury Department to give him six more rooms. And in January 1871 he asked the House Appropriations Committee for money to hire watchmen for F Street because the Treasury—providing them at the time—was pulling out at the end of the fiscal year.[27]

One aspect of the Justice Department reforms drew enthusiastic support from the cabinet: the requirement that Justice provide counsel to address complex legal issues. The department did not have the talent in-house but had nonetheless inherited the task of hiring expensive outsiders. By late 1870, Akerman was denying most of these requests—from cabinet colleagues, Congress, and from federal officials all over the country—because he had no extra money. During a four-month period in 1870–71, Akerman turned down requests from Iowa, Massachusetts, Mississippi, Tennessee, Virginia, and Texas. By late spring, the flow of begging letters had dropped off, partly, it is almost certain, because of Akerman. There was no point in asking for special counsel if the attorney general refused to hire them.[28] This posture, it can be assumed, did not win him any new friends.

One of his biggest problems, however, was developing behind his back and completely without his knowledge. Solicitor General Bristow was disillusioned with Akerman and thinking of resigning. In an April 25, 1871, letter to Louisville law partner John Marshall Harlan, Kentucky's Republican Party leader and a close friend, Bristow confided that he was "unpleasantly situated." He would stay on until the fall, but if matters did not change, he said, he would resign "at once."[29]

Both Harlan and Bristow, Louisville patricians and attorneys of considerable skill, were undoubtedly well aware of the beating Akerman had taken at the hands of Congress during the Union Pacific dispute and with the ridicule that accompanied it. From then on, Akerman's legal shortcomings became a constant theme in the letters exchanged by the two Kentuckians.

Akerman never seemed to have paid any attention to the damage the Union Pacific case had done to his reputation. And in May the Union Pacific's Central Branch came at him again but this time with hat in hand.

Interior Secretary Columbus Delano asked Akerman about an application by the Central Branch seeking a land and bond subsidy. And on May 9 Ebenezer Hoar, Akerman's predecessor, and former senator George Williams, who wanted his job, visited Akerman to argue the Central Branch's case.[30] The visit apparently did not go well because on June 3 Akerman issued an opinion opposing the railroad's petition.

The Central Branch was one of four railroads that had been granted subsidies to build separate lines westward from the Missouri River, eventually to rejoin the transcontinental trunk line. Congress had granted subsidies to the Central Branch for one hundred miles, after which it was to link up with one of the other three lines, which Akerman lumped together in his opinion as "the Kansas road."

The Kansas road had subsidies for a much longer distance but had applied to Congress to change its trajectory and take a new route. Congress had granted the waiver, and the Kansas road changed direction. Its subsidies remained intact.

The Central Branch argued that the Kansas road was in default for not building the original route and that its subsidies should now be granted to the Central Branch. Akerman disagreed, noting that Congress had given the Kansas road permission to alter its route and had made no change in its original subsidy. Essentially, he said, the Central Branch was asking for new money, but, since the original grants were still in place, there could be "no substitute for what still exist[ed]."

Akerman noted that the Central Branch—Hoar and Williams, undoubtedly, among others—had "impressively urged" on him that his ruling imputed to

Congress "a violation of the public faith pledged to the Central Branch" in the original railroad acts of 1862 and 1864.

This harked back to the Union Pacific case from the previous year, when Congress decided that the transcontinental railroad was a national treasure and did not have to pay interest on its bonds.

Akerman addressed this contention directly, noting that the "bounty" of the original acts gave Congress—and only Congress—the right to "alter, amend or repeal" the terms of the agreements. If the Central Branch wanted a waiver, that was the Central Branch's problem. The Central Branch should speak to Congress. As a cabinet secretary he had no authority to grant new subsidies. Congress had not changed its mind for him in the Union Pacific case; why should it change its mind now?[31]

This was not the finding that the Central Branch wanted, nor was it the finding that Delano, a favorite of the railroads, had expected. The Central Branch immediately appealed, and Akerman, contacted on vacation in Georgia, telegraphed the Justice Department that he had "no objection to a rehearing on new facts." But he would not be bullied again.[32]

CHAPTER SIXTEEN

"A Bad State of Affairs"

MAY 4, 1871

There were no names in Major Merrill's May 4 report, his first to General Terry in Louisville. York County had no telegraph or mail service of its own. To get out of the state, dispatches had to travel twenty miles south by rail to Chester, and Merrill had little confidence that they would get there without someone taking a peek. He was learning fast.

During the first weeks of his Yorkville assignment there was little activity, he wrote. He had no explanation. Perhaps the Klan was on its best behavior, reluctant to test Merrill until it had a chance to get used to him.

Things changed in mid-April. Between fifteen and eighteen Ku Klux started raiding out of Clay Hills in northern York County, near where the Catawba River crosses into North Carolina. The first time was around 2:30 a.m. on Saturday, April 8, or maybe it was Tuesday the next week—Merrill wasn't sure. The riders stopped by Dr. Lowry's plantation first, but the man they wanted wasn't there, probably laying out in the woods so they wouldn't find him.

No matter. Six of the riders pulled the man's father out of bed and beat him for not raising his son properly. They used ramrods. Then they rode off, looking for other "offenders" who had voted Radical, joined the Union League, marched with the militia, or had simply drawn their wrath.

The next Saturday, April 15, the same set of Ku Klux raided the Bryant plantation and beat a black couple who lived there. They used whips this time—probably hickory switches but maybe rawhide. The riders made other stops afterward to deliver warnings, but there were no more beatings.

The day after that they rode into North Carolina to hunt down a York County man who had been attacked so many times that he left the state. They found him and beat him so badly that he probably would have died had he not managed to crawl away and eventually reach the U.S. Army outpost in Yorkville where he was hospitalized.

Merrill had spoken with as many as ten of the people targeted that month, all of them black, he told Terry. Four of them, "at places distinct from each other," identified three of the attackers, and all of them identified one man who did not even bother to wear a disguise. He was probably the boss, a "physician" who had tended to the black community for years, Merrill wrote. They knew him by his voice and general appearance.

And now Merrill knew him too. He said as much in his dispatch, probably deliberately. Whoever looked at his mail would learn that Merrill was shadowing the physician and other Klan leaders.

Merrill told Terry he had no doubt that the April events occurred exactly as he had described them, but only one victim was willing to give evidence. The others were terrified: "While they have to live and work where they do, it would be worth more than their lives are worth to testify to the facts," he concluded. "This is a bad state of affairs."[1]

THE ABSENT son at Doctor Lowry's plantation was Richard Wilson and the father was Dick Wilson, who claimed he had no idea where Richard had gone. Dick Wilson was "a damned liar," the raiders said. They badgered him about his Radical politics and his Union League activity and condemned him and other "damned niggers" for "ruining the country," Dick Wilson said later. They made him drop his trousers and lie down on the ground.

"We'll make a Democrat of you tonight," one of them said, and three of them beat him so severely he was laid up for two weeks. "I couldn't walk. I couldn't sit down, and when I lay down, I would have to lay right flat down on my stomach," he said. He identified six of his attackers, including "Doctor Parker."[2]

The man who escaped across the river to North Carolina was Hampton Hicklin, a black farmer targeted by the Klan since the beginning of the year. He never saw the faces of his attackers but knew virtually all of them from their voices, their mounts, their weapons, and their physical characteristics. He had dodged them repeatedly, spied on them, listened to their plots and reported them to York County sheriff R. H. Glenn, who, he found out later, had told his pursuers everything.[3]

Merrill nevertheless told Terry he had "excellent relations so far" with Glenn, whom he described as "a good man disposed to do his duty." Still, Merrill's confidence had limits. "[Glenn displays] the characteristic shiftiness of the officials here generally, letting his chance slip or failing to follow up intelligently the trail of these fellows."[4]

While Merrill had found out about Dr. Parker and had undoubtedly heard about Dr. Bratton, he was also probably interested in yet another Klan physician-chieftain. This was Dr. Edward Avery, the brother of York County Klan leader J. William Avery. In late March, just as Merrill was arriving in Yorkville, Dr. Avery led a series of brazen raids near Rock Hill, in the eastern part of the county.

Dr. Avery's targets included Isaac Postle, a lay preacher known as "Isaac the Apostle," and his wife, Harriet, eight months pregnant. Two others were Abraham and Emeline Brumfield, an elderly couple. Isaac Postle was a respected local leader, and Abraham Brumfield was a Union League stalwart. All four victims had known Avery for years—"ever since he was a little boy," Emeline Brumfield said later. They identified him immediately by his voice and his withered hand, the result of a war wound.

Avery's men burst into the Postles' cabin, knocked Harriet Postle to the floor, panicked their six children, and set off in search for Isaac until they discovered him hiding under the house. They grabbed him by the hair and took him into the woods where they beat him and choked him in a mock hanging.

At the Brumfields', Abraham and Emeline got an early warning when their dog started barking in the yard in the middle of the night. Abraham had been worried about a possible Ku Klux visit for some time and had been laying out for weeks, but rheumatism had finally driven him inside that night. He was in his sixties. He fled out the back door as the raiders called for him.

"He ain't here," Emeline yelled back.

"You're a God-damned liar," one said.

"If I am a God-damned liar, you may come in and get him," she replied, throwing open the front door.

"Now you have got to tell me where he is," her tormentor said. "If you don't, I will blow your God-damned brains out."

Emeline was unimpressed: "Then you will have me to shoot to-night."

The raiders searched the house and found Sam Sturges, an elderly houseguest roughly the same age as the Brumfields. They put a noose around Sturges's neck and stretched it until he choked. Then they released him.

Avery turned to Emeline, whose head he had slammed against the bedpost earlier: "You tell that old man, Brumfield, that I came here to-night to send him to hell, for I am just from hell myself, and I came to send him there."

Emeline shrugged: "When a soul dies and goes to hell, it can never come back here again."[5]

MERRILL TOLD Terry he and his men were gradually learning their way around the county and had a good idea where the dens were gathering. He was also accumulating evidence from black refugees at the Yorkville garrison and from a small number of informants, both white and black, who periodically approached him in the field.

"[I have] some hopes of being able to trap some of these scoundrels," he wrote. "[There is] so much good to be accomplished by the punishment of even five, or three, that I shall spare no effort to accomplish it."

But he was seething. "[Finding and arresting the offenders] would be the merest child's play if I had the authority to go about it as I see fit," he said, but the task was nearly impossible. He could not provide help unless civilian authorities asked for it, and they never did. He could not arrest anyone without an arrest warrant, and civilian authorities never issued one.

He was "well satisfied" that there were many more Ku Klux in York County than was generally thought, including "a large number of the most reputable people" who were "more or less intimately connected with it." He certainly knew of Parker, Bratton, and the Jim Williams lynching, and he was also watching plantation owner John W. Mitchell, whose marauders prowled the western edge of York County between Broad River and Bullock's Creek. Mitchell's men had beaten and subsequently murdered blacksmith Charley Good, like Williams an influential black community leader, about a month before Merrill's March arrival.

And even though the number of actual night riders was relatively small, Merrill added in his dispatch to Terry, the leadership could not control them and did not really care. "The debauched sentiment of the old slave-holding communities is not up to the mark of seeing any great offense in 'whipping a nigger' for being a Radical."

"I fear much here that the result shortly must be a general emigration of one race or the other, or a series of burnings and murders," Merrill concluded. "The prospect of a peaceable future here is gloomy."[6]

HE DID NOT exaggerate. The day after Merrill mailed his dispatch, six Ku Klux broke into the home of Elias Hill, one of Merrill's best sources of intelligence. Hill, a preacher, schoolteacher, and Republican political activist from Clay Hills in the eastern part of the county, was a public figure of considerable renown. Afflicted with what he called a "rheumatism," his limbs and muscles had started to seize up when he was seven years old. The condition had progressively worsened, and at fifty-two his limbs were badly withered, and his jaw clenched so tightly that he was able to feed himself only after a pair of his teeth had been removed.

White schoolchildren had more or less adopted him when he was a child and had helped teach him how to read and write—Merrill knew of only one other literate black person in the county. Hill's father bought his freedom for $150 around 1840. Friends used what he described as a "spring wagon" to drive him to church, and he was a leading figure in York County's Republican Party, which he revered as "nearer the laws of God than any other party."

Hill heard the dogs barking outside between midnight and 1:00 a.m. on May 5 and lay awake listening as the raiders broke into his brother's house next door. His sister-in-law screamed as they dragged her into the yard. He could hear her attackers lashing her with a whip until she told them where he lived.

"You is at his house," she said finally.

One of the men opened Hill's door.

"Who's here?" one shouted.

Hill was going nowhere. He could move only by tugging himself along the floor with the aid of what he called his "pry stick."

"I am here."

There were six of them, all hooded or otherwise disguised. Two grabbed him by the arms, dragged him into the yard, and dropped him to the ground. They began yelling at him, recounting his supposed sins: He had ordered the gin houses to be burned. He had ordered black men to rape white women. He was a member of the Union League.

He admitted he was the president of the local Union League, but he had not held a meeting since the fall. They accused him of bringing Jim Williams to Clay Hills to make a speech. No, Hill said, he did not even know Jim Williams, "upon honor." You have no honor, they said, and they started beating him, pulling up his shirt and lashing him about the hips because it was the only part of his body that was solid. Every accusation was nonsense, parroting the fictions that Klan aristocrats used to stoke the hatred of the minors who did the dirty work.

Then one of his attackers, probably the leader, asked him if he had been corresponding with Alexander Wallace, York County's white Republican U.S. congressman, a Radical hated by the county's white opposition. Yes, he had, Hill said, but "only tidings."

"You were writing about the Ku Klux," the questioner said. "And haven't you been preaching and praying about the Ku Klux?" They wanted the Wallace letter. Hill told them to check the shelf by his bed. They found the letter and continued rummaging around the house. When they came out again, they pointed pistols at Hill's head. Was he ready to die?

"I would rather live."

They beat him again with a horsewhip, then put a leather strap around his neck and threatened to throw him in the Catawba River. Where was it?

"East," Hill said.

"I don't know no east," one of them said. "Where is the damned thing?"

Eventually they relented. If he stopped preaching, put a notice in the paper renouncing the Republican Party, and cut off his mail-order subscription to Charleston's Republican newspaper, they would not kill him. If he did not comply, they would come back the next week and finish the job.

"Don't you pray against Ku Klux," one of them added. "Don't pray against us. Pray that God may bless and save us." And then they went away.[7]

DURING HIS first days on the job Merrill noticed that the Klan had a habit of raiding a particular neighborhood over three weekend nights beginning Friday. Seeking to take advantage of this tendency, he set up ambushes in the affected locale on Saturday after the Friday night raid. His adversaries immediately figured this out, and different raiders would raid a different neighborhood on Saturday, comfortable in the knowledge that Merrill was far away and out of reach.

This was "exactly" what he would have done, he later told congressional investigators, and by early May these tactics and other insights had convinced him that he was dealing not with random bands of unlettered thugs and thieves but instead with a highly disciplined and dangerous organization that was operating "in concert" throughout the county.

He took a special interest in the attacks that occurred subsequent to his arrival, probably because he regarded them as personal insults and undoubtedly because some of them, like the outrageous beating of Elias Hill, happened after passage of the Ku Klux Klan Act and could be prosecuted one day in federal court. The Clay Hills whites could have stopped the April terrorism "immediately if they chose," he said, but they remained silent. "I never conceived of such a state of social disorganization being possible in any civilized community as exists in this county now."[8]

MERRILL SOON got a chance to act on some of his frustration. On May 13, Secretary of War Belknap sent a presidential directive by telegram to General Terry and field officers in South Carolina, ordering them to arrest and "break up" bands of "disguised night marauders."[9]

That same day Merrill summoned York County's leading white citizens to a meeting at his headquarters "[to] confer upon the subject of the disorderly and turbulent spirit which [had] prevailed in this section of the state," the *Yorkville Enquirer* reported.

Merrill was fed up with York County's white power structure and made no effort to hide his disgust. In stark language undoubtedly honed during years of service on courts-martial, he delivered an unvarnished dressing-down. Judging from the *Enquirer*'s stilted recounting of the event, the guests, who arrived "by invitation," got the message.

"Major Merrill expressed his regrets that bands of disguised men had recently been whipping and otherwise maltreating white and colored citizens of this section," the *Enquirer* said, even though there was no confirmed record at that time of any attack on a York County white citizen. Merrill described recent incidents in detail. "[This] impressed those present with the idea that he is kept informed as to the operations of disguised persons in this county."

Merrill also said he had evidence "amply sufficient to convict some of the persons before any impartial jury," and "seemed to be amused at the idea that the names of the guilty parties were not known to the people." Merrill said he could furnish the names whenever he wished "and have such persons arrested in a few hours."

Huge numbers of people were forced to lay out at night to avoid the night riders, he continued, "and such a state of affairs would no longer be tolerated," the *Enquirer* reported. He did not blame local officials for allowing the violence to persist, because the victims were too scared to file complaints. Local lawmen had no warrants to enforce.

It was therefore up to York County's influential citizens "to adopt prompt and decisive measures to suppress any further disturbance," the *Enquirer* said, "and thereby avoid the consequences of military interference."

Merrill "daily expected" habeas corpus to be suspended in York County, he said, something to be avoided. If the "good people" took action, he finished, "[the outrages would stop] at once."[10]

With this meeting, Merrill had drawn a line. He knew what was going on; he knew who was doing it; and he knew he was staring directly at the men who were giving the orders. Not only did he rebuke them, he threatened them directly: Make it stop. If you don't, the army will.

On May 15 Terry and Merrill received a letter from army headquarters in Washington echoing the president's May 13 communiqué and again directing units in the field, in Grant's words, "to arrest and break up disguised night marauders."[11]

There was no guidance, however, on how this should be done. This directive was followed shortly by the army's General Order 48, dated May 15. It called attention to the Ku Klux Klan Act and called on "all good citizens, and especially upon all public officers, to be zealous in the enforcement thereof," and it warned "all persons to abstain from committing any of the acts thereby prohibited."[12] This directive was signed and dated by Grant on May 3 and in essence was the proclamation drafted by Attorney General Akerman the same day. Now it was codified for military application.

A week later many of those Merrill had taken to task produced an initial list of county leaders who agreed to renounce violence. The signers, a roster that Yorkville lawyer I. D. Witherspoon later said eventually grew to over three hundred citizens, included Klan stalwarts like Samuel G. "Squire" Brown, doctors Love and Avery, and several participants in the Jim Williams lynching. Major Avery and Dr. Bratton, perhaps finally reaching the limits of their cynicism, did not sign.[13]

On May 25 Merrill telegraphed Terry's headquarters in Louisville asking if he could make arrests and hold prisoners even though civil authorities had given him no authority to do so. The next day he wrote a long dispatch to Terry, explaining his dilemma in detail.[14]

He had sought no arrest warrants, he wrote, because he had no confidence in local authorities, who are "so swayed by public opinion" that any case he brought to them "would almost certainly be discharged." This would simply "embolden" offenders to "other acts of violence."

He also had "grave reason" to believe that some lawmen were "in complicity" with the Klan. "This situation is daily becoming worse," he added, "with no apparent reason [to expect any improvement]."

Then he turned to Grant's telegraphed directive to "make it [his] duty to, in all cases, arrest disguised night marauders and break up the bands." He had no doubt about arresting "the fanatics" when they could be caught in the act, but was "not clear" how to arrest "without civil warrant" offenders "well-known to be of this class when not caught flagrante delicto."

He had no idea how "to break up the bands." He suggested that he had plenty of evidence to go after the Ku Klux Klan, but without help from local authorities he would need federal arrest warrants, almost a logistical impossibility. He would have to send a written request by railroad from Yorkville to the telegraph office in Chester, but if he did not get a reply from Chester the same day he would have to wait three days, and without a writ of habeas corpus "no civil or U.S. authority would hold the prisoner [for that long]." He told Terry he had "twenty or more" pending cases of this type.[15]

This, after two months, was the crux of Merrill's dilemma. He had everything he needed: manpower, weapons, and information. His men were professionals, they were horsemen, and they could move fast. The Klan was afraid of him. He knew it, and his men knew it. Yet his hands were tied.

He was supposed to catch the Klan in the act, an almost impossible task when the majority of the raiders on any given night had no idea where they were going or what was planned. To be successful Merrill needed to be the initiator.

He needed to be the one making the raids, rousting the offenders in the middle of the night and frog-marching them to the stockade. He knew who he wanted, but without permission from civilian authorities all he could do was react.

MERRILL SOON realized that his misgivings about the local mail service were not misplaced. It turned out that his May 25 telegram to Louisville inquiring about arrests had been leaked by the Chester telegraph operator to Yorkville's white establishment. I. D. Witherspoon, the loquacious attorney, described Merrill's behavior as "rambunctious." Several prominent whites thought about addressing "a very respectful note" to Merrill.

Instead, a group of hotheads decided to raid Merrill's encampment. It never took place, but the next day Witherspoon and the rest of Yorkville's respected whites approached Merrill and asked what had happened. Merrill passed it off, saying he had heard some "reckless youth" planned to shoot into the camp.

Who was it, Dr. Bratton asked. He and Major Avery were both among the delegates. From Witherspoon's account—whether Witherspoon understood it or not—Merrill apparently had decided to regard this incident as a Klan warning.

He could not have cared less. He told Bratton and his companions that three men were involved in the incident, and one had been caught skulking around the camp. He nevertheless had all three names, he said, and could arrest them any time he wished. Bratton asked him for the names. Not a chance. Merrill did not want to endanger his informants, and there was no way he was telling Rufus Bratton or J. W. Avery anything.[16]

Merrill's account of this incident, related later to congressional investigators, added further details. He indeed had information from an informant—these were known in York County as "pukes"—that some Ku Klux "young bloods" were going to "try it on," and fire into the camp. He apparently had plenty of advance notice and was not particularly worried.

He sent a few additional troopers to sleep in the stable and be ready to fight if necessary. He also posted a "silent sentry," with instructions to fall back if any attackers approached "and let them come" toward the stable. He thought no more about it until Witherspoon and his delegation showed up the next day.[17]

IN LOUISVILLE, General Terry mulled Merrill's dispatches, Grant's telegram, and General Order 48. On June 11 he sent Merrill's reports to army headquarters in Washington along with a long cover letter of his own.

If the army had any doubts about Major Merrill in the aftermath of his dustup with Custer at Fort Laramie, Terry dispelled them immediately. Merrill, stuck in the "most disturbed district" of South Carolina, was "an officer of great intelligence," he wrote. "I think that the utmost confidence may be placed in his representations."

Terry then offered his own views on "the general subject of the suppression of the Ku Klux organization." It was so large that it would be "manifestly impossible" to deal with it everywhere at the same time.

"Fortunately, it is not necessary, as I think, to attack the organization at every point," he continued. "If in a single state it could be suppressed, and in that state *exemplary punishment* meted out to some of the most prominent criminals, I think that a fatal blow would be given to it everywhere, or at any rate the task of suppression elsewhere would thereafter be an easy one."

There was no need to use extreme measures in an entire state, but only to "act vigorously" in a "small district," Terry continued. His said his own experience had shown the effectiveness of this strategy, and he recommended using it again now—in "one of the most disturbed districts in South Carolina"—in a powerful and overwhelming effort.

Still, military power would not be enough, he said. He cited Merrill's reports describing "the great unwillingness of the people to give sworn information upon which arrests [might] be made, or to testify against members of the Klan." This unwillingness, he said, arose from "their fears of revenge." He saw no solution to this difficulty except by hiring "an *efficient corps of skillful and efficient detectives*" to infiltrate the Klan hierarchy and gather evidence.[18]

With this letter Terry had paid Merrill the ultimate compliment a military superior can bestow on a subaltern. He had read Merrill's reports and thought about them for two weeks. He had lauded Merrill's professionalism and Merrill's insights, and he had made it obvious that his own thoughts derived from Merrill's belief that if he could arrest and punish "even five, or three" Klan members, York County's troubles would end.

He had recommended South Carolina's upcountry as the focus of any military intervention and made it obvious that Merrill's York County was the "small district" he had in mind. And his suggestion to hire undercover informants to infiltrate the Klan dovetailed neatly with the efforts of Attorney General Akerman and Senator Pool in Washington.

The original of Terry's letter, together with Merrill's reports, went to War Secretary Belknap June 17. General of the Army William T. Sherman received the package four days later. General Henry Halleck, Terry's immediate superior, asked the high command for instructions "on the points suggested by General Terry and Major Merrill."[19]

CHAPTER SEVENTEEN

The Long Hot Summer

By mid-June U.S. Marshals and troops in the field had had a month to implement President Grant's General Order 48 "to arrest and break up disguised night marauders" in the former Confederacy, and nothing substantive had happened. Unable to act without permission from local authorities, federal lawmen, as Major Merrill had explained, were hamstrung. They needed guidance from the Grant administration—Attorney General Akerman and Secretary of War Belknap—on how to get around this restriction. None was forthcoming.

On June 23 the *New York Herald* suggested that Grant was waiting for Klan terrorism to ripen "until, in the judgment of the President, the condition of affairs in that section of the country shall require [instructions]."[1]

Less forgiving was the Philadelphia *Evening Telegraph*, which blamed Akerman, "a Georgian [who] thinks he knows best how to deal with the people of that section of the country, and does not believe in precipitating matters." Since Akerman had issued no order, the Ku Klux Klan Act might as well have "never passed."[2]

Akerman's failures, however, were no worse than the War Department's. If Grant was simply waiting for the mere existence of the new law to bring the unrepentant South to heel, it came as little surprise that the Klan disdained the Ku Klux Klan Act just as it had disdained the first two Enforcement Acts.

But what both the South and North had ignored were the two serious pieces of legal artillery that the new law contained. The first, as Merrill had explained to Yorkville's "best people" in May, was suspension of habeas corpus. This would give him carte blanche to chase down suspected Ku Klux, throw them in jail, and leave them there. The second was the Ironclad Oath for jurors. In trials there would be no more automatic acquittals.

The *Cincinnati Enquirer*, no friend of the Grant administration, had figured this out, albeit with some impolite exaggeration. With Congress's help, the *Enquirer* wrote on June 28, Akerman now had "the power to order the reconstruction of any state." Congress decided to empower the blacks, so "they could use them for party purposes," to "take away the free choice of the white people" and to "strike down the white population."[3]

The Ku Klux Klan Act, as the *Enquirer* recognized, was a powerful law. Its only sticking point, at this juncture, was Grant's failure to apply it. But events—and the attitudes of the principal actors—were moving in that direction. General Terry, the U.S. Army high command, Belknap, and Akerman were pushing hard.

BUT IT WAS summertime. Congress was in recess; Grant was vacationing in Long Branch, New Jersey; and, after filing his opinion in the Central Pacific case on June 3, Akerman left town for Georgia, the last cabinet secretary to depart.

His absence heralded a new round of insults—probably ginned up by the Central Pacific. The Lancaster, Pennsylvania, *Intelligencer Journal* denounced Akerman for failing to pay attention to the cases before him and noted "a great deal of consternation among high officials," because of his ill-prepared appearances before the Supreme Court. Two of the "high officials," were unnamed "fellow cabinet ministers," one of whom was undoubtedly Interior Secretary Delano—the railroads' special friend. The *Intelligencer* predicted that Akerman would be gone shortly.[4]

The *Cincinnati Commercial*, whose reporter obviously had attended the same news conference, went further. Akerman "materially retard[ed]" the business of government by his procrastination. "In some cases large sums of money have been lost, because he would not act," the *Commercial* said. "[He is] incompetent, and all the cabinet officers are convinced of it." Some had approached the president, and the "Solicitor General [Benjamin Bristow] and one of the assistant Attorney Generals" were ready to resign. Grant, the *Commercial* concluded, was upset with Akerman and might soon "invite him out."[5]

By the end of June, with Congress gone and no one paying attention, the overt slurs died away, but the gossip lingered. Akerman's departure was a given, the *New York Herald* reported on June 25, and he would be replaced, according to "cabinet rumor," by either Solicitor General Bristow or John Harlan, Bristow's Louisville law partner. Nearly identical reports appeared elsewhere, always with the Kentuckians prominently featured.[6]

DESPITE HIS alleged woes, however, the *Herald* found Akerman "much invigorated" when he unexpectedly returned to Washington the evening of June 24 after two weeks with Matty and the boys.[7]

His task was to render an opinion on whether Grant should pardon former South Carolina congressman Christopher Bowen, convicted of bigamy in June in a Washington trial whose scandalous revelations had caused a nationwide sensation. Grant wanted to hear what his attorney general had to say before making his decision.

Bowen, sentenced to two years in prison and fined $250, was in jail awaiting transport and leaving his fortunes in the hands of the remarkably capable Susan Pettigrew-King, "Mrs. Bowen No. 3," who had won broad public sympathy with a tearful and dramatic courtroom plea for mercy for her disgraced "husband."[8]

Pettigrew-King, described in the *New York Times* as "a lady belonging to a prominent and wealthy southern family" in Charleston, South Carolina, had remained in Washington after the sentencing to gather support for a petition pleading that the president grant clemency.[9] She had gotten "hundreds of signatures," the *Buffalo Commercial* wrote, including several from people "very prominent in business and politics."[10] She had also wangled an appointment to speak with Akerman.

Bowen's friends, the *New York Herald* reported, were not particularly sanguine about Bowen's chances, given Akerman's "prejudices."[11] These were not described but probably had something to do with the similarities between the biographies of the two men and their very different ethical compasses.

At the time of his June 13 conviction, the supplicant was thirty-nine, a flamboyant fellow "of fine personal appearance," according to the *Buffalo Weekly Courier*. He was born in Rhode Island, but had moved to Georgia in 1850 and to South Carolina in 1862, where he studied law and was admitted to the bar. During the war he served as a captain in the Confederate Coast Guard, but he became a Republican after the surrender. He was twice elected to Congress before losing his seat in 1870.[12]

There was no doubt Bowen was guilty of bigamy, and he was probably guilty of perjury and fraud—and perhaps bribery and forgery. In 1852 he had married Frances Hicks, the first Mrs. Bowen, in Augusta, Georgia, but had abandoned her when he moved to Charleston. At some point in the next few years he married the second (unnamed in the national press) Mrs. Bowen, whom he also eventually abandoned. She moved to Kentucky and apparently tried to sue him, but her case did not prosper. Hicks, the first wife, was the complainant in the current trial.[13]

Bowen married Pettigrew-King in August 1870 and claimed to have divorced Hicks in New York in 1865. His lawyers produced a divorce decree during the trial, but it turned out to be a forgery. Bowen had actually obtained a divorce in New Haven, Connecticut, but only in November 1870, after his third "marriage" to Pettigrew-King.

Bowen's July 13 conviction set up what the *Buffalo Weekly Courier* described as "an extraordinary scene" at sentencing five days later.[14]

The judge invited Bowen to speak, and, as he rose, "Mrs. King-Bowen convulsively clung to him," the *Courier* reported. He had married Pettigrew-King believing he was divorced, he said, and blamed "false friends" in New York for deceiving him.

"Much has been said about my abandoning a woman in Augusta," he continued. He did not want to "plead an extenuation," he said, but then he proceeded to do so. He was "a boy" of eighteen at the time of his first marriage, while the first Mrs. Bowen was "a mother of thirty." He was working, "toiling every day," he said. "Was I to sit down there in that little town and starve to death?"

So he left for Charleston. At one point, he said, he sent a messenger to find Frances, but she told the messenger "take the letter back, I want nothing more to do with him," Bowen said. Time passed, and she never came forward, he said, even after he got into politics. He thought she was dead.

"[As for this prosecution], if you are pleased to call it that," he continued, "[it grew out of political involvement] and this alone. . . . I stood in the way politically, of someone. I must be gotten out of the way."

"I am tired and worn out with this pursuit of me," he concluded. "I married that woman last August in good faith," he said, pointing to Pettigrew-King. "Though the laws of the country may annul that, I have a firm belief that the laws of God never will."

At that point Pettigrew-King stood up and grasped his hand, then clung to him until he asked her to resume her seat. Then the judge read the sentence.

Pettigrew-King rose again: "If he did it, I did it," she sobbed. "If he is to be sentenced, please sentence me . . . Oh! Sentence me, I cannot part from him."[15]

"Bowen, after a pause, addressed Mrs. King, saying when his term expired he would return to her," the *Chicago Tribune* reported. "Whereupon Mrs. King extended to him her hand, which he grasped as in pledge of faith. She appeared deeply affected."

The *Tribune*, no friend of Bowen's, nevertheless acknowledged that this final act found its way into newspapers all over the country and that "the people of Washington, regardless of politics," were signing Pettigrew-King's petition in droves.[16]

Akerman saw Pettigrew-King on Monday, June 26, and reportedly told her he would pay close attention to her case.[17] But Bowen's friends were right in thinking that Akerman had little interest in furthering Bowen's cause. By Thursday, June 29, Grant apparently had decided not to pardon Bowen, and Akerman had concurred.[18]

This news, however, was not yet public, and Pettigrew-King, undaunted, decided to spend her weekend rallying public support. "It appears she was successful," the Nashville *Republican Banner* reported, saying that the president had telegraphed Akerman Saturday afternoon, July 1, asking him to draft the pardon and send it to Long Branch.[19]

Akerman dutifully wrote the pardon and sent it to Grant, but he also attached his opinion, agreeing with the judge and prosecutor who handled the case that a pardon was not justified, the *Republican Banner* reported. Grant pardoned Bowen Monday, July 3, just in time for the "Bowens" to celebrate Independence Day.

Grant's motives were not known. He may have succumbed to the pleadings of Pettigrew-King, or he may have concluded that public sympathies had shifted to the supplicant. Much later the New York *Sun* reported that Grant had no intention of pardoning Bowen until Grant's wife Julia stepped in and induced him to change his mind. This report was never confirmed.[20]

AFTER THE Bowen affair, Akerman remained in Washington to begin marshaling his forces for the coming confrontation with the Ku Klux Klan. He had a $50,000 congressional appropriation to spend.

On June 28 he wrote to H. C. Whitley, the chief of the Secret Service, which now came under the purview of both the Treasury and Justice Departments. The letter was intended to formalize a conversation he had had earlier with Whitley, probably in Atlanta. Akerman had known Whitley since his Georgia days.[21]

Congress had given him new money, Akerman wrote, and he wanted Whitley to have some of it ("on account of your expertness in the detective system"). "I have also reason to believe that Congress at the same time had particularly in view certain sorts of crimes which are reported to be more frequent in the southern states than elsewhere," he continued. He noted that the Ku Klux Klan Act was focused on "the provisions of the Fourteenth Amendment."

Whitley was to hire "capable and trusty persons" to "detect" violators, gather evidence, and report [to Akerman]." The general field of operations would be the southern states, but Whitley could pick the specific locales. He urged Whitley to consult with Senator Scott's select committee if he needed ideas. Whitley could spend up to $20,000.[22]

Akerman, however, did not intend to rely exclusively on Whitley's agents. He also sought to strengthen U.S. Marshals and U.S. Attorneys in affected states, either by hiring new men or encouraging existing staff. In July Akerman began sending letters and secret directives to his U.S. Attorneys in the South, instructing them to arrest offenders and prosecute them in federal court under the Ku Klux Klan Act.[23]

Like Grant, his focus was shifting to the South Carolina upcountry, where violations were occurring in all the northern border counties. In early June, before meeting with Whitley, he wrote to D. H. Starbuck, his U.S. Attorney in North Carolina, and directed him to "take such action as . . . necessary to bring the supposed offenders to a speedy trial."

Starbuck was not one of his favorites. The previous year Akerman had pushed Starbuck to rid the state government of officials who could not take the Ironclad Oath, and in his June letter he reminded him: "Prompt and intelligent investigation of all these cases, and vigorous prosecution of the guilty parties are expected from you."[24]

Efforts to stiffen federal law enforcement in the South continued sporadically through the summer. Akerman did not make a substantial push in South Carolina, an odd oversight perhaps. But he had seen Terry's reports and knew that Merrill, at least in York County, already had an unmatched network of informants. South Carolina also had U.S. Attorney Corbin.

He remained concerned about his home state and in July hired two "special assistants" to work with the U.S. Attorney's office in Georgia. Victims of Ku Klux violence were often "ignorant, poor and timid," he wrote in a letter to one of them, and had no way of bringing their suffering to the notice of federal authorities.

"Knowing your energy and courage, and your readiness to defend the oppressed, I desire to employ you." He wanted the new assistants—he sent almost identical letters to both—to go into affected neighborhoods and gather evidence. The investigators could choose whether to identify themselves. The job, Akerman said, would take about two months. Akerman would pay $250 per month, plus expenses.[25]

These efforts began to bear some fruit in August when U.S. Marshals chased down hundreds of suspects all across the region. Predictable problems, however, immediately arose. Although the Ku Klux Klan Act was being put to use, it had not been fully implemented.

Grant had not suspended habeas corpus anywhere, making it impossible to jail suspects long enough to give prosecutors time to cajole terrified witnesses into coming forward. The army had no orders and was still held hostage to the whim of local law enforcement. Klan detainees refused to give evidence because of their oath-taking, their fears of reprisal by their erstwhile comrades, and the certainty that they would get no mercy from federal juries in the South.

Late in July Congressman Ben Butler wrote Akerman a long letter suggesting a possible solution. Why not ask the president to offer amnesty to all Ku Klux who renounced the organization and gave evidence?[26] Not yet, Akerman replied. Instead, he wrote, he preferred to have U.S. Attorneys and prosecutors "discreetly plant" the idea that amnesty would be given to offenders who showed "reasonable penitence."

Amnesty appealed to Akerman as a reward to individual Klan members for turning state's evidence, but it was still too early for general amnesty or presidential proclamations, he told Butler. "The scoundrels" needed to "get more extensively alarmed," he wrote. And they were, at least in South Carolina. Informants there, he said with something approaching glee, had told him that whites wanted the prosecution stopped lest there be starvation because so many white landowners were hiding in the woods to avoid arrest. Now it was Klan members who were laying out.

"[Though] they are well scared in certain parts of South Carolina," he added, "in other states we have not made much impression.[27]

Akerman, at this point, was intransigent. On August 18, he wrote a private letter of encouragement to U.S. Attorneys E. P. Jacobson and G. Wiley Wells in Mississippi after Jacobson had described the limits of the Ku Klux Klan Act's reach. Akerman sent a vintage reply: be firm, and don't wait for apologies from the Ku Klux. "It is my individual opinion that nothing is more idle than to attempt to conciliate by kindness that portion of the southern people who are still malcontent," he wrote. "They take all kindness on the part of the Government as evidence of timidity, and hence are emboldened to lawlessness by it."

The government would not win converts, but it could command respect "by the increase of its power," he added. "It is the business of a judge to terrify evildoers, not to coax them." He offered the two prosecutors $1,000 each to investigate violations of the Ku Klux Klan Act, and he suggested they spend it on detectives.[28]

THERE WAS little for Akerman to do in Washington except wait for animosity toward the Ku Klux Klan to mature, and in mid-July he returned to Georgia. On his way, however, he stopped in Weldon, North Carolina, a black Republican stronghold in the northeastern part of the state, to give a speech about the General Assembly's efforts there to call a constitutional convention.

The state's Republicans, of which there were a significant number, regarded the convention as a thinly disguised effort by the assembly's recently elected Democratic majority to rewrite the state's 1868 constitution, stripping out many of the reconstruction provisions it contained as a condition of North Carolina's readmission to the Union.

Early in 1871 Democratic assembly members had tried to summon a convention but had failed to win the two-thirds majority required by law. Now the Democrats were trying to sidestep this provision with a referendum, with which a simple majority could call the convention.[29]

Supporters said North Carolinians had nothing to fear, but opponents were skeptical, especially about the possibility that the convention would void the "homestead" provision of the 1868 constitution, which made it illegal to attach the property of smallholders in payment for debts. "The homestead" was a favorite of blacks, but there were also plenty of whites who had taken advantage of it.[30]

Akerman's July 16 speech lasted for more than two hours before a largely black audience. He was not conciliatory. Congress would not like to see "overturned" the 1868 constitution it had approved. Even less would it like to see the creation of a new government. "When a president is called upon to protect a state against domestic violence [because of competing governments,] "it is his duty . . . to determine which party is the lawful government and which is insurgent."[31]

Akerman left no doubt that "the present national executive," would support the one "Congress had recognized." His implied advice was easy to understand. Vote no on calling the convention—or face the consequences.[32]

Reaction to Akerman's speech was sparse in North Carolina. The Raleigh *Tri-Weekly New Era,* a Republican paper, gave it ample display, albeit with considerable editorializing. The object of the convention's supporters was to bring about a "collision between the convention, if called, and the United States government." North Carolina did not need any more of this, the *Era* concluded. "If you wish to prevent another revolution, go to the polls and vote 'No Convention.'"[33] Elsewhere, Akerman's speech played to mixed reviews, focusing on its political implications rather than its substance. The *New-York Tribune* described a "statesman-like effort," remarking that Akerman's clear support for the Grant administration "should put an end to the frequent criticism of some journals, which have doubted his republicanism," and clamored for his removal from the cabinet on political grounds."[34]

The New York *Sun,* however, castigated "ex-rebel Major Moses T." Akerman for leaving his job to go stumping in North Carolina. It was "humiliating" to see Akerman "belittle himself," the *Sun* reported. "Every loyal man in the country blushes at the thought that a man who but a little while [before had] armed himself to assist in destroying this government and severing this Union" should have more prominence than "gallant union men."[35]

In Memphis, the *Public Ledger* wrote on August 24, 1871, that Akerman ought to be "indicted" for interfering in North Carolina's election. It called the Weldon speech "a threat." Which it was.[36]

The coverage appeared somewhat surprising for several reasons. Akerman, languishing in political limbo for most of the year, had suddenly increased his visibility as an opposition target, this time not because of his perceived legal incompetence or his fights with the railroads but instead because of his civil rights advocacy.

The *Sun*'s screed was perhaps the first time Akerman had been seriously vilified for his Confederate background, even as the *Tribune* celebrated him for demonstrating his loyalty to the Grant administration and the Republican Party.

The Weldon appearance had also shown northerners that Akerman was quite likely unique in the Grant cabinet in that he not only lived in the South but was also comfortable working in the South—and communicating with blacks. He brought the federal government into southern parlors, a skill not to be taken lightly.

And this reemergence was different from his first flirtation with political relevance. In North Carolina, as in Georgia, he had taken a hard partisan line, but in this case his cause triumphed: "No convention" won a solid ten thousand–vote victory in the August 3 referendum.[37]

Success in North Carolina, however, won him no friends in his ongoing dispute with the Central Branch of the Union Pacific. Upon his return from Georgia in early August, Kansas senator Samuel Pomeroy inquired about further consideration of the Central Branch's claim for bonds, prompting a courteous but terse response from Akerman. "I can have no further connection with the matter unless the Secretary of the Interior should request a reconsideration," Akerman wrote. He assumed Secretary Delano would not ask for a new hearing unless new information came to light. Akerman undoubtedly knew that Pomeroy had served as the second president of the Atchison, Topeka & Santa Fe Railroad.[38]

The "new facts" were forthcoming August 25 in a letter from the Central Branch's lead attorney, Effingham H. Nichols, to Delano. Far from containing fresh information, Nichols rehashed the railroad's earlier contacts with Akerman, larded the text with good wishes from important politicians, and intimated in hackneyed legalese that the attorney general, as the Union Pacific had said before, was incompetent.

"And when subsequently certain questions were propounded by the Honorable Secretary [of the Interior] to the Honorable Attorney General at the suggestion of the President," read one part of a run-on sentence, "it was supposed that such questions were pro forma, and not only so, but I was personally requested to make but a brief statement before the Attorney General." The statement was apparently so brief that the attorney general could not "gather therefrom any clear understanding of the case."

The conclusion to be drawn here was that Akerman did not know what he was doing, had no interest in giving Nichols—and others, presumably—a fair hearing, and had shown Nichols the door almost immediately.[39]

Akerman was enraged. On September 5 he wrote to Delano, dispensing with the customary format when one cabinet secretary wrote to another ("I have the honor . . . ") and denouncing Nichols as being "entirely mistaken as to the amount of attention" he had given the Central Branch during the spring.

"I heard Mr. Nichols two hours on one day, Judge Hoar one hour on another day, and another hour on a third day," he wrote. Then he listed fifteen different documents he had consulted—affidavits, opinions, arguments and letters—from the likes of Pomeroy, Nichols, Hoar, and others.

"Though I entered upon the investigation with strong personal sympathies in favor of the company," he continued, "I was unable to advise that its application was well found in law." He was still willing to hear "further argument" on new "material facts," but he had other things to do. Akerman said he would give the Central Branch one more chance to make its case—"any time" during the following week—and would meet "for up to six hours." That would be the end of it.[40]

Akerman heard nothing until six weeks later when Delano announced that the Central Branch had abandoned its application. Failing to win approval from Akerman, the railroad had apparently taken its case directly to President Grant, who did not approve the Central Branch's initial proposal, because, as Akerman already knew, it contained nothing new. Late in October former attorney general Hoar, in a letter to Akerman, described the president's position as an "insuperable obstacle." Hoar wrote, "[Thus] you will be relieved from the trouble of giving an opinion, and from a further hearing on our part."[41]

Akerman, however, was under no illusions. In late August, as he fumed over Nichols's letter, he wrote Matty to let her know that "powerful interests"—which he did not name—were quite likely not going to go quietly. Hoar's letter had all but confirmed that the Central Branch was finished with Akerman and would seek redress elsewhere.

He told Matty he had "a close secret" and needed her to understand "the dimensions of a new effort which I am satisfied is going on to oust me from office." Akerman did not particularly care about his own fortunes, he said. "But I have a delicacy on the point of exposing the President to annoyance [and perhaps] censure and dislike."

"I believe I am right in my views of the law," he wrote, "[but if my opposition is] serious in its strength, I have a disposition to get out of the way by resigning."[42]

CHAPTER EIGHTEEN

Bearing Witness

JULY 27, 1871

Hamp Hicklin had been living in York County for about fifteen years when it started. He was a talkative, engaging fellow who knew all his white neighbors and practically everyone else in York. He had a farm about seven miles outside Yorkville, he told congressional investigators. "But then I had to leave."

That was after the Ku Klux started to "visit" him in January 1871. Seven times in all. He was sleeping in the woods, he said, and managed to escape each time, but they beat his wife, wrecked his house, and shot his turkeys. After that, he "went away"—over the river to North Carolina.

They came after him anyway, which he did not expect, and found him on a Sunday, probably sometime in April. He couldn't remember exactly. He had gotten in late that night after spending the day in Charlotte. He thought he was safe outside York County. They caught him in bed.

"Then they whipped me. They had my hands tied, and they whipped me and whipped me and whipped me until they cut me all to pieces." Eighteen men, all in disguise, but Hicklin recognized some of the horses: the one with the white right hind foot and white left forefoot was Jimmy Jones's; the leopard mule belonged to Henry Williams.

Afterward they walked him for about two miles. They accused him of telling Sheriff Glenn about how they had been hunting him. They said that he gave Glenn their names. "I didn't tell him nothing," Hicklin insisted. But when they started repeating everything he had told Glenn, using Hicklin's own words, he was trapped.

"Sheriff Glenn told us to kill you," one of them said.

He managed to escape. He crawled thirteen miles back across the border and down to the U.S. Army encampment in Yorkville. It took him two days. Major Merrill put him in his field hospital. Hicklin had been living in the garrison ever since.

Senator John Scott asked him whether he had gone back to North Carolina. He had not. "They would kill me."[1]

SENATOR SCOTT, a Republican from Pennsylvania, was chairman of the Joint Select Committee to Inquire into the Condition of Affairs in the Late Insurrectionary States, consisting of seven senators and fourteen House members. Scott was leading a three-man subcommittee that interviewed Hicklin on July 27, 1871, in Yorkville, the last stop on a South Carolina fact-finding trip that had lasted almost a month. The subcommittee was leaving the next day.

The joint committee had won easy approval from Congress in April despite the misgivings of President Grant and outright opposition from Radical leader Ben Butler, who scorned the idea as an excuse for Congress to do nothing about the Ku Klux Klan except call witnesses and write reports.

The committee had begun its work in early June in Washington. Its brief was to explore Ku Klux atrocities throughout the former Confederacy, but their chief priority was South Carolina's upcountry.

At first the naysayers' prophecy appeared to be coming true. Early testimony came from well-spoken, well-to-do whites—witnesses who could afford the trip to the capital. Among them: former South Carolina governor James L. Orr, the apostate who had converted to Republicanism during the 1870 state elections; Richard Carpenter, the 1870 Reform Party gubernatorial candidate in 1870; state attorney general Daniel H. Chamberlain; U.S. Attorney David T. Corbin; and Yorkville businessman Joseph Herndon.

One witness who did not appear was York County Klan chieftain J. W. Avery. Summoned to attend, he checked in to Washington's Hotel Boston but then abruptly left town, whereabouts unknown. He was believed to have gone to Canada. Having ignored the committee's invitation, he was a fugitive.[2]

The Washington witnesses were engaging, articulate, and frequently informative, but their appearances took place behind closed doors, and their testimony lacked excitement. At the end of June, Scott decided that the investigation needed to go on the road if it wanted to dive deeply into South Carolina's troubles.

He appointed a subcommittee composed of himself and two Ohioans, Congressmen Job Stevenson, a Radical Republican and an attorney by profession, and Democrat Philadelph Van Trump, a former judge. They reached Columbia, the South Carolina capital, on July 3.

A significant number of the Columbia witnesses, unlike the Washington crowd, were working people, both black and white. But Columbia was still something of a special place: a Radical-dominated government outpost and safe haven for about one hundred refugees who had escaped the Ku Klux.

After a few days, the subcommittee wanted to get still closer to the action, so it headed for the upcountry, arriving in Spartanburg July 6 for an anticipated visit of three or four days. They stayed for eleven days.

The panel still did not talk publicly about the proceedings, but word of the committee's arrival got out, and would-be witnesses, most of them black, most of them country people, streamed into town from all over Spartanburg County. Once this happened, the committee ceased being an excuse to do nothing. Spartanburg was a national event—and the committee was a national story.

The public clamored for information, and news reporters struggled to provide it. Unable to approach committee members directly, the easiest way to find out what was happening, apart from pure speculation, was to interview the witnesses. Predictably, white viewpoints dominated.

In a dispatch dated July 10 from Spartanburg, the New York *World* dismissed the subcommittee's "evidence so far" as unimportant, except as it disclosed "the miserable condition of the state government." It cited former U.S. senator and Confederate general James Chestnut by name as one of its principal sources.[3]

Chestnut, the husband of noted Civil War diarist Mary Chestnut, blamed South Carolina's unrest on ignorant whites, political corruption, carpetbaggers, black militias, and black suffrage. These were standard grievances, but they accurately conveyed the bitterness and confusion of the white South.[4]

With no committee members to dispute their distortions, some reporters claimed knowledge they could not possibly have. In a July 22 dispatch from Spartanburg, the solidly Democratic *San Francisco Examiner* declared that "careful sifting of the entire batch of statements"—there was no transcript yet—had produced "a solid refutation" of the Klan's "alleged existence." Witnesses "of unquestioned veracity" blamed the carpetbaggers and scalawags: "[These] meet in secret dens at midnight and conspire to poison the minds of the negroes and organize schemes for perpetrating feuds and bitter jealousies."[5]

The *Carolina Spartan* said the hearings were designed to produce "a campaign document" for 1872, so the federal government would have an excuse to send enough soldiers "to place bayonets at every voting precinct in the South."[6]

The Columbia *Daily Phoenix* acknowledged that it knew nothing about the Spartanburg hearings, but "someone gave out that witnesses who could give any information on Ku Klux matters would be allowed two dollars a day and ten cents mileage." This word "spread like wild-fire," the *Phoenix* continued, "and the yard in the rear of the hotel was quickly filled with willing colored witnesses."[7]

Black witnesses were never quoted. Many were undoubtedly fearful of further retribution should their testimony or even their presence at the hearings become known. But it was also apparent that white reporters—northerners as well as southerners—were not accustomed to speaking with blacks.

The Columbia *Daily Union*, the lone Republican voice among the Democratic papers that dominated South Carolina's public discourse, told a different story. "Evidence in about three hundred cases of outrages has been taken, consisting of all grades of horror and cruelty," the *Union* wrote. "Many cases have been before the committee where backs that have been lacerated and other bodily injuries received from the hands of the Ku Klux have spoken louder than words." Scores of witnesses had to be turned away. "The mass of evidence adduced is undeniable and horrible."

The *Union* may have spoken with black witnesses or may have managed to get Scott or Stevenson to summarize the proceedings. The likeliest source, however, was probably white Republican U.S. congressman Alexander Wallace, an unalloyed Radical hated by the white establishment. He had accompanied the subcommittee throughout its tour. After all, the upcountry was his district.

Perhaps most significant for readers in South Carolina, the *Union* said that threats made against the witnesses had so alarmed Senator Scott that he had "plainly indicated" that renewed violence would end up with Spartanburg County being put under martial law.[8] The *Union* did not say where or to whom Scott had made this remark.

The *Union's* report and Scott's warning were reprinted elsewhere in the state. The *Charleston Daily News* disguised its dispatch as a letter to the editor about the "reliable (?)" *Union*, but carried it in full. One out-of-state paper said Scott had delivered the warning during a meeting with leading Spartanburg citizens who had assured him that violence would cease.[9] It was not clear that such a meeting had taken place.

The verbatim transcript of the hearings, released many months later, showed a businesslike atmosphere with only sporadic political digressions. Both Scott and Stevenson were restrained and matter-of-fact. Van Trump, outnumbered by his Republican colleagues, was more belligerent and impatient, sometimes bullying.

For the most part, however, the witnesses simply talked, and their testimony was extraordinary. Black farmer William Moss had been "knocking about" since "ten or twelve" Ku Klux ran him off his farm in May, he told the subcommittee, the same night they murdered his neighbor Wally Fowler. Tenant farmer Elias Thomson was tending his sick wife and sleeping with two of his small children when fifteen gowned Klan members rousted him. "Are you ready to die?" they asked. Then they pushed him outdoors, threatened to hang him, threatened to shoot him, and ended up beating him with tree limbs.[10]

The committee left Spartanburg July 16, spent two days in Unionville, and then spent three more days in Columbia, hearing from mostly black witnesses but also from two former Confederate generals—cavalryman and Southern Life executive Wade Hampton and Matthew Butler, Richard Carpenter's erstwhile Reform Party running mate.

THE COMMITTEE arrived in Yorkville, its last stop, on Saturday, July 22. The county appeared to be making an effort not to offend its distinguished visitors. The *Enquirer* had reprinted the *Daily Union* story in its entirety two days before the committee's arrival—without comment. A number of the county's leading citizens were prepared to offer testimony.[11]

Politeness, however, only went so far. The same *Enquirer* that printed the *Union* story also reprinted a denunciation from the *Spartan*, which described the select subcommittee's labors as little more than an election maneuver.

The elusive J. William Avery had apparently returned home briefly to Yorkville after fleeing Washington but was long departed by the time the subcommittee came to town.[12] And potential Ku Klux witnesses—several had been summoned—had been reminded by the leadership that death awaited them ("Death, death, death!") if they told the visitors anything about raids, rituals, or regulations.

Yorkville's tentative hospitality fell apart immediately. On their first night in town Scott and Stevenson entered the dining room of Yorkville's Rawlinson's Hotel to have supper with Congressman Wallace. The "semi-official version" of what followed, issued in a statement by the committee at the end of the trip, was first reported by Washington's *Evening Star* and then reprinted in one form or another all over the country.[13]

"They were just seating themselves at the table, and not a word had been spoken," according to one rendering of the semi-official version, when a Major James Berry—a complete stranger—grabbed a pitcher of milk off a nearby serving table, intending to empty it over Wallace.

The hotel owner spotted what was happening, however, and jogged Berry's arm. Wallace emerged unscathed, but Stevenson apparently caught a substantial dousing. Both men stood up.

"Mr. Wallace jerked out a revolver and raised it to shoot Berry—the ladies screaming," the report continued, but the owner stepped between the two men "and Mr. Stevenson coolly caught Wallace's hand" before he could do any damage. Stevenson ordered the owner to "take that man out of the room."

Half a dozen friends gathered around Berry and led him out, the report said.

Over the next hour "several citizens of prominence" arrived "to apologize in the amplest manner on behalf of Berry."

But there were no regrets about the hated congressman, known throughout his district and maybe throughout the state thereafter as "Buttermilk Wallace."[14] "It was subsequently ascertained that the ambush had been discussed by the assailant and his friends during the afternoon," the semi-official statement said. "Berry was to use hot coffee, but had finally concluded on milk."[15]

Unfortunately for York County, the night was still young. After dinner the sodden Stevenson and his companions removed to the hotel porch where a brass band composed of black musicians began to serenade them.

"An immense crowd" gathered on the sidewalk, the *Yorkville Enquirer* wrote, "collected partly by the music of the band, and partly, perhaps, to create a demonstration in honor of the members of the committee."

Town marshals were trying to keep the crowd off the sidewalk, presumably to let pedestrians pass unmolested. As the concert was coming to an end, Marshal William M. Snyder confronted Tom Johnson, one of the musicians, who would not move out of the way, the *Enquirer* said.

Snyder then attempted to arrest Johnson, apparently poking him with his baton. Johnson insisted on moving to the head of the crowd, the *Enquirer* continued, with Snyder in pursuit. The third time Snyder poked him, Johnson jerked the baton away, causing Snyder to fall down.

"Snyder then drew a pistol and fired five shots at the belligerent darkey, wounding him in the face, shoulder, hand, arm and back," the *Enquirer* wrote, "each shot taking effect, but not inflicting dangerous wounds."

At that point Major Merrill arrived. He was able to calm the black musicians and told Snyder to get the white audience out of the street. Johnson was never in danger, but the town council convened a special investigation that exonerated Snyder, ruling that he was simply doing his duty.[16]

The *Enquirer*, however, left out a few details, which were highlighted later in the "semi-official" statement. As the music began, a crowd of rowdy young white men gathered on the Rawlinson's porch to shout insults and catcalls, the statement said. So much for a demonstration in honor of the committee.

Also, the committee reported, both Snyder and Yorkville mayor Frank Harris—leader of the town council—were Klan members. Summarizing their stay, and certainly their first evening, the committee reported "a bitter spirit" prevailing in Yorkville.[17]

OFFICIAL HEARINGS began Monday morning, July 24, at Merrill's headquarters in Rose's Hotel. The conference room and its environs were jam-packed, "stairs, halls and perches," with witnesses waiting to testify, the committee statement said.[18]

In Columbia, Spartanburg, and Unionville the hearings had had a first-come, first-served feeling, with the committee taking statements from anyone who wished to testify. There was little information on how the committee actually chose its witnesses in those three places. The *Charleston Daily Courier* suggested that Wallace was doing "the dirty work" for the Republicans by finding black victims and vetting them.[19]

The Yorkville hearings were different, displaying a significant amount of witness organization. This was almost certainly due to Merrill. He had plenty of legal experience and had been asking questions, collecting informants, and writing notes to himself for months in hopes of putting the Ku Klux on trial. He had probably spent Sunday briefing the committee. He knew the Klan—both the chieftains and the foot soldiers—and now he could finally make them squirm.

Yorkville druggist John Tomlinson, suspected ringleader in the March 7 death of Anderson Brown, apparently considered the threat of retaliation from his fellow Klansmen more powerful than the risk of perjuring himself. He denied knowing anything about the murder, and, asked where he was that night, he tried to demur: "That is a delicate question."

So what? Scott asked, unimpressed.

"For a young man and single, he might be in places where he would not want to tell where he was," Tomlinson replied. "It is a little delicate. I was in town. I will tell you that."[20]

Rufus McClain, the purported leader of the Black Panther Klan and a town marshal like Snyder, said nothing. Named by informants as a member of the Jim Williams lynch mob and a participant in the Yorkville ammunition raid, he claimed repeatedly to have "no opinion" about Ku Klux activities or even to know that the Klan existed.[21] John Hunter, a clerk in a dry goods store and another Black Panther at the Jim Williams lynching, seemed smarter than McClain and said even less.[22]

On Tuesday, the panel applied pressure. The predominant witness was J. Rufus Bratton, and his testimony, lasting several hours, was something of a sparring match in which he appeared to be taking the measure of his questioners—how much they knew about the Jim Williams raid and the York County Ku Klux Klan in general, while denying any "personal" knowledge of any of it.

"I merely hear rumors and reports," he said. These, however, he was willing to share at some length. He had come armed with old editions of the *Yorkville Enquirer* describing the Tom Roundtree murder. He had also heard of "a negro up here named Brown" who was killed—"a farmer, renting land, I presume."

And then there was "Williams," a militia captain: "[He] was hung about twelve miles below by some persons, who I cannot tell."

He also had *Enquirer* editions describing his "peace meetings," along with copies of the Klan's published manifestos. He spoke about other things he had read, all designed to support his contention: "I am no member of the Ku Klux, and know nothing of their proceedings."

He acknowledged that in "many cases" he did not believe blacks' reports of whippings. Why don't they show their scars and name their tormentors, he said. "A great many of these people dislike to work, and if they can get the protection of the state or the United States to relieve them from work they will do it," he added. "I have no faith in their testimony."[23]

It was an impressive performance. While never denying the existence of the Klan, he had strictly limited his acquaintance with it to the public record while highlighting his position as a peacemaker and as a knowledgeable, informed member of the Yorkville establishment. He had managed all this with apparent frankness and confidence.

His difficulty, which he could not have failed to recognize, was that the committee knew who—and what—he was, and did not believe a word he said. Scott, in particular, had been relentless, asking the same questions over and over despite Bratton's repeated nonanswers and professions of ignorance. The committee knew he was lying. To them, his performance came across as brazen arrogance.

Bratton's smooth claims of ignorance, however, were quickly dispelled by the next witness. This was erstwhile Klan member William K. Owens, who had participated in both the Rose's Hotel raid and the arms theft at the Yorkville probate judge's office.

Owens was obviously a Merrill informant and had come before the committee at least in part so Merrill could make sure its members understood who Bratton was and what he had done with the help of Tomlinson, McClain, and Hunter, among several others.

Owens was cocky and smart, despite describing himself sardonically as a "poor mechanic." He had joined the Confederate army at fourteen in 1861, served four years as an artilleryman, and ended the war in a Union prison camp. At twenty-four he was a journeyman carriagemaker who worked alongside Rufus McClain at "Kerr & Roach" in downtown Yorkville. He did chassis; Rufus made wheels.

Owens had joined the Klan late in 1870 at McClain's behest because he was a Democrat, he said, but quickly became disillusioned by the violence. Nevertheless, he stayed on because there was no way to leave.

Owens testified for twice as long as Bratton. He summarized the Klan oath and described the secret hand signals, passwords, and disguises. He listed several of the raiders at Rose's Hotel and all of the raiders at the probate office, named Bratton and Major Avery repeatedly as York County Klan leaders, and put Bratton, Tomlinson, McClain, Hunter, and others at the scene of the Jim Williams lynching and a half-dozen other raids.

So blunt and unequivocal were his answers that the committee may have wondered how Owens expected to get out of the hearing room alive, let alone continue to live and work in his hometown.

He had obviously thought about this, but his responses veered between prudence and recklessness. At one point he acknowledged that men were pledged to deny their Klan membership "under penalty of death," and he said that testifying in court would not be "profitable" or safe for him.

But he also told the panel that he broke the Klan oath and decided to testify because he did not consider the oath "valid." "[Despite having done this] I don't think I am in danger of my life." When Mayor Harris had confronted him about it in the street, Owens had threatened to give him "a decent, genteel punching," he said. "That is the only way I take satisfaction out of a man, and I generally do that with interest if he fools with me."

Van Trump's restraint frayed badly at this point. He could not hide his intense dislike of Owens, who seemed almost to welcome the animosity and returned it effortlessly. It was clear that Yorkville's leading citizens knew what Owens was going to say and had briefed Van Trump, who came armed with a barrage of accusations intended to discredit the witness.

Owens never flinched. He acknowledged stealing a horse in Chester in 1865 and subsequently escaping from jail and hiding out in North Carolina for a few months. He had been "falsely" accused, he told Van Trump, and broke jail because his arrest happened right after the war, and he did not trust the justice system.

He told Van Trump he had known that the theft would come up during his testimony. "I have been used a tool by these men in town as long as they can, and now they want to go back on me, on my past life," he said. "I wouldn't hesitate to denounce them in the public square."

Van Trump also asked him about rumors that Merrill had paid him between $1,000 and $5,000 to testify and whether Merrill and Governor Scott had promised him a pardon and free passage to Canada. It never happened, Owens said. He had heard a "report" on the street saying Merrill had given him $3,500. "I went up the street the other day to buy some goods, and I said, 'This is the last cent I have of the $3,500.' . . . I said that to aggravate them."[24]

Despite the length of his appearance, Owens's testimony offered few clues about his plans. His brash self-confidence and willingness to defy Van Trump—and also Avery, Bratton, and the other Klan "aristocrats," suggests that he may have been physically intimidating. He admitted he was something of a brawler—a "wild chap," he told Van Trump. He was clearly not someone to be pushed around.

But was this enough to save him from retaliation? The other obvious explanation for his swagger was, as Van Trump intimated, that Merrill had paid him to testify and Owens planned to leave town as soon as he was excused from the hearing room. Merrill almost certainly was asked about this, but there is no record of what he might have said.

Regardless of his fate, Owens's information was almost flawless. In what might have been another scheduling manipulation to establish his bona fides, the panel the previous day had heard barkeep Dave Russell talk about the Rose's Hotel raid in great detail. Owens's account, told from the Ku Klux perspective the following day, was indistinguishable. And months after Owens's testimony, witnesses under oath confirmed his account of Klan rituals and the Williams lynching in every essential particular.

Finally, it became instantly clear that York County's white establishment, as Owens had told the subcommittee, regarded him as a dangerous witness and were trying to do everything they could to discredit him.

On July 27 the *Yorkville Enquirer* cited "street reports" that the committee, with help from "the military and other influences equally potent," had found in Owens a witness who "knew a number of persons who had been engaged in the Ku Klux outrages, and gave the names of eighteen gentlemen from this vicinity—persons of high respectability."

The *Enquirer* said Owens accused the eighteen of "a wonderful amount of deviltry," including the Brown and Williams lynchings, Rose's Hotel, the ammunition raid, and "other crimes equally heinous." He also admitted stealing a horse, the *Enquirer* added, and was "generally a bad man."

"The statements of this witness were so palpably false in every particular as to cause little concern to those whose names he has used," the *Enquirer* said, even though his story may have been "sufficiently credible" for use in Washington as a campaign document."[25]

The *Enquirer* report, published and probably read by the committee the day it left town, undoubtedly benefited from a surreptitious interview either with Van Trump or with the secretary charged with transcribing the testimony.

But such a gratuitous insult did York County no favors. What mattered was that Owens's evidence was good, and the Ku Klux Klan knew it. The crimes were facts, and the *Enquirer* contributed further to York County's dishonor by pretending it was all "palpably false."

Dr. Bratton, among others, quickly understood that peace meetings and bluster were not going to mute the effect of the hearings, and he decided to leave Yorkville, then leave South Carolina, and finally flee the country altogether, following Avery to Canada. Hundreds more South Carolina Klan members were leaving the state, and thousands more elsewhere in the South were doing the same thing.

This time, many southerners suspected, the Grant administration was not governing "by proclamation." Despite the best efforts of Bratton, Witherspoon, and others of Yorkville's "best people" to clean up the image, and despite the committee's efforts to speak softly in public, the Yorkville hearings were transforming York County and the entire South Carolina upcountry into an object of national disgust.

"If the state has the force necessary to maintain its authority and protect its people, it is a disgrace to civilization that it does not use that force for that purpose," the ordinarily restrained *Chicago Tribune* commented. "The further continuance of these barbarities should not be tolerated, even if it be necessary to place a soldier in South Carolina for every Ku Klux in the state."[26]

EACH DAY of the Yorkville hearings was anchored by at least one unimpeachable witness. Monday featured Dave Russell, on Tuesday Elias Hill testified, and on Wednesday Major Merrill appeared.

Merrill was to summarize the extent of York County's distress, and he had brought with him a long opening statement detailing Klan crimes from the Roundtree murder forward. He drew substantially on the views he had expressed in his letter to General Terry the previous month. Six weeks later, his vision had grown even darker. The refusal of civil authorities to take any action showed a "diseased state of public sentiment." He found it "incredible" that a local jury had acquitted three white defendants in the Roundtree killing, then convicted William Wright the same day of perjury for accusing a white man of beating him.

His preparation was impressive. He had documented six murders of black men and sixty-eight cases of beatings, rapes, and robberies, and presented them one by one to the committee, in most cases naming the victims. He delivered these statistics after estimating that the Ku Klux Klan had committed "between three hundred and four hundred" acts of "personal violence" in York County since November 1, 1870.

How did he know that? Van Trump interrupted.

"It would be necessary to explain somewhat, in regard to that," Merrill replied.

He then did so, describing his investigative methods in exhaustive detail. He might hear of "some party" of Ku Klux crisscrossing the county in various directions. He would get a report of one beating, when he knew that many more took place. He constantly talked with Sheriff Glenn and other county officers and had had "conversations with various persons" on "various occasions": "[These] gave me an idea of the number of the outrages that occurred, besides those that I knew of myself."

How did he know he was not being told about the same cases "over and over?" Van Trump asked. Because Glenn told him the names of reported victims, he said, and Merrill knew where the raids were taking place. Sometimes so many cases were reported to him that he could not write them all down.

Merrill, as he had told Terry, did not altogether trust Glenn but probably left him alone because Glenn described incidents and gave him names, even as he dragged his feet as an investigator.

Merrill continued reading. He recounted his version of the hotel raid, noting that Ned Rose's barrage of gunfire from the balcony had preceded it and saying that I. D. Witherspoon had told him that this is what prompted the raid. Van Trump at that point interrupted again, suggesting that Merrill had not investigated the incident thoroughly because he "was known here as a pronounced Republican."

Merrill recoiled at this question, not something that a sitting congressman would normally ask a serving military officer. But Van Trump badgered Merrill until he acknowledged that his views coincided "decidedly with the Republicans"—no surprise given what he had observed during his four months in Yorkville. Still, he added, "I have engaged in no political discussion of any kind since I have been here."

Merrill continued. Yes, the fires set by the blacks were quite likely retaliation for "real and supposed grievances." He also noted that during the same period the Klan had burned down twenty-two houses, cabins, schoolhouses, and churches used by the blacks.

On several occasions Van Trump asked why Merrill did not dig deeper into incidents and come up with more names. Merrill was offhand, almost dismissive. Nobody asked him for the names; no one was ever arrested; no one ever went on trial. It was enough that he knew the participants. If he ever had a chance to bring the evildoers to justice, he would be able to identify them all.

The unspoken second reason, of course, was the same one that kept him from telling Bratton how he found out his encampment was going to be attacked. Why would he share his sources with the enemy?

He told the panel that black men and women from all over the county confided in him, but he was especially circumspect about the identities of "four or five" black "agents" on whom he relied. Elias Hill was one of these, he said, but he would go no further.

Van Trump suggested the blacks would get "considerable vainglory" by bringing him information, even if it were false. No, Merrill, replied, they approached him so "that justice may be done them."[27]

ON THE fourth and final day of the hearings, the panel heard from I. D. Witherspoon, who knew everything about York County. He minimized the bad and exaggerated the good, but he provided an enormous cache of information. Also appearing was Benjamin Gore, the former militiaman who came to recount the black version of the Chester riots. The committee had heard the white version from Chester physician Alexander Wylie the day before.

And then there was Hamp Hicklin. He wanted to tell the committee about Sheriff Glenn. Talking nonstop, he related how he had repeatedly trailed the Klan raiders after they left his home and overheard their conversations. He knew who they were—by their voices, by their horses, by who and what they talked about. He was able to identify one man because he was the only person in Clay Hill who had one arm.

"Because of the war?" Van Trump asked.

No, Hicklin replied. Lost it in a cane mill.

"Wait," Van Trump interjected at one point, furiously taking notes. "Do not talk so fast."

But Hicklin would not slow down. He named more than a dozen of his attackers, and he told the sheriff about each of his spying adventures, only to have Glenn tell his assailants that he was stalking them—they had all but admitted it.

"When Major Merrill has so much confidence in the sheriff, why do you doubt him?" Van Trump demanded.

"[Glenn] deceived me, and deceived more than me," Hicklin replied.

Van Trump pushed harder, but Hicklin only laughed: "You thought I didn't know these men," he said, and "[you] wanted to trip me up. I know them as well as you can make figures on that paper."[28]

CHAPTER NINETEEN

Nine Counties

On Friday morning, August 31, President Grant suddenly and unexpectedly returned to Washington. For a good part of the day he met with Senator John Scott, and then he visited various executive departments. There would be an extraordinary cabinet meeting the next day. Secretaries who were not already in town were expected to arrive on the morning trains.

Before Scott left South Carolina the previous month, he had warned that if he heard about Ku Klux Klan reprisals aimed at his witnesses he would be "obliged in honor" to tell Grant about it and recommend that the president take action under "the extreme powers of the Ku Klux bill."[1]

That moment had arrived. Within days of the congressional committee's departure from the state, Scott began receiving reports from contacts in South Carolina of Klan raids, beatings, and burnings throughout York, Spartanburg, and Union Counties. Spartanburg had ten new cases of beatings. In York, night riders had burned down a schoolhouse for black students, whipped two victims at Allison Creek, and shot up black neighborhoods across the county. Black men everywhere were hiding out at night in the woods.[2]

When Scott contacted the president at his summer residence in Long Branch, Grant left for Washington and directed Scott to meet him there. Scott made his case and handed Grant recently transcribed witness testimony from South Carolina, along with Merrill's York County report to the committee and a copy of General Terry's June 11 letter urging "vigorous" action in "a small district." Grant also asked Scott to write a formal cover letter describing the substance of their interview. Scott delivered it to Grant in time for the next day's cabinet meeting.[3]

SCOTT'S SOUTH Carolina expedition had had a huge impact, both on the senator himself and on efforts by Attorney General Akerman and General Terry to prod Grant into taking action against the Klan. The congressmen's visit had stoked public outrage like nothing that had come before. Senator Scott, now thoroughly radicalized, no longer needed John Pool to provoke his rage or translate his thoughts. He was both convinced and convincing. He had the president's undivided attention.

Scott already knew Akerman through Congress's efforts to obtain the $50,000 Akerman was using to hire spies. He had met and been impressed by Major Merrill in Yorkville and had given Merrill funds to hire spies of his own. This money almost certainly came from Akerman's $50,000, probably a contingency fund to be used if Scott saw an opportunity.

Merrill told Terry he had the funds, and Terry on August 4 told Merrill to spend them "as your judgment dictates." Furthermore, the general had applied for similar funds and had contacted Scott and given him copies of his June letter and of earlier reports from Merrill on the Ku Klux. When Grant sat down with his cabinet on September 1, he knew the identities and the views of all four of the major players pushing for intervention.[4]

Grant opened the meeting by reading Scott's cover letter, which recounted recent Klan offenses in the South Carolina upcountry and described the failure of local authorities to take any action. Despite promises to the contrary, Scott wrote, recent events "indicate[d] that the cessation of lawlessness [was] but temporary." The Klan in York and Spartanburg Counties were guilty of "crimes that ought not to go unpunished in any civilized country." The criminals had again "resumed their arms and their midnight raids of brutality and assassination."

Both counties should be "informed by proclamation that the limit of endurance has been reached," Scott wrote. It was time to invoke the Ku Klux Klan Act, Scott urged. The army should be allowed to intervene directly without deferring to local law enforcement.[5]

The only recorded description of the meeting was some hastily scribbled notes by Secretary of State Hamilton Fish, indicating that Grant was ready to follow Scott's advice and move against Spartanburg and York at that moment. Akerman then read a letter whose sender offered to meet him in Georgia to tell him the names of the York County Ku Klux leaders in order to "break up the whole organization." Fish's notes concluded, "[Akerman] is going to Georgia. He is to obtain information there."[6] There was no mention of any final decisions from the meeting.

News reports furnished more detail. The *New York Herald* had been cultivating Senator Scott and on September 1 had printed his version of South Carolina events after the congressmen's departure—a clear attempt by Scott to put Grant and the cabinet on the spot before their meeting.

For its September 2 edition the *Herald* had probably spoken with Scott again, and perhaps with cabinet members, many of whom—especially Fish—

had scant interest in a full-scale confrontation with the Klan. Instead of invoking the Ku Klux Klan Act, the *Herald* reported, the administration had decided to temporize. "The President evidently hopes that what now appears the necessity of proclaiming martial law may pass away."

Grant had handed over Scott's package of documents to Akerman and sent him on a fact-finding mission, a move that could have "no other meaning" except delay, the *Herald* continued somewhat bitterly, perhaps reflecting Scott's disappointment that the president had not acted immediately. Scott left Washington at midday on September 1, and Grant returned to Long Branch in the evening.[7]

Scott's credibility suffered a heavy setback less than a week later, when U.S. Army major Marcus Reno, Merrill's counterpart in Spartanburg, wrote to the senator, noting that the county had been at peace since his own arrival on July 19, shortly after Scott's subcommittee had left town. "There has not been to my knowledge any outrage."[8]

Reno, later to gain notoriety as General Custer's second-in-command at the Little Bighorn, sent a copy of the letter to Akerman but did not immediately release it to the public. The next day, however, twenty-six prominent citizens of Spartanburg, among them a U.S. commissioner, a federal tax assessor, a probate judge, and the county sheriff, published a similar but much more pointed letter.

The signatories had read Scott's allegations of continued violence and knew that he had "recommended the proclamation of martial law" in Spartanburg County. "We have made diligent inquiry, and have been unable to hear of a single outrage having been committed in this county since your Committee left it," the letter said. "On the contrary, the county is in a state of profound peace and quiet."[9]

Unfortunately for Scott, these critiques reached Grant in Long Branch. In a September 8 interview with the *New York Herald*, Grant laconically noted: "[Scott's report] tells its story, and there are contradictory reports on the heels of it."

When the interviewer mentioned the Spartanburg letter, Grant said that it was not the only denial: "There are plenty of others. All we can do is to wait further developments."

No immediate plans?

"None."[10]

York and Chester Counties, undoubtedly aware of the dampening effect the Spartanburg twenty-six had had on federal zeal, published similar statements over the next few days. Scott, somewhat chastened perhaps, was still convinced of his views and sent Akerman the correspondence he had received from his Spartanburg sources.[11]

SCOTT'S FLIRTATION with celebrity was over, but his initiative was not, although he may have thought so at first. Spartanburg was obviously off the table. With federal officials and the county's leading army officer contradicting Scott, a crackdown there would appear capricious and vindictive. Akerman had no intention of following up on Scott's Spartanburg reports.

Instead, he, Terry, and Merrill were already focused on York, and Grant was not ready to back away from a confrontation there. Grant had not sent Akerman to South Carolina as a stalling maneuver. Akerman, as Grant undoubtedly knew, had been eager to go after the Klan ever since he came to Washington—and he did not do whitewash.

Akerman left Washington on September 12, traveling on his own. His initial stop was Raleigh, North Carolina, where the first set of Ku Klux trials was taking place in federal court. He had summoned David T. Corbin, his U.S. Attorney in South Carolina, to meet him there, and both men stayed several days, the *Charlotte Democrat* reported. Neither Akerman nor Corbin participated in the proceedings.[12]

Akerman, however, did see the beginning of the Ku Klux Klan trial of Randolph Shotwell and eleven codefendants charged with the abduction and beating of a Republican state assemblyman the previous June. Shotwell, a rabble-rousing newspaper editor, was a major target of federal investigators. He was eventually found guilty of conspiracy, fined $5,000, and sentenced to six years in federal prison.[13]

Under the headline "Shame Has No Blush," the *Wilmington* (N.C.) *Journal* denounced both Akerman and the trials, deeming them a federal "invasion."

"Over one hundred peaceful men are dragged from their homes and carried to Raleigh for trial, on charges preferred [*sic*], in many instances, by negroes and irresponsible white men, worse than negroes," the *Journal* wrote. "Over one thousand people are taken from their labors and forced two hundred miles to testify in cases in which the Radical party are the prosecutors and the white men of North Carolina are the defendants."[14]

Despite the bombast, there were good reasons for Akerman to stop in North Carolina, because the Shotwell trial was the first test of the Ku Klux Klan Act. The prosecutors took a narrow approach. They did not attempt to extend the reach of the Fourteenth Amendment to include constitutional rights or to prosecute the common crimes that accompanied violations—Akerman's most coveted goals. Instead they focused on conspiracy, specifically actionable under the Ku Klux Klan Act. But while the case thus broke no new constitutional ground, the prosecution got a relatively easy conviction and made an example of Shotwell, a Klan favorite.

Akerman also probably wanted to take the measure of U.S. Attorney Starbuck. Senator Pool, like Akerman, had decided that Starbuck was "thoroughly intimidated and traumatized" by the Ku Klux Klan and feared he would free Shotwell.[15]

But Akerman need not have worried. Although Starbuck was theoretically the lead prosecutor as the sitting U.S. Attorney, courtroom action was handled by assistant U.S. Attorney Samuel F. Phillips, a rock-solid North Carolina Republican and a fierce civil rights advocate. Many Klansmen turned states' evidence during the trial, and Phillips made sure Shotwell and his codefendants were left with virtually no way to contest the prosecution.[16]

Akerman was also undoubtedly impressed with the performance of newly installed U.S. Fourth Circuit judge Hugh L. Bond. Defense counsel at the Shotwell trial's outset attempted to have the case dismissed or stalled by raising multiple procedural challenges, contending at one point that the jury was "stacked," which it undoubtedly was, given the jury requirements of the Ku Klux Klan Act. Bond listened to several hours of these arguments, waving them aside one by one with short, dismissive sentences. The trial would proceed. The Raleigh *Tri-Weekly Era* noted, "[Bond is] the object of our hate. Akerman is loved about as well."[17]

AKERMAN NEXT went home to Cartersville, Georgia, where he had moved his family eight months earlier. His old neighbors from Elberton were happy to see him go, and Akerman was probably happy to leave. Elberton had snubbed Matty when she was sick, and local tempers had probably grown nastier—and perhaps even dangerous—as Akerman's stature advanced.

"Attorney General Ackerman [*sic*] left this place (perhaps forever) on Wednesday last," the *Elberton Gazette* wrote in a January send-off. "We care not how long he may live, nor how far he may go. He carried his family with him."[18]

In Cartersville Akerman mulled his next steps. He found his task "perplexing," he wrote in a September 22 letter to Solicitor General Bristow—acting attorney general in his absence. He wanted to hit the Ku Klux Klan as hard as possible, but he doubted that the information he had at the moment was explicit enough to prove a conspiracy. As in North Carolina, conspiracy would have to be established to bring any federal Ku Klux case to trial. Only then could he and Corbin try to amplify the Fourteenth Amendment.[19]

In North Carolina he had seen how Phillips's turncoat witnesses had described in detail the rituals and gestures that defined the Klan there. He needed something akin to this for South Carolina—proofs that the baseline conspiracy existed. Finding them was why he was in Georgia.

Sometime in the next few days Akerman met with Kirkland L. Gunn, a professional photographer from York County who had been working in Georgia since May. Gunn had joined the Klan in York in January and was now a member in good standing in Georgia.

Gunn was undoubtedly the source of the letter that Akerman had read to Grant and his cabinet colleagues on September 1. The sender had offered intelligence about the York County Klan, and Akerman had traveled to Georgia to get it.

Details of Akerman's meeting with Gunn were not made public, but Gunn left a signed statement with Akerman before he departed. Later, in federal court testimony, Gunn described its contents. He was a reluctant Klansman who had joined for his "personal safety," he said. "[Members told me] it would not be good for me if I refused to join the order."

He described his initiation ceremony, the Klan "constitution" and bylaws, and Klan rituals, weaponry, disguises, and hand signals. Only after his initiation did he learn that the real purpose of the Klan was "killing off the white Radicals" and "whipping and intimidating the negroes to keep them from voting."[20]

With most of this information at hand, Akerman, still in Cartersville or perhaps already on the road, telegraphed General Terry in Louisville seeking a meeting. On September 26, 1871, Terry replied succinctly: "Your telegram received. I shall be here all the week."[21]

There is no record of what transpired in Louisville, but the substance of Terry's June 11 packet of dispatches had plenty for the two men to discuss. They also may have received a preliminary briefing from Merrill about his mid-September visit to the fall session of the state's district court, where he was summoned to present evidence of Senator Scott's contention that Ku Klux outrages in York County were serious and ongoing. If Akerman and Terry needed any further convincing that York was their target, Merrill provided it.

The major had not enjoyed the experience. District court judge William Thomas opened the session by delivering his charge to the grand jury. It was an oration of considerable bombast, but it had one substantive and important message. Martial law was on the way to York County, Thomas told his jurors, unless the court could show this: "*We are capable of self-government.*"[22]

The court did not rise to the challenge. "Whatever doubts I have entertained of the willful connivance of civil authorities at these crimes was entirely dissipated," Merrill wrote later in his end-of-the-year report to headquarters. "The courts were not only unable to prevent these outrages, but were unwilling to try to do so."[23]

Merrill said he soon learned from his sources that the grand jury's sole job was to discredit him. At one point the jurors contemplated arresting Merrill for suborning perjury from William Owens. Also, Merrill said, the Klan let it be known that the jurors would do nothing "in regard to the outrages" except to prove the falsehood of his statements.[24]

And that was what happened. Merrill went to court September 20 and handed over his notes, which described the beatings, arson, and vandalism in York County since the congressional committee's departure. The grand jury, he said, spent six days of its ten-day session examining these "in a belabored effort" to discredit him.[25]

The grand jury's final report found two minor crimes among those alleged to have occurred since the departure of the committee. It ignored earlier crimes like the Rose's Hotel raid and James Porter's subsequent whipping—disclosed at the committee's hearings—even though Porter named two of his assailants, and it brushed aside older crimes, including the murders of Anderson Brown (evidence not "sufficiently definite"), Jim Williams (not "sufficiently definite") and Tom Roundtree (evidence "insufficient").[26]

That was all the state press needed. There had been no serious crimes since the committee visit, Merrill's evidence was fraudulent, and Senator Scott was simply looking for an excuse to intervene in South Carolina's affairs. The *Charleston Daily News* dismissed the whole affair in a short piece under the headline "Bursting a Ku Klux Bubble."[27]

Merrill noted later that none of the evidence he had offered received more than a passing glance, and jurors who wanted to act properly were excluded from caucuses convened by compromised jurors.

"The whole conduct of their duty was so broad a farce that it was very distasteful to be forced in contact with it," Merrill said later. "[Subsequent developments] show it to have been the most ghastly mockery of justice that it is possible to conceive." One-third of the white grand jurors and petit jurors were Ku Klux members, he said. "A number were of high grade in the order," and "at least two" were "accessories to Ku Klux murders."[28]

IT IS NOT clear whether Akerman and Terry had Merrill's new information for their Louisville meeting, but, even without it, Akerman's stopover undoubtedly cemented his partnership with the general and Merrill and their determination to choose York County to test the Fourteenth Amendment. With Kirkland

Gunn's statement, Akerman had concrete proof of Klan conspiracy, and Merrill would find more. Conspiracy may have been the starting point, but he could take it further with Merrill and Corbin working with him.

It was time for Akerman to see the boss.

Grant, on his way back to Washington after a trip to Chicago, stopped over in Dayton, Ohio, to visit a home for disabled soldiers. Akerman met him there on October 3 and accompanied him to the home.

The event, the *New York Herald* reported, was "an imposing affair," with local dignitaries, banners, bands, soldiers passing in review, and cannons firing a twenty-one-gun salute. Grant spoke briefly before some 1,750 disabled veterans, lamenting that "circumstances" had prevented him from visiting sooner and thanking his audience for the cordial welcome. The soldiers gave him "nine cheers."

Akerman spoke next and was equally brief. It was clear from his remarks, however, that the president had given him the vote of confidence he had sought. There was peace "in most of the states, but not altogether," he said. "Rebels in some of them . . . have not yet learned to submit gracefully to the inevitable." But he added, "It is hoped [that] there will soon be a unanimous acquiescence in all the results of the war."[29]

After the Dayton ceremony, Akerman returned briefly to Cartersville, and on October 7 he wrote to Bristow. He had seen the president, he said, and had suggested the possibility of suspending habeas corpus in "certain parts of South Carolina." He planned to draft a presidential proclamation to that effect as required by the Ku Klux Klan Act and send it to Bristow "for use if the occasion should be forced to exist."

In the meantime, he enclosed a draft warning proclamation aimed at Chester, Spartanburg, Union, and York Counties as South Carolina's worst offenders. The warning was to precede by five days the suspension of habeas corpus.

The habeas corpus proclamation would be sent in military cipher, he continued, because the Ku Klux "have a machine and sometimes tap the wires." Akerman intended to travel to Yorkville in the next few days and to remain there if Grant decided to take action—clearly viewed by Akerman as a foregone conclusion.[30]

Three days later, on October 10, Akerman, Corbin, and Merrill were in Columbia to meet with Governor Scott and state attorney general Daniel H. Chamberlain. This was a courtesy call, contemplated by Akerman only after he realized that he and Grant were about to authorize armed U.S. Marshals and the U.S. Army to turn a significant slice of South Carolina into a battleground.[31]

Akerman knew Chamberlain from Chamberlain's visit to Washington earlier in the year, and he had taken Corbin's measure in North Carolina. He had never met either Governor Scott or Merrill, although he had closely read many of the dispatches Merrill had sent to Terry.

The Columbia meeting went well. Governor Scott was supportive, and, after the consultations concluded, Merrill encoded a telegram from Akerman to Bristow. To the original four counties named in Akerman's October 7 letter to Bristow, Akerman on October 10 added five more: Chesterfield, Fairfield, Lancaster, Laurens, and Newberry. This expansion undoubtedly came about at Scott's suggestion or at least with his acquiescence.[32]

Most important, however, Akerman, Corbin, and Merrill at Columbia found that they worked well together and were seeking the same goal: to use the Ku Klux Klan Act and the Fourteenth Amendment to destroy the Klan. This bond of like minds formed the basis of a collaboration that never faltered. The three men left Columbia together and reconvened in Yorkville on October 11 to plot strategy.

AKERMAN HAD made only one misstep so far, and he was completely unaware that he had done so. When he named the first four targeted counties in his October 7 letter to Bristow, "Union" in Akerman's handwriting was hard to read. Bristow decided it was "Marion," a county where the Klan was virtually nonexistent.[33]

Bristow knew nothing about South Carolina. But if Akerman's handwriting confounded him, he could easily have checked the counties list with Senator Scott or examined the Justice Department's official correspondence or read the newspapers. Only Union County competed with York and Spartanburg as a locus of Klan savagery.

Bristow never took even partial ownership of the error. By the time he received Akerman's October 7 letter, he was already embarked on a personal quest to get Akerman fired.

For several months, in correspondence with his Louisville partner John Harlan, he had expressed dissatisfaction with the Justice Department, his job, and Akerman. Solicitor general pay was so low that his whole salary would not cover the rent, he said, and Washington was unpleasant and boring. He disagreed with personnel changes and wanted to resign.[34]

In late September, probably during the same railroad journey when Grant met Akerman, Harlan had sought out the president during a stopover in Compton, Illinois, ostensibly to discuss Klan activities in Kentucky. During the conversation, he also noted in a letter to Bristow, the president told him that he had "an excellent opinion" of Bristow: "You can obtain at his hands almost any promotion whenever an opportunity presents."[35]

On October 7, perhaps bolstered by this news, Bristow sought out Grant for the specific purpose of denouncing Akerman. "I have 'gone and done it,'" he wrote Harlan the next day. "Perhaps I have done wrong, but I couldn't help it. After making up my mind to stay here a while longer, I thought it was not peculiarly my duty to say anything to the President, but as the time for [the Supreme] Court to sit drew around, I couldn't tolerate the idea of going through another term *under him*."

Akerman needed to be gotten out of the way. Bristow went to Grant "to tell him *plainly* all about it." He expressed "respect for A personally," but Akerman was "altogether too *small* for the place in every particular." The Supreme Court and the profession generally ridiculed him; he was "a *dead weight* on the administration" and "*could not* organize the department." Hiring was "badly done," and "there was absolutely no hope of improvement" under Akerman.

He offered to resign, he told Harlan, but Grant told him that was "out of the question." Bristow said that Grant told him that while Akerman "had not come up to his expectations," he was surprised to learn "that he had failed so disastrously." Akerman was "earnest and thoroughly honest," Grant had said, and it was "delicate thing to ask him to resign without giving a reason."

Bristow told Harlan he would resign in December if Akerman had not left, and although it could be construed that he was putting himself forward as Akerman's successor, he wrote, "I care not a fig for that." He thought Grant would name George Williams, not Bristow's choice but "a good lawyer and a strong man."[36]

AKERMAN, CLOSETED with Corbin and Merrill in Yorkville, had no inkling of these machinations and never learned they had taken place. The criticisms were justified up to a point. Akerman had never professed expertise in federal law and had undoubtedly allowed his mammoth postwar caseload to languish.

As far as organizing the Justice Department, however, he took his cues from Congress, which would not give him the money he needed to hire more attorneys and pay them properly. And he also took his cues from Grant and his cabinet colleagues, who had no interest in losing their patronage prerogatives.

Bristow had no apparent interest in the campaign against the Ku Klux nor did he appreciate the fact that Akerman and his Yorkville colleagues were about to undertake one of the most ambitious expansions of federal legal power ever attempted.

Bristow's appreciation of the pressures facing Akerman and his team was negligible. "A is in South Carolina and, in my opinion, doing no good," Bristow wrote in an October 14 letter to Harlan. Bristow was "satisfied," he said, that a change would be made "before December," and Akerman would be gone.[37]

Two days earlier, on October 12, Akerman had sent a coded telegram to Bristow via the War Department to recommend release of the warning proclamation. Grant did so the same day, targeting "unlawful combinations and conspiracies" in South Carolina that were depriving "certain portions and classes" of people of their constitutional rights.

These "combinations and conspiracies" were too powerful for state and existing U.S. authorities in South Carolina to handle. "I, Ulysses S. Grant, President of the United States, do hereby command all persons composing the unlawful combinations and conspiracies aforesaid to disperse and to retire peaceably to their homes within five days of the date hereof."[38] He named nine counties, including Marion.

THE CLOCK was ticking, and the Ku Klux Klan finally understood that "war by proclamation" was over. "On the very day of [Akerman's] arrival, many of the Ku Klux leaders, suspecting that measures were being devised to bring them to justice, and with the cowardice that defined all of their infamous crimes, fled," Merrill later recalled. Left behind were "their poorer followers and ignorant dupes."[39]

Five days later, as mandated by the Ku Klux Klan Act, Grant issued his second proclamation. He declared the nine named counties "to be in rebellion against the Government of the United States." The "unlawful combinations and conspiracies . . . have not dispersed and retired peaceably to their respective homes [but rather] do still persist." Thus, his proclamation continued, "In my judgment . . . to the end that such rebellion may be overthrown . . . [I] do hereby suspend the privileges of the writ of *habeas corpus*."[40]

CHAPTER TWENTY

The Hammer Falls

OCTOBER 19, 1871

Troop K of the U.S. Seventh Cavalry had been in Yorkville for almost eight months, sent by President Grant after Governor Scott warned of a "state of war" in upcountry South Carolina. The troopers were a motley lot: a large number of immigrants—mostly Irish and German—and a sprinkling of Civil War veterans, among them Major Merrill and several of his noncoms. Merrill and his family lived in Rose's Hotel while the troopers bunked in A-frame tents nearby, their mounts tethered in a stable next to the hotel. Most of the officers took rooms elsewhere in town.

Troop K had fought Indians on the western plains. They were heavily armed dragoons, mounted infantry carrying Sharps .50 caliber breech-loading carbines along with .44 caliber revolvers and sabers. As trained guerrilla fighters, they were perfectly suited to hunt the Ku Klux in South Carolina, but Merrill worried about readiness. For eight months the troopers had spent their time riding about, ignoring insults, listening to horror stories, and taking care of the beaten and bleeding black men and their terrified families who staggered into their encampment.[1]

At first, like most whites everywhere in the United States, Troop K viewed the blacks they were charged to protect with contempt or indifference, but as time passed their respect grew, along with their appreciation of the hardships they had to endure.

The only opportunity for Troop K to vent its frustration fizzled out when the Klan decided to call off its ill-advised June raid on the camp. "Our troops laid on their arms ready to receive them, but they are too big of a coward to come and let us see them," wrote one sergeant in his diary.[2]

EVERYTHING CHANGED on October 17, when President Grant invoked the Ku Klux Klan Act and suspended habeas corpus in York County. Instead of waiting for local civilian authorities to ask for help—which never happened—Troop K could finally go after the Klan.

Attorney General Akerman and U.S. Attorney David T. Corbin had come to Yorkville to plan strategy with Major Merrill. Akerman knew whom he wanted to arrest, and Merrill knew where to find them. On October 19, Troop K mounted up, along with two other cavalry companies sent by General Terry the previous week.[3]

There may have been nine counties involved in Grant's decree, but the focus was on York, mostly because of Merrill. General Terry respected and trusted him. Merrill had amassed a huge amount of intelligence, and he had an easy and seamless relationship with Akerman and Corbin.

Merrill's readiness concerns were unfounded. Troop K was "so disposed that a large number of arrests were effected simultaneously over the county," Merrill wrote later.[4]

There were no pitched battles, burnings of houses, beatings, or torture. Troopers without incident arrested Klan chieftains targeted by Akerman: Samuel G. "Squire" Brown, a Klan elder statesman; John W. Mitchell, from Bullock's Creek, wanted in the murder of Charley Good; Dr. Edward Avery, brother of county Klan boss J. W. Avery; and Elijah Ross Sepaugh, wanted in the Tom Roundtree murder. They also swept up a bunch of the raiders who participated in the Jim Williams lynching: Milus Smith Carroll, Elias Ramsay, John Caldwell, Robert Hayes Mitchell, and the four Shearer brothers. J. W. Avery and J. Rufus Bratton were both believed to have fled to Canada. Rufus McClain was also a fugitive, as was John Tomlinson, wanted in the Anderson Brown killing. Tomlinson escaped pursuing troopers by jumping from his horse and running into the woods.[5]

In an exhaustive report sent to his superiors early in 1872, Merrill described a careful, ruthlessly efficient enterprise. Once the Ku Klux leaders were in jail or on the run, the rank-and-file mass of Klan soldiers were left "bewildered and demoralized," Merrill wrote. Without guidance or resources of their own, there was mass surrender. "Day after day for weeks, men came in in such numbers" that he and Corbin could do little more than jail the major offenders and send the rest home "on their personal parole."[6]

The *Yorkville Enquirer*, perhaps because it knew that it sat in the bull's-eye of the government's offensive, provided a remarkably unbiased account of the events.

"Squads of soldiers were returning at all hours, having in their custody citizens of the county, embracing men of all stations," among them five black allies of the Klan, the *Enquirer* wrote. Most of the arrests were being made in daylight, and there was no resistance. "Major Merrill assures that no innocents will be arrested."

There was, however, no denying that the uproar had fostered "a depressing influence on the county," the *Enquirer* continued. Crops were unharvested, and business was at a standstill. "The future of our section, we are forced to confess, is now more gloomy than it has been at any time since the close of the war."[7]

In the rest of South Carolina, newspaper coverage of events in York differed markedly. "Innocent, unoffending citizens are dragged from their homes at the dead hour of night and thrown into jail with common felons," read one typical account in the Winnsboro, South Carolina, *Fairfield Herald*. "We have heard of men being torn from their families at midnight without being allowed to make any preparations for their journey, or provide for their loved ones during their absence; forced to ride ten, twenty and thirty miles, and then confined to loathsome dungeons."[8]

The only "outrage" the papers could put an actual name to was the October 21 arrest of John Mitchell, "highly esteemed as a straightforward, upright man by all who know him," the Columbia *Daily Phoenix* reported. Mitchell came to Yorkville the evening of October 20 for a Masonic meeting and was arrested the following morning by "a common soldier," who, "after cocking his musket and putting on a fresh cap, ordered [Mitchell] to hold up his hands, and told a negro to search his pockets and disarm him."[9]

The Klan, the papers insisted, was not the problem. This was all about politics. The *Anderson Intelligencer* denounced the raids as "the beginning of a reign of terror" to preserve Republican hegemony in anticipation of Grant's reelection campaign.[10]

Reaction in much of the rest of the country was more muted but still skeptical, except in the most fiercely pro-Republican newspapers.

Suspending habeas corpus was "a dangerous precedent for exercising arbitrary power," the *New York Herald* editorialized October 21. The Klan disturbances, the *Herald* said, resulted from "the lawlessness of a few individuals."[11]

The most comprehensive analysis in the opening days of the intervention appeared in the *Herald*, which interviewed Governor Scott during a visit to New York to try to refinance South Carolina's public debt.

Scott was not feeling charitable to his fellow Carolinians. Had "the best citizens" of the upcountry made "a slight effort," they could have "prevented three-fifths if not more of the outrages that have been perpetrated," Scott told the *Herald*. "These gentlemen are suspected of actual affiliation with the lawless combination known as the Ku Klux."

He acknowledged that upcountry violence had abated only insofar as murders. "Whippings and similar outrages have been practiced . . . almost nightly."

Only one thing puzzled Scott during his *Herald* interview. Why had Union County—"the worst Ku Klux county in the state"—been omitted from Grant's proclamation, and why had Marion County—"one of the most quiet"—been named? "I presume it was a clerical error," he said.[12]

It was, and Akerman was not pleased. In an October 20 coded telegram sent through the War Department to Bristow, Akerman referred to the proclamation published by the *Enquirer* the previous day. "I intended Union," he wrote, "which is in the original."[13]

The same day, Akerman wrote Bristow a personal letter. "I am sure that you misread my writing," he said. "But no matter how it happened, the mistake has been made, and the question is whether it should be corrected." Noting that it would take two proclamations and ten more days to put Union on the list of upcountry offenders, he recommended "forbearance." They should let it go for the time being, and they could issue a supplementary proclamation if fugitives started taking refuge in Union County.[14]

THE ASSAULT left the Klan reeling. In an exultant October 27 telegram, Merrill wrote to Terry in Louisville: "Operations not only successful, more than one hundred arrests [and] surrenders and confessions so numerous that it is difficult to find time to hear them. Many of chief men and worst criminals in custody, some of leaders fled upon arrival of attorney general before proclamation issued, evidence overwhelming, all my reported information fully confirmed and verified, numerous crimes including four or five murders heretofore unsuspected now brought to light [commas added to the original]." He predicted the "complete destruction of the organization."[15] In a second telegram the next day he told Terry that he and the U.S. Marshals had 127 prisoners, while 160 "lesser criminals" had to be paroled on their own recognizance because he had no room to hold them.[16] By year's end, Merrill reported to his superiors, he had 195 men in jail and estimated another 500 had surrendered. Adding in the fugitives, he estimated that there had been about 800 wanted men in York County.[17]

In Spartanburg the day after the offensive began, 100 men voluntarily surrendered to U.S. Marshal Louis Johnson, including an entire "den" of 20 men who said they had been forced to form their group to avoid Ku Klux reprisals.[18]

The Klan's "secrecy or death" vow didn't hold under pressure. Suspects "were silent" at first, recalled Louis F. Post, a young lawyer brought by Corbin to Yorkville to transcribe prisoners' testimony. "But as hope of release died out and fears of hanging grew stronger," the weaker ones confessed. Their evidence led to more arrests and more confessions until confessions became "quite the fashion."[19]

AKERMAN STAYED in Yorkville for the first ten days of the roundup and left on October 27, arriving in Washington the following day. Grant had said nothing about the raids during Akerman's absence, and neither had Bristow, who was interested in these events only insofar as they hastened Akerman's exit and perhaps opened the door for Bristow to replace him.[20]

Akerman's ability to promote the federal government's cause had been severely limited in Yorkville by the need to send encoded military dispatches.[21] As soon as he returned to Washington, however, he gave a long press conference, seeking to dispel misconceptions, stress the need for federal government intervention, and herald its effectiveness. Troopers had made more than one hundred arrests in York County alone, along with countless surrenders. Of the two hundred fugitives that had fled York County, he said, most were prominent in the organization. The prisoners, by contrast, came mostly from "the poorer class of whites," who expressed "great indignation" at their leaders for "leaving them to suffer the burdens of fine and imprisonment," he said. This outcome was just what was desired, he said: "It breaks up the order by arraying the rank-and-file against the leaders."

He described local law enforcement as a "farce" that ought to make the South Carolinians "blush for shame." Finally, he said that "numbers" of prominent whites had assured him of their desire to put an end to "a condition of affairs, which, unchecked, was blunting all the moral sense of society."[22]

The picture Akerman painted was a bit too bright. He and his Yorkville associates—especially Merrill—would have liked nothing more than to get their hands on J. W. Avery, J. Rufus Bratton, and John Tomlinson, among others.

On November 3 Akerman traveled to New York to deliver a ninety-minute speech to Brooklyn Republicans at a campaign rally four days before local elections. His words were paraphrased by reporters covering the event. The South, having lost the war, "needed to surrender all that was involved," he began, to reconcile itself with the national government and to reconcile itself with the end of slavery. It had done neither.

Even though he was speaking in the northern heartland of the Democratic Party, he did not tread lightly. Victims of the "outrages" committed against South Carolina's blacks, he emphasized, "in every instance" were told that they would be revisited if they continued to vote for Republicans.

He enumerated some of the worst crimes: Elias Hill, Tom Roundtree, and Jim Williams, the last lynched in the woods, he said, by raiders led by "a physician" who felt "the pulse of the victim and informed the murderers when he was dead."

In each of these cases, local law enforcement "let it pass." This was why President Grant had suspended habeas corpus, so "the guilty would not have the opportunity of fabricating stories to defeat the ends of justice."

What had happened in the nine counties was not martial law, he stressed. The prisoners would be tried in federal civilian courts, and Akerman was "morally certain" that all of them had committed crimes. "They are to be convicted," he said. "Some would be fined, some would be imprisoned, some sent to the penitentiary and some would be hung." This last remark was greeted with prolonged applause.[23]

TRIALS FOR the Klan prisoners were scheduled to open the fall term of the U.S. Fourth Circuit District Court in Columbia on the fourth Monday of the month—November 27.

On November 3 President Grant issued a warning proclamation removing Marion County from the list of nine offending counties and replacing it with Union County.[24] There appeared to be some doubt whether Grant would actually suspend habeas corpus in Union, perhaps because of the overwhelming caseload elsewhere in the state. The five-day waiting period expired November 8 with no action taken.

The following day, however, Merrill telegraphed Akerman from Yorkville. He had been hunting Ku Klux fugitives and probably had information that some had sought sanctuary with their western neighbors. "If it is asked whether habeas corpus should be suspended in Union County, it is answered in the affirmative," he wrote.[25] On Nov. 10 Grant suspended habeas corpus.[26]

Merrill's telegrams marked the first time he had sent dispatches directly to Akerman. Terry had undoubtedly given him permission to do so, and both he and Corbin—sometimes both at the same time—were in constant contact with Washington.

On November 10 Merrill sent Akerman a copy of the "Constitution and By-laws of the KKK." One of his cavalry lieutenants, obviously working with information obtained from a Merrill informant, found it in the desk of Klan chieftain Samuel G. "Squire" Brown. "This copy," Merrill said, "was traced directly to [J. W.] Avery."[27]

This was a key piece of evidence that proved the existence of a conspiracy as described in the Enforcement Acts. Kirkland Gunn had given Akerman details of the rituals and perhaps an outline of the constitution in Cartersville in September, but Merrill's original was decisive evidence.

LATE IN October U.S. Fourth Circuit judge Hugh L. Bond and U.S. district court judge for South Carolina George S. Bryan were named jointly to oversee the Klan trials. Bond, a founder of the Maryland Republican Party, was a staunch supporter of black rights. Bryan was an anti-secessionist South Carolinian, a Democrat, and a former slaveholder esteemed by the state's white elite. Federal prosecutions of Ku Klux earlier in 1871 had gone nowhere under Bryan, ending in acquittals and mistrials, with juries failing to convict. Bond, under no illusions, accused the Democrats of trying to persuade Bryan "to be a stick between our legs at every step." But juries this time would be chosen under terms of the Ku Klux Klan Act—the Ironclad Oath of no ties to the Ku Klux and heavy penalties for those who lied about it.[28]

Corbin would lead the prosecution. Working through a prodigious number of cases to produce the state's agenda, he wrote to Akerman on November 20 asking if he planned to attend the opening session.[29] Akerman could not, but he promised to get help. On November 24 he sent Corbin a commission to hire South Carolina attorney general Chamberlain to assist.[30] Corbin later fired his own deputy U.S. Attorney and hired William Stone, his Charleston law partner and brother-in-law, to replace him.[31]

Finally, Corbin on November 23 asked Akerman to get permission for Merrill to attend the trials. His "services would be invaluable" as an expert on the York County Klan, he said. Akerman immediately made the request of the War Department, and the request was granted.[32]

THE KLAN put its defense in the hands of a committee led by Wade Hampton, the former Confederate cavalry commander, Southern Life executive, and South Carolina favorite son. The guiding principle was to produce a forthright, law-abiding image by finding the most prestigious counsel available.

Hampton's committee hired former U.S. attorneys general Reverdy Johnson and Henry Stanbery.[33] Johnson, who served under President Zachary Taylor, had argued for the slave-owning defense in the prewar Dred Scott case, even though he personally opposed slavery. The *Charleston Daily News* described him as a "man of eminent ability." He, like Judge Bond, was a Marylander, and the two men were close friends. And Louis Johnson, the seventh of Johnson's eight surviving children, was the U.S. Marshal for South Carolina.

Reverdy Johnson's most recent public service as ambassador to Great Britain under President Andrew Johnson had ended badly, however, when the Senate ignominiously voted down 54–1 his proposed treaty to resolve wartime disputes with Britain. He was criticized for being too cozy with the British and for drinking too much and accomplishing nothing: "He sits here with his tongue lolling out, or picks his teeth with his fingers," one of his subordinates noted in a diary.[34]

Stanbery, attorney general under Andrew Johnson, had resigned in 1868 in order to join the defense team during Johnson's impeachment trial. He was a vehement opponent of reconstruction and of all federal encroachments on states' rights.[35]

Once hired, Hampton's committee needed a way to pay its "eminent counsel from the North." The committee began dunning local leaders, county by county, to collect $15,000. This, its circular said, "is deemed a public duty."

To emphasize the urgency of the endeavor, The *Charleston Daily News* quoted Akerman's Brooklyn promise of convictions and his assurance that some of the Ku Klux "WOULD BE HUNG."[36]

It was clear that Akerman's hopes of support for the intervention from right-thinking white South Carolinians was misplaced. White South Carolina backed the Klan.

THE PROSECUTION'S first priority would be to seek justice for blacks' grievances, but Akerman and Corbin knew that the constitutional validity of both the Ku Klux Klan Act and the Fourteenth Amendment itself would also be on trial. They welcomed the challenge posed by their illustrious opponents, both of whom had vast experience interpreting constitutional law.

"Is the professional strength of the prosecution adequate in view of the force on the other side?" Akerman asked rhetorically in a letter to Corbin in early December. "My impression is that it is sufficient."[37]

Akerman and Corbin had a strong relationship and, with help from Merrill and Chamberlain, unfaltering familiarity with the evidence. Corbin, thirty-eight, and Chamberlain, thirty-six, had known the Ku Klux Klan for years. Defense counsel may have known plenty about constitutional law, but they knew little or nothing about South Carolina or about the crimes to be tried.

BY MID-OCTOBER, northern newspapers finally had firsthand glimpses of the army and the Akerman team at work. At the end of October in Yorkville, *Cincinnati Commercial* correspondent "H. V. R." caught up with U.S. Commissioner Samuel T. Poinier, a fellow Ohioan who took him to visit Merrill so he could see some affidavits.

"I read several; read enough to brand the Ku Klux forevermore in my eyes as murderers, organized murderers," H. V. R. wrote. Merrill would not let him publish the actual material while fugitives were still at large, "but some of the operations of the midnight raiders would be altogether too revolting for publication even if it was allowed."

On a Sunday morning Poinier took H. V. R. to the jail during visiting hours. Forty or so visitors were allowed in at a time, then swapped out. "Quite a crowd and a large number of ladies," H. V. R. noted. Those accused of the most heinous crimes were in cells on the third floor—rich, poor, ignorant, educated, all mixed.

"The prisoners are considered martyrs to a military despotism by their friends," H.V.R. wrote. The food was good. The gifts were good. Nobody was suffering, and "flowers were hanging from all the cells."[38]

Two weeks later a correspondent from the *New-York Tribune*, a fierce supporter of Grant, watched Corbin and Merrill interviewing prisoners. If the prisoner was just a "passive member," Merrill would parole him and send him home.

But if he made up a story, Merrill put him in jail. "You're just the man I've been looking for, you live on the Howell's Ferry Road, belong to the Rattlesnake Clan and participated in the Jim Williams raid," the reporter quoted Merrill as saying. "I don't ask you to tell anything, but if you want to make a statement here's your chance." The *Tribune* described the Jim Williams lynching in detail, named J. Rufus Bratton as the ringleader, and mentioned the Roundtree murder, the Unionville jailbreaks, the Chester riots, and the raid on Rose's Hotel.[39]

Even opposition papers abandoned the pretense that prisoner treatment in Yorkville was somehow inhuman. But they raised two important points, which cast doubt on the army's intervention. The New York *Sun* succinctly summed up these views in a Yorkville story on November 16. "Not a half-dozen" acts of conspiracy had been committed after April 20 passage of the Ku Klux Klan Act," the *Sun* said. Most of the cases fell under the first Enforcement Act of 1870, which covered denial of voting rights but did not authorize suspension of habeas corpus.[40]

Notwithstanding the contention by Merrill and Governor Scott that beatings and burglaries continued unabated since April 20, evidence indeed showed a sharp decline in violence.[41] The Grant administration, however, had a ready answer. The U.S. Army was all over the upcountry, and a large number of Klan chieftains—the plotters—had departed. It would have been a surprise if raids and beatings had not all but disappeared.

As far as the arrests being illegal, Corbin and Merrill took care of that somewhat cavalierly. Just as the trials were starting, Merrill sent a list of 172 prisoners arrested and held for trial, along with the charges against them. Virtually all of were named in the Elias Hill raid—which took place May 5. The reasoning was defensible: since the Klan conspiracy existed after April 20, as Squire Brown's documents proved, outrages committed before passage were covered by the same conspiracy.[42]

AS SOON AS he returned to Washington, Akerman was confronted with a pile of letters from federal authorities throughout the South describing how they were swamped by the caseload of Klan arrests. Clearing the docket, they warned, was hopeless. In a private letter to former U.S. Attorney Benjamin D. Silliman on November 9, Akerman acknowledged the problem and estimated there were between five thousand and ten thousand cases throughout the South.[43]

The next day he wrote to Corbin. So many prisoners were being held in South Carolina that it would be impossible to try them all "with the present judicial force," he wrote. It was time to divide the prisoners into three categories.

"Leaders in the conspiracies" and other major criminals should be held prisoner and brought to trial. Lesser criminals should be released "upon light bail," to be tried later. Reluctant participants and those forced to join the Ku Klux should give written statements in writing and be released, but they would be recalled if they failed to "bear themselves as good citizens."[44]

As early as November 3, Corbin had warned Akerman that it would be logistically "impossible" at that time to try anyone except York County's Klan. "I have no doubt that will occupy the whole term of the court to the exclusion of business from other counties."[45]

On November 15, five days after Union County was added to the list of offenders, Akerman cautioned Corbin about undertaking "vigorous operations in other counties," despite the temptation. "It is certainly desirable that nothing could be done which looks like faltering."[46] Corbin had already decided to give Union a pass.[47]

JUDGE BOND and Reverdy Johnson left Maryland on November 23 and arrived in Columbia two days later as companions on the same train. Corbin and Judge Bryan arrived the next morning. Stanbery was handling a case in Kentucky and was expected in town November 27—opening day.[48] Corbin had seventy-seven defendants sorted out for trial, along with thirty-six witnesses. Defendants and witnesses were all from York County.[49]

"Act vigorously" in only a "small district," General Terry had advised his superiors in June. Do it once, and the Ku Klux Klan everywhere will collapse.

CHAPTER TWENTY-ONE

Great Questions

The fall session of the U.S. Fourth Circuit Court convened at 10:00 a.m. Monday, November 27, 1871, in the conference hall of the Nickerson House hotel in downtown Columbia. It was a long room with a raised dais set up at one end for presiding judges Bond and Bryan. Reporters sat in rows of chairs on either side so they didn't have to strain to hear.

Below the dais, the courtroom was arranged in a T-shape composed of wooden conference tables. At the crossbar, immediately below the judges, sat the clerk of the court, U.S. Marshal Louis Johnson, and other courtroom officials.

A long table extended from the crossbar toward the far end of the room. U.S. Attorney Corbin, South Carolina attorney general Chamberlain, and their aides sat on one side, and defense attorneys Henry Stanbery and Reverdy Johnson were on the other, along with their aides. Ku Klux Klan benefactor Wade Hampton also appeared for the opening, sitting with the defense. Double rows of seats set against the wall on opposite sides of the room served as makeshift jury boxes for the grand and petit jurors.

Spectators filled the rest of the space, beyond the jurors on either side and clustered at the far end of the chamber. Blacks and whites sat apart from each other.[1]

The *Charleston Daily News* immediately dismissed the proceedings as "a horrible farce," noting that Louis Johnson and his father Reverdy were opponents in the trials, while partners from the same prominent law firm were also sitting across from one another. The only object of the trials, the *News* concluded, was to "make money for the lawyers and political capital for Mr. Grant."[2]

This analysis was seriously mistaken. The stakes in Columbia were high, and both sides knew it. Corbin, Chamberlain, and Akerman in Washington had three goals. The first was straightforward: get rid of the Ku Klux by using the First and Third Enforcement (Ku Klux Klan) Acts to prove conspiracy to violate the voting rights of freedmen.

The other two goals were far loftier. Following Akerman's lead, the prosecution wanted to establish two Fourteenth Amendment precedents: first, that under the amendment federal jurisdiction could trump state law whenever states refused to protect the constitutional and civil rights of citizens; second, that federal courts could try as federal violations the common crimes that frequently accompanied Klan terrorism.

Stanbery and Johnson had an easier job: to show that the federal government had no business ferreting out conspiracies, defending citizens' rights, or prosecuting common crimes in South Carolina or any other individual state. They were reaffirming a status quo that had existed since the days of the American Revolution.

The vast majority of York County's Klan raids had occurred before passage of the Ku Klux Klan Act, so the prosecution's cases were based on the First Enforcement Act's prohibition against interfering with the voting rights of citizens—male citizens. Misdemeanor convictions applied to individual offenders and carried a maximum prison sentence of one year and a $500 fine. Felony convictions involving two or more conspirators carried prison terms of up to ten years and fines up to $5,000. The act, at least in theory, could also be applied to any violation intended to "prevent or hinder any right or privilege granted or secured" by "the Constitution or laws of the United States." This was the door Corbin and Chamberlain needed to open.[3]

Both prosecution and defense understood that the trials would be divided into two parts. The constitutional questions would be decided first. These outcomes would dictate the course of the criminal prosecutions to follow.

In a November 13 letter, Corbin told Akerman he had begun to shape his schedule. He had about three hundred confessions and a similar number of statements from black victims and witnesses, detailing "a catalogue of crimes probably never surpassed, if equaled in the history of any country." Merrill had told him that between fifteen and twenty of the prisoners were implicated in murders.

In bringing his cases to trial, Corbin would indict for conspiracy and charge "that in the act of committing that offense" other crimes took place. These, he said, would include murder and beatings—common crimes—as well as confiscating weapons and breaking into homes—constitutional violations of the Second Amendment right to bear arms and Fourth Amendment protections against illegal search and seizure. What did Akerman think?[4]

Akerman responded two days later. He was "inclined to the opinion" that the Fourth Amendment was intended to keep government from invasions of citizens' privacy but probably did not apply to "an irregular and unofficial seizure." Still, he was not sure, and there was no harm in trying it out. On the right to bear arms, however, "I think you are impregnable."[5]

THE FIRST days in court were consumed by tedious bureaucratic hassles, mostly about jury composition. On Friday, December 1, Judge Bond swore in the grand jury, first reading to them the Ironclad Oath required by the Ku Klux Klan Act—that they had never participated in or abetted a Klan conspiracy. Of the twenty-one grand jurors, only six were white.[6]

The jurors returned two indictments over the weekend. The first named Allen Crosby and codefendants for conspiracy to deny the voting rights of Amzi Rainey, a young father in his late twenties who lived along the Pinckney Road only six miles from Yorkville.

On March 22, Klan raiders had broken into Rainey's cabin, beaten his wife, who had a baby in her arms, shot and wounded his ten-year-old daughter, raped his oldest daughter, and took Rainey into the woods and threatened to hang him, freeing him only after he pledged never again to vote for the Radical party.[7]

Crosby was not a major Klan chieftain, but this, Corbin hoped, would be the test case. The eleven-count indictment had everything: denial of voting rights, illegal search and seizure, assault and battery, burglary, rape, and the attempted murder of a child. Corbin described Rainey as "a most respectable mulatto" who had "always sustained an excellent character." He was well-spoken, he told Akerman, and would be an "excellent" witness, along with his wife and daughter.[8]

His second, more ambitious case was the Jim Williams lynching. This indictment named several of York County's "best people," among them J. William Avery, J. Rufus Bratton and his brother John J. Bratton, and Yorkville town marshal Rufus McClain. Corbin charged conspiracy to deny Jim Williams's voting rights, with murder as the accompanying common crime.

"[Stanbery and Johnson] will attack my indictments furiously on constitutional grounds," Corbin wrote in a letter to Akerman, "an amusement I trust we shall live through."[9]

It was not so amusing. No sooner had Bond gaveled the Monday session to order than Stanbery moved to dismiss all eleven counts of the Rainey indictment. Then, in a presentation that lasted the entire day, he demonstrated his talents by systematically shredding Corbin's case. He started by denigrating Corbin's credentials as an attorney. The first count of the Rainey indictment charged a conspiracy to deny voting rights but named no one as a victim, prescribed no penalties, and did not specify a particular election where rights were denied. The second count named Amzi Rainey as the victim but described him only as a U.S. "citizen," Stanbery said. If the Enforcement Act gave Rainey the same voting rights as any white man, he had to comply with South Carolina's requirements. The indictment did not say whether Rainey lived in South Carolina, let alone in York County, nor did it even specify that he was twenty-one years old.[10]

Stanbery then moved on to several counts that spoke to core concerns of both prosecution and defense. The indictment charged the accused with threats and intimidation against Rainey, denial of his voting rights, illegal search and seizure, denial of equality before the law, and burglary, all of these portrayed as corollaries to the basic conspiracy.

Stanbery focused on burglary, the common crime, arguing that it occurred independently of any attempt to deny Rainey his voting rights. But though it was unrelated, federal jurisdiction over the offense was a "great question" requiring "the most mature consideration." He hinted that Bond and Bryan might wish to refer the issue to the Supreme Court.

Here Stanbery was tipping his hand, but it was not unexpected. Should the two judges disagree with one another on the propriety of trying this count or others, they had to ask the Supreme Court for a ruling. This was crucial for both sides since it would also require the court to decide the constitutionality of the First Enforcement and Ku Klux Klan Acts and, by extension, the reach of the Fourteenth and Fifteenth Amendments. This was the key question for both prosecution and defense.[11]

Stanbery's viewpoint was clear. The burglary and the other supplementary counts were legitimate complaints, he acknowledged, but they did not belong in federal court. "I will fight to the last ditch against federal usurpation," he said.

Corbin, perhaps somewhat shaken, admitted that Stanbery's motion to dismiss was unexpected and was granted an adjournment to prepare a response. Still, Corbin and Akerman, like Stanbery and Johnson, had undoubtedly discussed a court referral and perhaps welcomed it. Regardless of the verdict in Columbia, the supplementary counts, if they remained in the indictment, would demand that the Supreme Court settle the constitutionality question.[12]

The battle was joined.

Chamberlain spoke first the following day, dismissing Stanbery's objections to the basic indictment. The case simply alleged a conspiracy under the First Enforcement Act, he said. Everything else was "surplusage." There was no reason to name either a victim, a punishment, or a specific election. Chamberlain could not "conceive how such an objection [could] seriously be taken to this indictment."

He was also satisfied that Amzi Rainey, as a "citizen," had all the qualifications necessary to vote. He would not otherwise have been named in the indictment. Also, his right to vote was clearly "hindered" by the raiders, who demanded he take an oath never again to vote the Radical ticket. He noted that punishments were fully described in Sections Four and Six of the Enforcement Act, another reason Stanbery's objections were groundless.

Then he addressed the supplementary counts. Stanbery's "elaborate" argument against the federal government trying a "domestic crime" was groundless. Under the Enforcement Act, if a separate felony were committed during the violation of a victim's voting rights, the federal court could use state sentencing guidelines to prescribe punishment.

He also asserted federal jurisdiction over illegal search and seizure and other violations of the Bill of Rights. Stanbery had said that only states could protect these rights, but state courts and laws were not working for Amzi Rainey "and many others," Chamberlain said. Congress had passed the Fourteenth and Fifteenth Amendments to give the government the power to enforce constitutional rights for "large classes of citizens" like Amzi Rainey who were "not secure," he said. To do so, Congress implemented the amendments with the Enforcement Acts.[13]

After a short recess, it was Corbin's turn. He spoke directly to the court. At conception, he acknowledged, the Bill of Rights was intended to keep the federal government out of states' affairs, but since the Civil War "states [had been] disposed to encroach upon the rights of newly enfranchised citizens."[14]

"And how are they to be protected?" By the Fourteenth Amendment and the Enforcement Acts, he said, which gave the federal government the authority to use the Bill of Rights to protect the "immunity and right" of citizens against state encroachments.

"I am aware that this is new law," Corbin said. And he was aware that the Court had "a solemn duty" to interpret it. Without specifically saying so, he appeared to agree with Stanbery—if the judges had doubts, they should refer their questions to the Supreme Court and see what happened.[15]

The following day Reverdy Johnson closed for the defense. Like Corbin, he focused almost exclusively on the conflict between federal power and states' rights. Neither the Fourteenth nor the Fifteenth Amendment conferred the right to vote, he said. They simply said that citizens, in different situations, could not be discriminated against because of race, color, or previous "condition of servitude."

The right to vote, "whatever that may be," is conferred by individual states, not the federal government, he said. As far as Johnson was concerned, Congress had no authority to pass either the First Enforcement Act or the Ku Klux Klan Act, both of which, in his view, were "void"—unconstitutional.

For this reason, he said, it was impossible to sustain the corollary counts.

The government was seeking to punish people "by means of laws they have no constitutional power to pass." Yes, if the federal government were threatened by rebellion, Congress could send troops to put down the insurrection and could grant the president the authority to suspend habeas corpus. "[But] are we in rebellion now . . . within the limits of South Carolina?" he asked. He did not think so but agreed that the entire matter raised "serious questions." These, he said, should be resolved by "the ultimate judicial tribunal."[16]

THE SESSION adjourned so Bond and Bryan could confer. The next day, December 7, Bond read their opinion. The judges sustained the prosecution on the conspiracy count, agreeing with Chamberlain that failure to name the victims, the penalties, and the disputed election were frivolous complaints.

Also sustained was the count that the prisoners conspired to prevent Rainey from voting in a future election. The conspiracy was ongoing, the court said, and the indictment was valid for the same reasons as the first count. The practical effect of this ruling, however, was that it put the defendants under the restrictions imposed by the Ku Klux Klan Act—denial of habeas corpus—as well as the provisions of the First Enforcement Act.

The judges agreed with the defense on the failure to describe Amzi Rainey's qualifications to vote, and they dismissed the second count. They also dismissed the counts related to constitutional privileges and rights, as either too vague or, in the case of illegal search and seizure, as a recognized common law right even before the Constitution was written. It had no place in federal court.

On two counts that referred to the burglary—the ability to impose sentence for a common crime committed as part of the conspiracy—Bond agreed with the prosecution that the Enforcement Act covered this, but Bryan dissented. These counts would be sent to the Supreme Court.[17]

AKERMAN AND his prosecutors had taken quite a beating at the hands of the two constitutional experts. States' rights had prevailed over their attempts to extend the reach of the Fourteenth Amendment, and Akerman's goal—to use the Fourteenth Amendment to protect the civil rights of those oppressed by hostile state governments—would not get a hearing with this indictment.

The prosecution, however, had not lost the war. The judges had left the conspiracy count intact, and by doing so they had legitimized the First Enforcement Act and left in place the possibility that Klan prisoners, if convicted, could pay heavy fines and end up in federal prison for a long time.

This may not have been Akerman's first choice of weapons, but he had watched Bond rule against the Klan in North Carolina and could have been confident that he would do so again. Also, in ruling that the Klan was an ongoing conspiracy, the judges had endorsed the Ku Klux Klan Act—ensuring that the worst offenders would languish in jail as long as the government wished. The deterrent effect of this finding could not be underestimated.

Finally, Bond's refusal to dismiss the burglary counts in the Rainey case left open the possibility that the Supreme Court would endorse the prosecution of "domestic crimes" in federal conspiracy trials. Should this be the case, the Klan would be held accountable for rape, battery, and other crimes against women and children. The First Enforcement Act focused only on voters—men.

So what to do next?

Akerman and Corbin certainly expected and may have even welcomed a referral to the Supreme Court, but Corbin was worried that the burglary counts were too vague. He would have trouble proving burglary in trial even if the Supreme Court ruled in his favor. He wanted to withdraw the burglary counts from the indictment and asked Bond to do so.

The defense objected, but Bond agreed with Corbin and pulled rank on Bryan. The burglary counts were removed, and nothing would go to the Supreme Court, because there was no longer anything about common crimes in the indictment.

For the rest of that day and the next, prosecution and defense argued about procedures for what had been the Amzi Rainey case and was now simply a conspiracy case against Crosby and his codefendants. In the end, prosecution and defense made a deal, and the defendants changed their pleas to guilty.[18] Ringleader Crosby was eventually fined $300 and sentenced to serve eighteen months in federal prison.

The Jim Williams lynching case came next. Corbin provided two different indictments. Both sides agreed that the first, alleging murder in conjunction with conspiracy to deny Williams's voting rights, would go to the Supreme Court for the ruling on whether a common crime—murder in this case—could be prosecuted as part of a federal conspiracy trial. J. William Avery was the lead defendant.

Both sides hoped that this strategy would elicit the definitive ruling that Johnson sought regarding federal jurisdiction over domestic crimes but without the uncertainties that Corbin feared with the Amzi Rainey burglary. Williams's lynching was a fact.

The second indictment was the same as the first but without the murder. This was fundamentally a conspiracy trial, and the lead defendant here was Robert Hayes Mitchell, a Klan underling who tended the horses of the men who actually killed Williams.

IN WASHINGTON Akerman was closely following events in Columbia, but the ground was shifting under him even as he watched his long-sought objective take shape. Suddenly the support he had enjoyed from President Grant for eighteen months was fraying. His first hint probably came during a December 1 cabinet meeting when he read a request from Georgia's governor to send troops to deal with Klan unrest. Grant was not interested.[19]

Then, when the second session of the Forty-Second Congress convened on December 4, Grant's third annual message disposed of South Carolina in a few paragraphs buried beneath a mountain of numbing detail about foreign and economic affairs. The message also suggested the possibility of granting amnesty for all but the "great criminals" of the former Confederacy: "This subject is submitted for your [Congress's] careful consideration." The unrepentant South was no longer a subject of major administration concern.[20]

The implications for Akerman were obvious. The *Buffalo Commercial* on December 5 predicted that he was about to be ousted "because of a disagreement between him and the President on the subject of the Ku Klux."[21]

The *New York Herald* said Akerman wanted to take a harder line on the Klan and that the president did "not seem to agree." Moreover, rumors of personal disagreements in the cabinet had "finally settled upon" Akerman as the offender. "[He] is quite self-opinionated, tenacious of his own views and rather disagreeable in considering those of others," the *Herald* reported. Nobody liked having him around.[22]

As days passed, speculation traveled other avenues. The *Richmond* (Va.) *Dispatch* blamed Akerman's fall from grace on his "failure to give the Radical party any strength in Georgia," noting that he had "but few friends in his own party." Akerman would be gone shortly, the *Dispatch* added, to be replaced by former Oregon senator George Williams.[23]

The New York *Sun* said Senate "hostility" to Akerman was growing because of the "inevitable damage" his presence would cause during the 1872 election. Making at least two errors in one sentence, the *Sun* said: "[There is no room for] a rebel general [wrong rank] in the Cabinet, especially a man from Andersonville, Ga. [wrong home town] who never raised his voice against the horrors of that prison."[24]

And in a gossipy piece a bit over a week after the president's annual message, The *New York Herald* raised the possibility that Benjamin Bristow, with serious support from "mostly" southern lawmakers, would shove ex-senator Williams aside and get the attorney general job at the last minute.[25]

Unlike earlier spurts of speculation about Akerman's imminent departure, these rumors had teeth. Akerman had plenty of friends in the Republican Party, but they were all in Congress. In the cabinet he had never been popular.

Akerman knew this. As he told a friend in a private letter, he was "chronically garrulous on the Ku Klux" and continued to belabor his cabinet colleagues with horror stories during its biweekly meetings:[26]

"He has it on the brain," Secretary of State Hamilton Fish wrote in his diary. "He tells a number of stories, one of a fellow being castrated, with terribly minute and tedious details of each case. It has got to be a bore to listen twice a week to this thing."[27]

He had also earned the enmity of Interior Secretary Delano, whose efforts to cozy up to the railroads had encountered a solid wall of opposition at the Justice Department. The *Baltimore American*, owned by Delano, said neither Delano nor Treasury Secretary Boutwell could "conduct the business of their departments" as long as Akerman was attorney general. And members of the Supreme Court, the *American* said, had also expressed a lack of confidence.[28]

And in his own shop, of course, Solicitor General Bristow had smeared Akerman during an audience with the president himself. In an administration filled with professionals and, increasingly, cronies, Akerman was still the outsider. His friends in government were in Columbia and Louisville, not Washington.

And certainly, whatever utility he may have had as a political actor on behalf of the Grant reelection campaign had been badly compromised—perhaps fatally—by the Georgia election results. Grant needed to focus on winnable states.

On December 10 Grant asked for Akerman's resignation. The next day he sought out Fish in his office and told him he would "be obliged to make changes in the office of Atty General" and would appoint "Judge Williams of Oregon."[29] Two days later Grant told Fish he had received Akerman's resignation. Akerman would leave January 10, and Williams would replace him. Grant had offered to make Akerman an ambassador or a district judge, but Akerman declined.[30]

Akerman's resignation letter was bare-bones and brief, but he added a short addendum: "[I] express my grateful sense of the kindness which I have uniformly received from you during my service in the office, and my ardent wishes for the continued success of your administration."[31]

Grant responded in kind: "[I have] high regards for you personally, and . . . appreciation for the zealous application which you have brought to the office which you have so honorably filled." He also praised—perhaps not altogether honestly—"the uniform harmony" that existed around Akerman: "[not only] between us, but also between yourself and colleagues in the Cabinet."[32]

And that was all. The *Philadelphia Inquirer* quickly dismissed the event by noting there was not "a single dissenting voice to Mr. Akerman's removal." The postmortem offered little of interest, focusing yet again on Akerman's legal limitations, the national weariness with reconstruction, and Akerman's political incompatibility with Grant in an election year.[33]

Grant's decision to back away from aggressive reconstruction policy was probably due mostly to political considerations. His commitment to the rights of black citizens never wavered, but a breakaway faction of his party—known as the Liberal Republicans—was moving toward an alliance with the Democrats. Weariness with reconstruction was a key element of the Liberals' disagreements with Grant. They were tired of military interventions to prop up corrupt state governments in the South. They favored amnesty for former Confederates and had little remaining sympathy for the plight of freedpeople.[34]

Akerman offered little in the way of explanation for his departure, but he was well aware that enthusiasm for reconstruction was waning. "The real difficulty is that very many of the northern Republicans shrink from any further special legislation in regard to the South," he wrote in a late December letter. "The Northern mind being active and full of what is called 'progress' runs away from the past."[35]

The only mention he made of his firing was an oblique reference in a personal letter to Corbin on December 15: "You have doubtless learned by this time that I have resigned the Attorney generalship." He added, "The reasons for this step I would not detail fully without saying what perhaps ought not to be said."[36]

These reasons likely had something to do with his railroad battles. These were largely ignored following the resignation, until the Lancaster, Pennsylvania, *Intelligencer Journal* wrote on December 23 that Akerman had to be shoved out because he was "in the way of the Pacific Railroad ring." The railroads "wanted a tool that would serve them without limit." They favored the Oregonian.[37]

This theme was amplified in a long appreciation of Akerman written in the 1880s by Cartersville, Georgia, essayist Rebecca Felton. "Certain railroad interests," she wrote, "discovered his honesty to be in their way." At one point, Felton wrote, "the railroad company approached a friend of Colonel Akerman's to know if $50,000 would cause him to reconsider." Not a chance, the friend said.[38]

Felton was a neighbor and confidante of the Akermans and undoubtedly got much of her material from Matty, whom she clearly knew quite well. The bribery story cannot be confirmed, but Matty apparently put enough stock in it to have it appear in print.

In the end, however, no one knew exactly why Akerman was fired, just as no one could know exactly why he was hired in the first place.

CHAPTER TWENTY-TWO

"Cradle to Grave"

DECEMBER 18, 1871

On December 12, 1871, Robert Hayes Mitchell went on trial in federal court for conspiracy to deprive "diverse male citizens of African descent" of the right to vote. Among them was militia captain Jim Williams, lynched by Ku Klux Klan night riders the early morning of March 6.[1]

Mitchell, a forty-two-year-old laborer, was no murderer, but Klan chieftains J. W. Avery and J. Rufus Bratton, the ringleaders in the Williams killing, had fled to Canada. Mitchell was one of some sixty men who had ridden out that night. If prosecutors could convict one conspirator, no matter how insignificant, then they could convict them all.

As the proceedings began, the clerk of the court called January Simpson, "colored," to be sworn as the first juror. Had he formed an opinion about the case? No. Had he ever served on a jury? "This is the first time." He was sworn.

Next came William Smith, also "colored." Where did he live? "In this place." Had he formed an opinion about the case? No. He was sworn.

Defense attorneys Reverdy Johnson and Henry M. Stanbery had twenty-two peremptory challenges. They used several, mostly, it appeared, to exclude white men from distant counties. U.S. Attorney David T. Corbin, the lead prosecutor, had only two challenges, but on several occasions he told prospective jurors to "stand aside." Johnson had no idea what that meant, and Stanbery said Corbin had no right to use such a maneuver.

Actually he did, Judge Hugh L. Bond explained. Defense had more challenges, but the government could pass on prospective jurors in the initial phase and re-interview them later if the jury still needed members once the entire pool had been questioned. That was the way federal court worked.

Vetting continued. In the end, the court empaneled two white and ten black jurors. Joseph Taylor, "colored," was the foreman.[2]

Corbin opened the case by calling Lieutenant Godfrey, a platoon leader in the York County army garrison, to recount how he had obtained a copy of the Ku Klux constitution and bylaws from the private desk of Samuel G. "Squire" Brown in October.

The defense, openly combative from the moment Bond first gaveled the court, immediately disputed Godfrey's right to take the document. Godfrey explained that Brown had given him a written authorization, and Brown's daughter Jennie had unlocked the desk. Where's the authorization? Godfrey gave it to Jennie. Did he record the event? Yes, Godfrey said. He had endorsed the document and had brought it with him. He read it to the court. No further questions.[3]

Corbin then called Albertus Hope, a former Klan chieftain, who testified that he had given the constitution and bylaws to Brown after receiving them from J. William Avery in 1868. When Hope became a Ku Klux leader in March 1871, he said, members were worried about gin house burnings and "threats" being made by York County's blacks. Did Hope ever hear any threats, Corbin asked. No, he did not.

Never mind, interrupted Reverdy Johnson. Hope's testimony showed that the Klan was a "self-defense" organization, not a band of cutthroats.

Then who was raiding the county, Corbin asked, ignoring Johnson. "The raids were generally made by white parties," Hope replied. "They were generally called Ku Klux."[4]

Kirkland Gunn, Attorney General Akerman's informant from Cartersville, came next. When he took the oath to join the Klan in January, had he understood the obligation, the constitution, and the bylaws, Corbin asked. Yes, he had. Corbin prepared to read the obligation and constitution.

Reverdy Johnson interrupted again. Don't put words in the witness's mouth. Have him tell what he thought his obligation was. Corbin had no objection and asked Gunn for his understanding of the obligation. "It was for the purpose of putting down radical rule and negro suffrage," Gunn said.

Corbin then read the entire Ku Klux document—obligation, constitution, and bylaws—into the record. The obligation opposed "the principles of the Radical party" but said nothing about black suffrage.[5]

At this point it was clear that Stanbery and Johnson, for all their erudition on constitutional matters, were totally unprepared to handle a criminal trial, and they had immediately put their ineptitude on public display, falling into every trap set by Corbin. They had ended up with a nearly all-black jury, they had not examined the evidence and did not know that Lieutenant Godfrey could easily prove the legitimacy of his document seizure, and they had allowed the prosecution to name J. William Avery as the long-time leader of the York County Klan.

They had described the Ku Klux Klan as a self-defense organization, only to have the next witness tell them its purpose was to bring down the Radical party. Then, as an added dividend for Corbin, Johnson prodded Gunn into saying the

Klan wanted to suppress black suffrage. Corbin's case was premised on conspiracy to deny Jim Williams's voting rights. Gunn—with a nudge from Johnson—had confirmed it.

Gunn continued, describing rituals and hand signals, detailing Klan raids and naming Klan leaders, among them Squire Brown. Reverdy Johnson interrupted yet again, claiming that Gunn's testimony in this regard was all hearsay. He badgered Gunn for some minutes to explain how he knew of Brown's Klan membership.

Gunn told Johnson he had overheard Brown boasting to another Klan chieftain, "I can kill and whip more damn niggers with my Klan than all the rest of York County."[6] This within earshot of the nearly all-black jury.

The defense recovered somewhat, discovering during cross-examination that Gunn had visited Akerman not only in Cartersville but also in Washington, where Akerman's clerk had given him $200 for expenses. This suggested that Gunn was a "detective" working for Akerman, Stanbery said. Gunn denied it.[7]

So why did Gunn join the Klan, Stanbery eventually asked. If he had refused, "it would probably go hard" with him, Gunn replied.[8]

How hard? The next witness, storekeeper Charles Foster, had the answer. He had joined the Klan after they shot up his house. "[If I didn't sign on, they had] cold steel prepared for my carcass." His raiders, he said, also visited Elias Ramsay the same night to deliver the same warning.[9]

Corbin next turned to the Jim Williams lynching. Gadsden Steel, kidnapped to point the way to the Williams cabin, Rose Williams, the victim's widow, and Andy Tims, Williams's fellow militiaman, took turns detailing the events of March 6. Their testimony began with the arrival of the hooded mob outside Steel's door and finished with Tims's discovery of the victim hanging dead from a tree with a placard around his neck.[10]

The courtroom, so noisy that reporters sitting practically alongside the witness stand could barely hear the testimony, fell silent when Rose Williams was sworn in. No one made a sound as she was questioned. She described the Klan break-in, how she peeked through the window when they took her husband into the woods, and how she waited, terrified, with her children. She finally went outside at noon the following day.

CORBIN: Did you see him?

ROSE WILLIAMS: Yes, sir.

CORBIN: What was his condition?

ROSE: He was hung on a pine tree.

CORBIN: With a rope around his neck?

ROSE: Yes sir.

CORBIN: Dead?

ROSE: Yes, sir; he was dead.

Corbin nodded imperceptibly toward the defense: "The witness is yours."[11]

UNABLE TO dispute the facts of the raid, the defense instead quizzed witnesses about Jim Williams and the militia—their guns, their ammunition, their drilling, and Williams's refusal to disband his company. Rose Williams acknowledged that her husband kept "a little paper box" filled with nine or ten minié balls in the house and that, while he had orders to return his company's guns, "he said he didn't allow to do it."[12]

Corbin inquired what purpose the defense had in pursuing these questions. Stanbery was straightforward: "We expect to show that he [Williams] was a very dangerous man, and that he had made threats over the county of what he was going to do with the white people."[13]

The following day Corbin called John Caldwell, Elias Ramsay, and two other Klan members as witnesses to detail how the Jim Williams raid was carried out—from the Brier Patch muster to the breakfast picnic at John Bratton's plantation.

They identified about forty Klan members by name. Caldwell, a prisoner undoubtedly seeking leniency, described how he had approached Bratton in the woods and told him "you ought not to have done that," after Bratton admitted "We hung him."[14]

Elias Ramsay detailed the Shearer brothers' initiations and tracked the expedition from its beginning to the post-lynching festivities. He had downed a shot of whiskey and eaten crackers but missed out on the ham and cheese.[15]

Reverdy Johnson handled cross-examination. He was mostly interested in the well-spoken Caldwell, who thought the Williams raid was about confiscating guns. He heard nothing about voting. Yes, he knew about the burning gin houses and had heard about a threat to burn down Yorkville. He had also heard that Williams intended to attack the white people of the county—that he "intended to kill from the cradle to the grave."[16]

The prosecution had heard this before. Louis Post, Corbin's stenographer, said much later that many prisoner statements and confessions had quoted Williams as having said this. And even as the trials began, it had been repeated so often that it was fast becoming part of white South Carolina's Reconstruction folklore.[17]

Corbin was having none of it. Had Caldwell ever heard any black person make these threats. "No sir, I never heard them." Did he know of any white person who had heard a black person make the threats. No. How about burning down Yorkville. No. Was this all rumor? "Yes, sir, it was to me."

Corbin was almost finished. His witnesses had outlined the conspiracy and had described the murder of Jim Williams from the viewpoints of his friends, his family, and even of his attackers.

He lacked only one piece of testimony to finish presenting his case. What was it like to be a victim of the Ku Klux? Jim Williams could not testify, but Corbin's best witness had always been Amzi Rainey. His own case may have been moribund, but Rainey had endured the worst that the Klan could do and had survived.[18]

Rainey began: "It was about the last of March. . . . about ten o'clock my little daughter called me and said, 'Pappy it is time we are going to bed.'"

"Just as I got up and turned around I looked out of the window and I see some four or five disguised men come up." He could hear the raiders as he ran upstairs to hide in the loft.

"God damn you, open the door! Open the door!"

His wife unbolted the door, and two men burst inside, Rainey said, and one of them "struck her four or five licks before they said a word."

Reverdy Johnson arose: "We object to all this."

Overruled. "Let him go on," Bond said.

"They asked her who lived here," Rainey continued. Amzi Rainey, she told them.

One of the attackers "struck her another lick": "Where is he, God Damn him, where is he?"

"And she says 'I don't know,' and one said, 'O, I smell him. God damn him, he has gone up in the loft. We'll kill him, too.'"

They found Rainey hiding in a box.

"We'll kill him," one said.

"Don't kill him yet," said the other.

They went back downstairs, and the first man returned to Rainey's wife. "God damn her," he said. "I will kill her now."

He hit Rainey's wife "four or five more licks," Rainey said, then stepped away to hit Rainey before returning to his wife, drawing a pistol, and pointing it at her head.

"Now I am going to blow your damn brains out," he said.

"Don't kill her," the second man said. He drew his own pistol and swung it at

Rainey's head, but Rainey dodged. The blow hit him in the back. "[It] sunk me right down," Rainey testified.

"I'm going to kill him," the second man said.

Rainey continued: "My little daughter—she was back in the room with the other little children—[ran out]: "Don't kill my pappy; please don't kill my pappy."

The second man shoved her away: "You go back in the room, you God damned little bitch. I will blow your brains out." He opened fire and shot her, then he started shooting over the heads of Rainey and wife—maybe fifteen shots in all.

Rainey's wool jacket caught fire. His wounded daughter, her forehead only grazed, but her head and face covered in blood, tossed the smoldering jacket outdoors.

The raiders followed, forcing Rainey ahead of them. They walked him about 150 yards up the road where he was surrounded by Ku Klux—about twenty-five in all, Rainey estimated. He did not know any of them. They asked him how he had voted. Radical, he said.

"Well, now you raise your hand and swear that you will never vote another Radical ticket, and I will not let them kill you," one of his captors said. Rainey swore. Then they told Rainey to run. "[They] throwed two big rocks after me about the size of my fist." The rocks missed.

"Do you know what they did to your [oldest] daughter in the other room?" Corbin asked. She had been raped.

"Yes, sir," Rainey said.

"Did you see it yourself?"

"No, I have only her word for it."

"I won't ask you that then."

Rainey had said enough. Johnson had no questions.[19]

THEN IT WAS the defense's turn. Stanbery began with Julia Rainey, the earnest widow who had known Jim Williams for twelve years.

"I believe he was a servant in the family?" Stanbery asked.

"Belonged to my husband," Julia Rainey replied.

"To what?" Stanbery asked. He was way out of his depth.

Judge Bond: "He was her former slave."

"My former slave," the widow confirmed.

The witness did her best to cooperate. Williams's militia company "caused a great deal of disturbance," she said, and "they were under his control entirely."[20]

But it was obvious she had not been coached prior to her appearance and bore no malice toward Williams. Even as she related her and the neighborhood's fears of the militia, she also spoke about how Williams had dropped by the house after he got out of the army "to see his old master."

"He always felt at liberty to enter my kitchen to see the old family servants," she said. "Indeed, sir, for two months before his death, I suppose he averaged twice a week in my kitchen."

As far as his threats, she added, "they were very common to me—through the servants; I never heard him myself."

At that point Corbin arose: "I don't think, if the Court pleases, this sort of testimony will do."

The court agreed: "That won't do, sir," Bond said to Stanbery.

Stanbery continued, querying the witness about her fears of the black militia, fears of an uprising, and fears of arson. She became so upset, she said, that she left home and went to stay with her father in Union County.

Corbin politely but easily shredded the damaging parts of her testimony. Her direct contact with Jim Williams, she acknowledged, had resulted in nothing but "kindly" memories. As far as threats and disorder, she told Corbin, "I saw nothing, sir, with my own eyes."[21]

The defense continued the following day, albeit with a strange beginning. Stanbery's first witnesses were John Moroso, the newspaper editor who had covered the upcountry gubernatorial campaign the previous year, and Reform Party gubernatorial candidate Richard Carpenter, both of whom testified to the disruption and disorder caused by black militiamen at political rallies.

Neither man knew Jim Williams or anything about him, but never mind. Stanbery decided that the disturbances were all Jim Williams's fault. He was a "dangerous character and a violent man," Stanbery said. He was "preparing them for war." He had threatened "again and again injuries to the whites" and had threatened "that they should be destroyed from the cradle to the grave." So violent did he become that "there was nothing left but to disarm him and put it out of his power to follow out his evil intention."[22]

The prosecution objected. How could political disturbances between Radicals and Reformers during the 1870 campaign have anything to do with a Klan conspiracy to murder Williams?[23]

Williams and the militia had created a climate of fear, Stanbery replied, and his next witness, black Democrat Bill Lindsay, described how Williams had obtained ammunition for his company and told Lindsay on a trip to Yorkville that he planned "to kill from the cradle up."[24] Several more witnesses followed, both black and white, who had heard or overheard Jim Williams talk about killing "from the cradle up."

But Williams had never personally attacked or hurt anyone, the witnesses agreed when pressed by Corbin. And most conceded he was a highly respected leader among the county's black citizens. York County whites, by contrast, did not know quite what to make of him.

"A pretty bad boy," A. F. Hinson said.

Because he stood up for his rights? Corbin asked.

"Well, he claimed to do that," Hinson replied.

"And he was called, consequently, a pretty bad boy?"

"Yes sir, to the best of my knowledge."[25]

During cross-examination Corbin and Chamberlain noted that all the defense witnesses were either Democrats or had personal grievances with Williams. And after the defense rested its case, Corbin recalled Andy Tims, who told Corbin he had never heard "from cradle to grave" threats until after Williams was dead—"from white people and some few Democratic niggers."[26]

ON SATURDAY, December 16, Judge Bond called for closing statements. Chamberlain went first. The prosecution's case was not about Robert Hayes Mitchell, "this poor prisoner," he said. Mitchell was merely the symbol of a much larger and long-running conspiracy composed of many offenders, who were, "in the eye of the law, one man."

Chamberlain said the conspiracy was intended to put down the Radical party and deprive freedmen of voting rights. The Ku Klux Klan used beatings and murders—including the murder of Jim Williams—to accomplish these purposes.

He examined the Klan constitution, paying special attention to the provision that "no person of color shall be a member of this order." He then reviewed the evidence to drive home the point that the Klan "was political, it was against negroes, and that its purpose was killing and whipping and intimidating the negroes of that county generally, in order to control the elections."[27]

Stanbery came next. He began by paying the jury what he apparently thought was a compliment. "Grave doubts have been entertained whether, in consideration of your previous condition, you have arrived at this time at a state of improvement which would justify your receiving the right to sit in judgment upon your fellow-men," he said.

"You have shown a disposition to give undivided attention to the case [of the prosecution]." But could they listen to the other side? "[If so, then] I am ready to say that you, at least, are entitled to sit in the jury box."

Stanbery then embarked on a confused comparison of "general conspiracy" allegations against the Klan and "specific conspiracy" charges against Robert

Hayes Mitchell for threatening Jim Williams, whom he consistently described as "Jim Rainey," Williams's slave name.

Stanbery spoke about how Governor Scott in 1870 had "armed the blacks" and "left the whites defenseless." This was not fair, he said. "I hope you of the colored race will not expect or desire to rule white men," he said. "Let me tell you, if you go for anything like that your triumph will be short and your doom inevitable."

The court record does not describe any reaction to these remarks, either by the jurors or by the spectators. Stanbery, oblivious, continued: "If an organization of Ku Klux is dangerous, an organization of colored militia may be made even more so," especially "made ready for war as Jim Williams's company was."

"[Suppose] your enemy, armed, with a company of white men at his back under his influence, [threatened] that he would take your family from the cradle up, lay waste your property," Stanbery told the jury.

"Would you feel quite easy, gentlemen?" he asked, incredibly unaware that every black citizen in the room, including most of the jurors, had experienced these exact fears—many of them on several occasions or even on a regular basis.

Jim Williams was a "dangerous man," Stanbery said, a "champion of his race" with a "mission to fulfill"—to "vindicate his race" and to do so "by force."

"If I had lived there in the vicinity of Yorkville on a plantation with my wife and children," Stanbery said, "I would have joined the first squad that came along." Better to have "taken imprisonment . . . than for one single night to allow such a demon as that to be in my neighborhood."[28]

Judge Bond adjourned after Stanbery's extraordinary performance, leaving Reverdy Johnson to clean up the mess on Monday. Johnson, clearly aware of what was necessary, did his best, opening with a statement of his own antislavery views: "Slavery is gone, and I thank God for it."

Also, he noted, the defense was not trying "to defend, to justify, or to palliate the outrages" of the Klan. "I have listened with unmixed horror to some of the testimony that has been brought before you. The outrages proved are shocking to humanity; they admit of neither excuse nor justification."

Johnson said he had come to Columbia because he believed the Enforcement Acts were unconstitutional. He spoke at length about states' rights, then denounced the corruption of the Scott government. "Do you think it was any offense . . . if they should bind themselves together to put down the Radical party?" he asked.

Radical corruption, he said, was a blight. "You must wish that the prosperity and honor of South Carolina may be revived," he said, perhaps unaware that most of the jurors had never experienced either honor or prosperity in South Carolina. He concluded, "[Radical or Democrat], you will use your best efforts to redeem South Carolina from the sad plight in which she is now placed."[29]

Corbin spoke last, and he, like Chamberlain, knew his audience. He called the jurors "laboring men," and treated them with respect. "You, gentlemen, have sat with patience, listening day after day . . . to legal questions, about which you are supposed to know nothing."

"Gentlemen, we have lived over a century in the last ten years," he continued. The ballot, once "a symbol of oppression" for black Americans, had become a "symbol of power." The Ku Klux Klan, not only in South Carolina but also in adjoining states, has conspired to "rob" the newly emancipated of their rights as "American citizens."

The Ku Klux Klan, he continued, might respect the Constitution. "[But that is only] *as it was, not as it is now*, not with the Thirteenth, Fourteenth and Fifteenth Amendments in it." He described the Klan members' unrepentant intractability: "We reject the results of the war," "We trample upon these amendments of the Constitution, and we intend to destroy and defeat them."

He described the defense's argument that Jim Williams and the militiamen created a "state of terror and fear" in York County as "pretense." The Union Leagues never harmed anyone, nor did Jim Williams. Slaves never rose up against their masters during the war, and freedpeople had never hinted at a race war.

"In the name of God [the Klan must] disband!" he concluded. "This organization to defeat the rights of our colored fellow-citizens *must and shall be put down*."[30]

The jury met for thirty-eight minutes and returned a verdict of guilty on the specific conspiracy of denying Jim Williams his right of suffrage.[31] Mitchell, and most of his codefendants, were eventually fined $100 each and sent to federal prison for eighteen months.[32]

IN WASHINGTON, Attorney General Akerman received news of the trial's outcome in a brief telegram from Corbin. "Trial of Robert Hayes Mitchell ended verdict guilty."[33] It was a mixed result. His team had lost the battle to make the Fourteenth Amendment the federal guarantor of constitutional and civil rights, while the question of whether common crimes could be prosecuted as part of a voting rights violation remained in abeyance.

But forced to present the case against Robert Hayes Mitchell simply as a conspiracy, Corbin and Chamberlain had won easily. The Ku Klux Klan was an outlaw organization subject to federal prosecution under the Enforcement Act.

Public opinion was somewhat muted in the North, but an undercurrent of outrage was nevertheless gathering strength. Ironically, it was Reverdy Johnson who gave it the initial push. His closing statement denouncing Ku Klux outrages as "shocking to humanity" was reprinted in countless newspapers across the country. "Mr. Reverdy Johnson is heartily sick of the whole business and wishes he were well out of it," wrote the *Buffalo Morning Express*.[34]

The *New York Herald* compared the Klan to the Spanish Inquisition and agreed with Johnson that crimes had been "charged to the Klan of a nature too revolting and too disgusting to be mentioned even at the bar of justice."[35]

THE COURT had only two weeks left in its fall session, and hordes of defendants awaited trial or sentencing. The prosecution chose its cases carefully. Despite the absences of Avery, Bratton, and others, the government had a number of Klan leaders in custody.

First up were Klan boss John W. Mitchell and codefendant Dr. Thomas Whitesides, charged with depriving "diverse persons" of their political rights by leading or participating in raids in the western part of York County. The lead complainant was Charles Leach, attacked and beaten at his Bullock's Creek home by as many as forty night riders on a Monday night in January.[36]

Corbin led the questioning, bringing forth appalling testimony from multiple witnesses describing three visits by the Mitchell Klan. The first time they came, Mary Robertson told them her husband wasn't home. The second time they stripped her clothes off and beat her. She identified Mitchell as one of her attackers.[37]

Charles Leach was beaten by Mitchell's men on the second raid along with four others, among them political activist Charley Good, who in a subsequent raid was shot to death, his body weighted down and pinned with stakes to the bottom of Broad River.[38]

Johnson and Stanbery were no longer managing the defense, and Mitchell's lawyer, C. D. Melton, used a variation on the time-honored Klan defense that Mitchell could not have been at Bullock's Creek on January 9, when Leach, Good, and others were attacked. He and Dr. Whitesides were attending to Mitchell's sick mother, who suffered from epilepsy.[39] Unfortunately for Melton and Mitchell, the court transcript showed that the raid did not take place on January 9, but a bit over two weeks later. Chamberlain also showed that the Mitchell camp had attempted to fix the January 9 date in the minds of some witnesses who could not remember the exact day.[40]

At 9:00 a.m. on Saturday, December 23, the jury returned a verdict of guilty. Mitchell asked for leniency. He had a wife and seven children. Bond was having none of it: Mitchell had "never thought" about his victims' families. The court fined him $1,000 and sentenced him to five years in federal prison.[41]

Next was Samuel G. "Squire" Brown. He had pleaded guilty, probably hoping for leniency due to his age. At fifty-seven, he was perhaps the oldest Ku Klux prisoner. Appearing before Bond, however, he had little to say except to proclaim his innocence. Bond fined him $1,000 and sentenced him to five years in prison. When Brown started to protest, Bond cut him off: "You evidently don't propose to tell all you know, and I don't, therefore, propose to hear further."[42]

Dr. Edward T. Avery was the last defendant. The evidence was clearcut. He was accused of violating the voting rights of Sam Sturges, the overnight guest of Abraham and Emeline Brumfield, beaten the same night as Isaac and Harriet Postle. The court heard from each of the victims, Sturges and the Postles, all of whom had known Avery for years and identified him easily.

Avery tried another well-worn ploy to quash the case against him. The Reverend R. E. Cooper, his clergyman, drafted a false statement saying that Isaac Postle did not recognize his attackers, and he and Avery's wife Mary badgered Postle for days, finally threatening him with jail for "assault and perjury" if he refused to sign the statement. Postle finally signed on the understanding that it was Mary Avery—and not him—who claimed the attack had never occurred.

Cooper, cross-examined by Corbin, said he might have talked about perjury, because he "wanted to get the old negro to tell what I believed to be the truth." How did he know the charges against Avery were false? Because Mary Avery said so. "I know Mrs. Avery is a truthful lady."[43]

On New Year's Day F. W. McMaster, Avery's attorney, called Major Merrill to the stand to ask him about Isaac Postle. He got nowhere. Merrill unequivocally supported the Brumfields, the Postles, and Sam Sturges. He also told McMaster that he had arrested Cooper on charges of witness intimidation. Corbin interjected and said that the grand jury had just indicted Cooper, Mary Avery, and two Avery servants for witness intimidation.[44]

A bit later the defense rested, and McMaster began his closing statement.

Corbin interrupted immediately. Where was Avery?

"That's for you to find out," McMaster replied.

"Do you know where your client is, Mr. McMaster?" Bond asked.

"I beg the court will excuse me from answering that question."

Dr. Avery had used yet another well-known Ku Klux Klan tactic. He had followed his brother into exile.

On January 2, with Avery absent, the court heard closing statements, and the jury deliberated for fifteen minutes before returning a guilty verdict.[45]

THE SESSION ended three days later after assorted pleadings and sentencing. Only four trials had been held, and all five defendants had been convicted. In addition, forty-nine defendants had pleaded guilty.

Nearly 280 cases would have to be carried over to the next term, and Corbin said he had 472 prisoners in the nine upcountry counties, and estimated that another 160 suspects were fugitives.[46]

Akerman nonetheless pronounced himself satisfied with the results. And in a letter written two days before he left office, he told Merrill, "It is comforting to believe that I have borne some part in the exposure and destruction of that terrible conspiracy."[47]

EPILOGUE

"Not with a Bang but a Whimper"

This is the way the world ends /
Not with a bang but a whimper.
T. S. ELIOT

Late in November 1871 Major Merrill wrote a long letter to Attorney General Akerman, enclosing outstanding warrants for the arrests of J. William Avery, J. Rufus Bratton, Robert Caldwell, and other prominent Ku Klux Klan fugitives.

Merrill told Akerman he had received a telegram from the U.S. Senate sergeant-at-arms seeking information on Avery, believed to have fled to Canada after failing to appear before the Scott committee in Washington the previous summer.

The sergeant-at-arms had since learned that, in addition to being a "delinquent witness," Avery was a suspect in the Jim Williams and Anderson Brown murders. He suggested that these charges would give the Senate enough extra muscle to ask for Avery's extradition.

Merrill had tracked Avery to Washington, Baltimore, and New York, he told Akerman but had lost him in Ontario. He did not have a photograph, but enclosed a description. Secretary of State Hamilton Fish would work on the extradition. Akerman would notify the U.S. Marshals and the Secret Service.

Avery was forty to forty-five years old, five feet nine or five feet ten, with a "robust build, florid complexion, fair or light beard and hair," "bluish-gray eyes and a short neck," and a mustache and short beard under the chin." He weighed about 160 pounds and had a very "slight stoop in his walk." He was "a man of considerable intelligence and accustomed to good society." He was also known as "Major Avery" and "Bill Avery."[1]

On January 10, 1872, just as Akerman was leaving Washington to return to Cartersville, he received a second—and final—letter from Merrill. Avery was believed to be in London, Ontario, at the home of Edward Manigault, an expatriate Yorkville resident. A letter sent to Manigault was mailed from Columbia but was "believed to" be for Avery, perhaps under an assumed name."[2] Merrill did not explain how he obtained his information.

FIVE MONTHS later, on June 4, a cab stopped curbside on Waterloo Street in London, Ontario, around 4:00 p.m. Two men stepped out and accosted a pedestrian as he approached. One of them knocked the man down and handcuffed him with the help of the second, then tossed him into the cab and drove off.[3] Nine-year-old Mary Alice Overholt, playing with dolls in her front yard, was the only eyewitness. She told "Mrs. Dixon," who called the police.[4]

A few days later, the *Ottawa Daily Citizen* reported "a high-handed" violation of Canadian sovereignty. The assault victim, living since May under the name "James Simpson," was the "respectably connected" physician J. Rufus Bratton. He had been kidnapped by Isaac Bell Cornwall, a local "clerk of the peace," and turned over to U.S. Marshal Joseph Hester, who spirited him across the border to Detroit and took him to South Carolina to stand trial for the murder of Jim Williams.[5]

Bratton arrived in Yorkville on June 10. Judge Bryan released him on $12,000 bond two days later, and Bratton immediately jumped bail and returned to Canada, just in time to appear as a surprise witness against Cornwall, on trial for kidnapping. Cornwall's alleged violations were twofold: Bratton had been snatched from Canada without any official warning or notification by Cornwall to Canadian authorities. And the extradition warrant U.S. Marshal Hester presented to Cornwall—signed by Canadian authorities—was for the arrest of J. William Avery, not J. Rufus Bratton (aka Dr. James Simpson).[6] Hester, the glib emissary sent to get President Grant's approval to hire detectives to spy on the Ku Klux, had no photograph of either Avery or Bratton.

Cornwall was sentenced to three years in prison.[7] Bratton reopened his medical practice in London.

Secretary of State Fish was forced to endure what must have been an excruciating visit from the British ambassador—Canada had just become a dominion a few years earlier, but its diplomacy was still handled by Britain—and a formal apology and indemnification were in order.[8]

It is unclear whether Akerman's successor, Attorney General George Williams, nominally in charge of the U.S. Marshals, was working from Merrill's five-month-old information. Had he concocted a plot deliberately targeting Bratton, or did he simply have no idea what was happening in London? In any case, it was quickly becoming apparent that his general performance was found wanting.

Williams was chiefly known in Washington for the extravagance of his beautiful second wife, Kate, and his poor handling of the fraud cases that crippled the second Grant administration. In 1873 Grant, to considerable surprise, nominated him as chief justice of the Supreme Court, but the Senate refused to confirm him. Prominent attorneys found him lacking "qualifications of intellect, experience and reputation."[9]

Williams resigned two years later because of countless indiscretions—using Justice Department funds for private expenses during the panic of 1873, rumors of Kate Williams accepting $30,000 in bribes to fix a case for a New York firm accused of custom house fraud; and the Williamses' purchase of the most expensive carriage in Washington.[10]

CONGRESS IN 1872 passed an Amnesty Act removing the "disabilities" of most former Confederates. Exceptions included U.S. House members and senators, high government officials, and military officers who had left the U.S. government to join the Confederacy in 1860–62.

Grant swept to reelection in 1872—and did win Oregon, Williams's home state—but cronies were ascendant, and his second administration became mired in corruption, initially because of the Credit Mobilier scandal, a stock manipulation scheme run by the board of directors and stockholders of the Union Pacific Railroad—one of Attorney General Akerman's most dedicated enemies.

As time passed, Republicans' dissatisfaction—both in the North and South—with Grant's reconstruction policy deepened because of carpetbagger government corruption and the president's continued willingness, albeit reluctant, to send army troops to intervene in the bloody racial confrontations that continued everywhere in the South after the South Carolina trials and in fact never ended.

The Ku Klux Klan was gone, just as General Terry had predicted. After the prosecutions in York County, the Ku Klux disappeared, not to be resurrected until the early 1900s as a completely new organization. Still, in 1872 and beyond there were more than enough ad hoc, murderous white supremacist successors to carry the torch. Particularly vicious in this regard were the murders of more than one hundred freedmen and black militia in Colfax, Louisiana, by white gunmen led by Confederate veterans.

Grant, to his credit, sent troops to Colfax and elsewhere on occasion to quell some of the worst violence, but military intervention and Radical reconstruction were no longer political winners. By 1876, black citizens in the South had no one to advocate for them.

Interior Secretary Columbus Delano, a trusted supporter of the railroads, lasted until 1875, finally forced to resign for his involvement in numerous scandals. Secretary of War William Belknap resigned in 1876 for taking kickbacks from the operators of Indian trading posts. He was the first cabinet secretary to be impeached by the House but was acquitted by the Senate.

Benjamin Bristow became secretary of the treasury in 1874. He played a major role in persuading Grant to get rid of Williams, Delano, and Orville Babcock, Grant's personal secretary, involved in a number of shady deals. Bristow decided to resign in 1876 to run for president as a reform candidate.[11]

He and Speaker Blaine, among others, lost the nomination to Ohio governor Rutherford B. Hayes, who ran against Democrat Samuel L. Tilden, the governor of New York. Tilden won the popular vote, but neither candidate held a majority of the electoral votes, twenty of which remained contested.

Eventually congressional Republicans and Democrats negotiated a secret deal that gave Hayes the victory by a 185–184 electoral vote margin. In return, the Republicans agreed to withdraw remaining U.S. troops from the former Confederacy. The 1876 election was a heavy blow to reconstruction and set the stage for decades of apartheid in the United States. Only in 1954 with the decision in *Brown v. Board of Education* did the Supreme Court begin to treat this affliction, and it took another ten years for the civil rights movement to bring it to the forefront of public consciousness. And more than a half-century later there is still no cure for the disease.

IN CONGRESS, Radical doubts about Williams's zeal for pursuing—or ability to pursue—the Ku Klux Klan surfaced well before Akerman's departure. North Carolina senator John Pool wrote Williams on December 27 to inquire about his intentions once he became attorney general.[12] On New Year's Day, the *New-York Tribune*, probably based on a leak from Pool, speculated that Akerman might stay on as special counsel for Klan cases to show that the administration would "not recede." "[Akerman] is thought to be, therefore, the most capable of performing the duties which the government will require."[13]

Even though Akerman at this point held the unqualified admiration of civil rights advocates, there was no truth to the rumor. The *Tribune* dispatch, however, had the desired effect. Williams assured Pool, "The President is determined to use all the power which the constitution and laws have placed in his hands to protect the lives and property of peaceable citizens and maintain the supremacy of the laws."[14]

Akerman filed his annual report on January 9, 1872, his last official act. In it, he outlined all of the key issues the Grant administration, Congress, and the Supreme Court had to resolve if the fight against the Ku Klux Klan were to continue.

First, the sanctions of the Ku Klux Klan Act, specifically the president's power to suspend habeas corpus, were to expire in June. It was up to Congress to extend them. Second, there were so many pending cases that efforts to bring the offenders to justice would fail. "The judicial machinery of the United States must be increased," he said.

Finally, the Supreme Court had two questions to resolve in the Jim Williams lynching case: whether a finding of murder in a federal indictment could be used to impose punishment, and whether the Fourteenth Amendment could be used to prosecute a defendant for depriving a victim of his constitutional right to bear arms.[15]

The government faltered on all counts. The habeas corpus provision of the Ku Klux Klan Act expired in June and was not renewed. The Department of Justice did not get needed resources and remained woefully short of money and manpower. And the Supreme Court on March 21 dismissed the referral on the Williams lynching case, agreeing with Attorney General Williams, who personally argued that the court did not have jurisdiction. The decision was 8–1, with Chief Justice Salmon P. Chase dissenting.[16]

This nondecision satisfied neither the defense nor the prosecutors in the Ku Klux Klan trials. Henry Stanbery and Reverdy Johnson had wanted the court to throw out Corbin's indictment on grounds that it encroached on states' rights and that the Enforcement Acts were unconstitutional. Akerman and Corbin had wanted the court to expand the scope of the Fourteenth Amendment to enable federal courts to prosecute common crimes as federal violations of civil rights.

The *Yorkville Enquirer*, for one, however, reported that the court's dismissal caused "general rejoicing" among supporters of the Klan trials who did not want to risk testing the constitutionality of the Enforcement Acts.[17]

This was probably a correct interpretation of Attorney General Williams's role. Akerman and Corbin had gotten conspiracy convictions and put Klansmen in jail without a Supreme Court challenge. Why tamper with success?

Indeed, in 1872 the Fourth Circuit produced eighteen more conspiracy convictions and an equal number of guilty pleas.[18]

Also, a jury of six blacks and six whites in the spring session convicted Elijah Ross Sepaugh of murder in the shooting and throat-cutting death of Tom Roundtree. Like the Williams case, Sepaugh's went to the Supreme Court—another test of whether the Enforcement Acts and, by extension, the Fourteenth Amendment could be used to prosecute common crimes in federal civil rights cases. Two years later Williams ordered Corbin to inform the justices that the government no longer intended to pursue the murder charge. Sepaugh was fined $100 and sentenced to prison for a year.[19]

Corbin could barely contain his frustration. Early in 1872 he had attempted to school Williams on the "very demoralizing effect" the York County prosecutions had had on the Ku Klux and the desperate need for more resources to maintain the pressure.[20]

By the end of 1872 he had clearly figured out that Williams was a third-rater interested only in clearing the docket. His "success" rate may have looked good at cabinet meetings, but he was padding his reports with convictions and guilty pleas from low-ranking coconspirators—easy pickings. Corbin wanted to go after "a few" of the worst offenders, preferably murderers, to set an example. Slack off, especially now that the election was over, and white South Carolina would decide that the prosecutions were "purely political."[21]

Over the following three years, however, enforcement proceeded desultorily and all but collapsed with Williams's disgrace and resignation, followed by Grant's determination to recommend clemency for the remaining untried Klan members. In 1876 he issued a blanket pardon.

J. Rufus Bratton returned home soon after that to a hero's welcome and reopened his Yorkville medical practice. He was said to be the model for the lead character in Thomas Dixon's 1905 novel *The Clansman*, the inspiration for D.W. Griffith's classic white supremacist film *The Birth of a Nation*.

J.W. Avery left Canada and settled in Norfolk, Virginia.[22] Dr. Edward Avery returned to York County after Williams dropped his case in 1874.

DANIEL H. CHAMBERLAIN, South Carolina's attorney general and Corbin's assistant prosecutor during the first series of Klan trials, became South Carolina's last Reconstruction-era governor, serving between 1874 and 1877.

His bid for reelection in 1876, after a hotly disputed, violent, and corrupt campaign, ended when Hayes withdrew the U.S. troops who were protecting the statehouse. He was succeeded by his Democratic rival, Confederate war hero and Klan fund-raiser Wade Hampton.

David T. Corbin was briefly appointed U.S. senator during the waning days of the Chamberlain administration, but the incoming Democrats did not confirm him. In 1879 President Hayes appointed him chief justice of Utah Territory, but once again he failed to win confirmation from a Democratic Senate strongly influenced by South Carolina senators. In 1885 he moved with his family to Chicago, where he practiced law and served as a law professor until his death in 1905.[23]

U.S. Army major Lewis Merrill shared Corbin's disillusionment and in mid-1872 applied for a leave of absence. He waited for a year before his request was granted, and upon his departure he received a $20,000 award for his service. Accusing Merrill of bribing and bullying suspects and witnesses, Senate Democrats ordered up a congressional investigation.

This did not prosper, and Merrill returned to the Dakotas with the Seventh Cavalry and also served in Louisiana. He missed the Little Big Horn but by 1880 was suffering from chronic kidney inflammation and retired. He died unexpectedly of Bright's disease in 1896 and was buried in Arlington Cemetery.[24]

General Alfred Terry left Louisville in late 1872, went to the Dakotas, and served on the Great Plains until 1886. He retired in Chicago in 1888 as a major general and died in New Haven, Connecticut, in 1890.

UNFORTUNATELY, LITTLE is known about the many Ku Klux victims. Amzi Rainey, his wife Catherine, and Hampton Hicklin stayed in York County and were counted in South Carolina's 1880 census. The Postles and the Brumfields appear in the 1870 census but are not listed in 1880.[25]

Of Tom Roundtree's widow Harriet there is no information readily available, but in 1873 state senator Hannibal White was appointed guardian of the Roundtrees' six "orphan" children, whom he sent to school in Shelby, North Carolina.[26]

In 1893 Rose Williams, the widow of Jim Williams, applied for a military pension, but she never received it because she could not provide sufficient proofs of her dead husband's service. She became so desperate at one point that she asked Harriet Rainey Bratton, sister-in-law of her husband's murderer, to vouch for her. Harriet claimed to have no knowledge of Williams's service. Rose Williams died in 1920.[27]

Amos T. Akerman returned to Cartersville and resumed a prosperous private law practice. He had made few friends in Washington, but he had forged strong bonds with Terry, Corbin, and Merrill.

In mid-November he wrote General Terry in Louisville, thanking him for "personal courtesies" during his visit there and unburdening himself about the terrible "depravity" of the Ku Klux Klan. It was clear that in Terry he had found a like mind.

"Though rejoiced at the suppression of the Ku Klux gang even in one neighborhood, I feel greatly saddened by the business," Akerman wrote. "It has revealed a perversion of moral sentiment . . . which bodes ill to that part of the country for this generation."

He had nothing but praise for Merrill, "just the man for the work," he told Terry, "resolute, collected, bold and prudent, with a good legal head, very discriminating between truth and falsehood, very indignant of wrong, and yet master of his indignation."[28]

To Merrill he was equally effusive, telling him in November that he had mentioned him to Grant and would do so again. Some of his words would probably get into print, Akerman added. "[And] certainly they are of a character to which your friends will not object."[29]

He had had a seamless relationship with Corbin, but, in contrast with the two army officers, his communications were all business, whether discussing strategy, gathering evidence, or preparing indictments. The two men had such a clear understanding of their constitutional goals that they never had to discuss them. There was none of the goading that Corbin was forced to resort to in his interchanges with George Williams.

The formality of their relationship could well have simply resulted from the fact that Corbin was Akerman's employee. Also, Akerman's embarrassment at the salaries he had to pay to his U.S. Attorneys—he mentioned it again in his 1871 annual report—undoubtedly weighed on him.

Despite his summary dismissal, Akerman had nothing bad to say about anyone. George Williams, he wrote in a letter to Merrill just before he left Washington, was "an able and experienced man." "In administering this office [as attorney general], [he] will be free of some of the hostilities that have obstructed me."[30]

Akerman visited with Grant and Williams during a trip to Washington in 1874 and had "a pleasant conversation" with his predecessor, Ebenezer Rockwood Hoar.[31] He never knew that Benjamin Bristow had undercut him, and, when Bristow was named Treasury secretary, he simply remarked in his diary entry: "I think him able and honest."[32]

Akerman and Matty had another son in 1874. He remained active in Georgia's Republican Party and equally active in defending the civil rights of black Georgians. If he was dismayed at the way the Republican Party abandoned reconstruction after his departure, he never said so, and he never spoke a bad word about President Grant. If he remained "a bitter, uncompromising Radical," as the *Columbus* (Ga.) *Enquirer Sun* described him, the paper acknowledged nonetheless that he was "possessed of much ability."[33]

In 1875 in Sanderson, Georgia, he defended black activist Cordy Harris, charged with insurrection for leading a procession with a drawn sword after he and his followers were denied use of the local courthouse.

The court had recessed, then resumed after lunch to hear closing arguments. The *Columbus Sunday Enquirer* described the courtroom as "painfully quiet" when Akerman rose to speak. "There ought to be harmony between colored men and white men," he said. "[Black men's] interests and yours are identical," he said, addressing whites. "They have smiled over your cradles. They will weep over your graves if you will let them stay, and be your friends until you die. You cannot better show yourselves their friends than by refusing to strain the law into an unjust conviction of a representative man of their race."

The jury deliberated for two and a half hours and found the defendant not guilty.[34]

AMOS T. AKERMAN died at home in Cartersville, on December 21, 1880, from a sudden attack of rheumatic fever. He was fifty-nine.

As the reader has undoubtedly noticed, *Grant's Enforcer* relies almost exclusively on the participants to tell the story of York County and Amos T. Akerman. These include both the victims of the Ku Klux Klan and their tormentors, newspaper reporters, politicians, public officials, private citizens, and soldiers in the field. I bow deepest to the magnificent investigation conducted by the joint committee of the U.S. Congress investigating the Ku Klux Klan in 1870–72. The committee's efforts produced thirteen immense volumes of raw and courageous first-person accounts of mistrust, fear, anguish, and despair in the postwar South. It took only two minutes with the transcript for one longtime friend with years of Washington experience to remark to me: "Anyone who thinks congressional hearings are a waste of time should read this."

I also hope that I have helped lead the way toward the liberal use of digitized newspaper archives to broaden our understanding of events that occurred long before our own time. Instead of painstakingly scrolling through rolls of microfilm, researchers now need only a few keystrokes to find multiple sources for anything that interests them. Newspapers.com, my principal guide in this endeavor, routinely produced multiple responses to any search, simply by entering the name of a person, place, event, or trend. Using this technique to describe what the public said and thought as events actually occurred dramatically enriches and expands the breadth and context of any narrative. The reader—as well as the author—is "in the moment" as never before.

Besides those long departed, I owe sincere thanks to those who have helped and encouraged me over the several years that I needed to complete this project. My wife Carla Anne Robbins, the best editor I know, read every word, offered advice, and made me do rewrites, which I frequently performed with bad grace, even though she was always right. Computer problems required consultation with my daughter, Annie, a professional designer and illustrator who expertly coaxed me through these digital quagmires.

Catherine Clinton, the Denman Professor of American History at the University of Texas at San Antonio and a longtime friend, put me in touch with the University of Georgia Press, where executive editor Mick Gusinde-Duffy was unfailingly encouraging with enthusiasm that never flagged.

In York County, I took full advantage of the resources of the McCelvey Center in York (no longer known as Yorkville) and the good offices of staff historian Zach Lemhouse of the Culture and Heritage Museums of York County; Nancy Sambets, director of archives for the Historical Center of York County; and Rylee Aquilanti, reference archivist for the Historical Center. In Rock Hill, I benefited from the expertise of John W. Skardon, the genealogy librarian at the York County Library.

Washington would have been a lost cause without the help of associate historian Daniel S. Holt of the U.S. Senate Historical Office who seemed to conjure up transcripts of obscure congressional hearings, drafts of bills, amendments, and arcane snatches of floor debate out of thin air. He also knows as much about congressional procedures—150 years ago—as any parliamentarian.

At the National Archives in College Park, Maryland, archives specialist Michael J. Hancock unearthed packets of correspondence, letter books, old telegrams, and odd communiqués from the earliest years of the Department of Justice. He was able to find things even when I did not know if they actually existed.

Amos T. Akerman was my most difficult research task. Outside of Washington, his paper trail is remarkably skimpy. We owe a debt to Lois Neal Hamilton, a Columbia University student in 1939 who interviewed Akerman's then-living sons for her master's thesis, which today remains the best source of information on Akerman's early life. Great-granddaughter Laura Love Yates provided more recent insights.

The current guardian of Akerman's legacy is high school principal and great-great-grandson Mark Akerman. A kindly man extremely interested in his noted ancestor, he is the custodian of photographs, diaries, letters, and Akerman family lore available nowhere else. He directed me to the Bartow History Museum in Cartersville, Georgia, where archives assistant Sandy Moore made me copies of several Akerman documents. I also owe thanks to the University of Virginia Library in Charlottesville, where I read several Akerman letter books. I also visited the Trinity College Library in Hartford, Connecticut, to consult the Alfred Terry papers.

Although I emphasize primary sources, *Grant's Enforcer* would not have been possible without others who have gone before me. For the institutional history of Reconstruction, Eric Foner's work is indispensable. Allen W. Trelease's seminal study of the Ku Klux Klan is an awesome resource, invaluable for the bibliography alone. Ron Chernow's biography of Grant shined a light on Akerman's brief government career and inspired me to look further. Gregory P. Downs's study of the U.S. Army after the surrender kept me abreast of postwar racial violence and detailed Washington's ambivalence toward military intervention in the South. Charles Lane described Akerman's eagerness to use the Secret Service as yet another mechanism to expand the influence of the federal government in domestic affairs.

In South Carolina, Richard Zuczek in 1996 dealt substantially with the Ku Klux Klan in the upcountry. Lou Faulkner Williams's superb study of the Columbia trials served as a welcome framework for my own—and Akerman's—focus on the Fourteenth Amendment. Jerry L. West found invaluable new sources within the Klan and without. J. Michael Martinez's work is the last word on Major Lewis Merrill. Scott Farris dug more deeply into the Jim Williams lynching than anyone else ever has. There is, I hope, much more to come. There is, I know, much more to be done.

NOTES

PROLOGUE. NIGHT RIDERS

1. "Ku Klux," as both noun and adjective, was the customary term from the time, used by everyone from the lowest foot soldier to leading politicians. It is used here throughout to put the reader in the moment.

2. U.S. Congress, *Report of the Joint Select Committee to Inquire into the Condition of Affairs in the Late Insurrectionary States*, vol. 5 (Washington, D.C.: GPO, 1872), 1769 (John Fudge), 1775 (John J. Lowry). Hereafter in this chapter's notes: *Joint Committee.*

3. Milus Smith Carroll, handwritten memoir, 1924, held by the Historical Center of York County, first cited in West, *The Reconstruction Ku Klux Klan in York County*. See also *Yorkville Enquirer*, Feb. 18, 1921, where Carroll recounts the same events with some additions and subtractions.

4. Ibid.

5. *Joint Committee*, vol. 5, 1360 (J. Rufus Bratton).

6. Carroll, memoir.

7. *Joint Committee*, vol. 5, 1750 (Julia Rainey).

8. Farris, *Freedom on Trial*, 38.

9. *Joint Committee*, vol. 5, 1784 (Scott Wilson).

10. Ibid., 1796 (Lewis Howser). See also ibid., 1790 (Andy Timms), 1795 (George Witherspoon).

11. See Scoggins, *The Armament of Jim Williams' Militia Company*, for the best and most detailed description of the militia weaponry.

12. Reynolds, *Reconstruction in South Carolina*, 189–90.

13. *Joint Committee*, vol. 5, 1775.

14. Ibid., 1767 (John Fudge).

15. Ibid., 1781–82 (Minor McConnell).

16. Ibid., 1726 (John Caldwell), 1733 (Andrew Kirkpatrick).

17. Ibid., 1718–19 (Gadsden Steel).

18. Ibid., 1718–19 (Steel).

CHAPTER 1. THE GEORGIA QUESTION

1. *New York Herald*, June 25, 1870.

2. U.S. House of Representatives, *Condition of Affairs in Georgia*, 40th Cong., 3rd Sess., H. Misc. Doc. 52, 12.

3. Ibid.

4. See, for example, *Pittsburgh Weekly Gazette*, Dec. 22, 1868, for a Republican analysis of "the Georgia Question" and a denunciation of Georgia's political behavior.

5. See Republican governor Rufus Bullock's explanation in U.S. House of Representatives, *Condition of Affairs in Georgia*, 1–3. The Democratic view is well explained in Knight, *A Standard History of Georgia and Georgians*, 841–44.

6. Ibid., 7.

7. Ibid., 11.

8. *Philadelphia Inquirer*, Dec. 22, 1868.

9. *Evening Star* (Washington, D.C.), Dec. 19, 1868.

10. See Bradley, *The Army and Reconstruction*, 15, 34; Downs, *After Appomattox*, 188, 232; Trelease, *White Terror*, xxxiv.

11. U.S. House of Representatives, *Condition of Affairs in Georgia*, 13.

12. Ibid.

13. Ibid., 14.

14. Ibid., 16.

15. Ibid., 17.

16. Ibid.

17. Ibid., 22.

18. Ibid.

19. Ibid., 18.

20. Ibid., 19.

21. See, for example, U.S. Congress, *Congressional Globe*, 39th Cong., 1st Sess., 1866, 1033–34, one of countless examples of lawmakers' differences of opinion over the role of the federal government in the postwar United States.

22. For a detailed analysis of the 1866 Congressional debate, see Foner, *The Second Founding*, 55–95.

23. See, for example, *Congressional Globe*, 39th Cong., 1st Sess., 2764–67. See also Foner, *Second Founding*, 74–76.

24. U.S. House of Representatives, *Condition of Affairs in Georgia*, 22.

CHAPTER 2. THE GRAND WIZARD

1. *Yorkville Enquirer*, Apr. 2, 1868.

2. *Weekly Telegraph* (Macon, Ga.), Mar. 20, 1868.

3. *Daily Intelligencer* (Atlanta), Mar. 15, 1868, quoted in Hurst, *Nathan Bedford Forrest*, 295.

4. See Groce, "John B. Gordon"; Trelease, *White Terror*, 74.

5. *Atlanta Constitution*, June 22, 1868, has a story on Southern Life and a full list of its directors. General John B. Gordon is listed as the president and a director of the company in Atlanta. Forrest is named as a company director in Memphis and the overall "traveling agent." See also Hurst, *Nathan Bedford Forrest*, 294, for Gordon's salary.

6. Quoted in Thompson, *Reconstruction in Georgia*, 369.

7. *Atlanta Constitution*, June 22, 1868.

8. The account of the Ashburn murder was reprinted in the *Buffalo Express*, Apr. 8, 1868.

9. *Selma* (Ala.) *Messenger*, Apr. 18. 1868. See also *Times-Picayune* (New Orleans), June 18, 1868.

10. Hurst, *Nathan Bedford Forrest*, 159–75.

11. *Cincinnati Commercial*, Aug. 28, 1868, reprinted in *New York Times*, Sept. 3, 1868.

12. Ibid.

13. Trelease, *White Terror*, xliii.

14. Lester and Wilson, *Ku Klux Klan*, 55–57.

15. Ibid., 64.

16. Ibid., 74.

17. Ibid., 149.

18. See Hurst, *Nathan Bedford Forrest*, 285. See also *Nashville American*, Aug. 27, 1905, for a lengthy and frequently fanciful origin story of the Ku Klux Klan, written by Thomas Dixon Jr., the white supremacist author of *The Clansman*, adapted by D. W. Griffith for *The Birth of a Nation*, the 1915 film that gave new life to the Klan in the early twentieth century.

19. Quoted in Hurst, *Nathan Bedford Forrest*, 290.

20. All interview excerpts taken from the *Cincinnati Commercial*, Aug. 28, 1868, reprinted in *New York Times*, Sept. 3, 1868.

21. Reprinted in *Charleston Daily Courier*, Sept. 9, 1868.

22. U.S. Congress, *Report of the Joint Select Committee*, vol. 13, 2–23.

23. Ibid., 24–29.

CHAPTER 3. THE OUTSIDER

1. *New York Times*, June 24, June 25, 1870. See also Lois Neal Hamilton, "Amos T. Akerman and His Role in American Politics" (master's thesis, Columbia University, 1939), 65. Hamilton's thesis is the best source for information on Akerman's early years, in part because she had access to Akerman's still-living sons.

2. *Chicago Tribune*, June 18, 1870.

3. Quoted in *New York Times*, June 24, 1870.

4. *Daily Columbus* (Ga.) *Enquirer*, June 18, 1870.

5. *New York Times*, June 17, 1870.

6. Ibid., June 21, 1870.

7. Eugene Davis, transcriber, *Can a Negro Hold Office in Georgia? The Decision of the Court in the Case of Richard W. White vs Wm. J. Clements* (Atlanta: Daily Intelligencer Book & Job Office, 1869), 8–17.

8. U.S. Senate, *Journal of the Executive Proceedings of the Senate of the United States of America*, 1869–1871, 318, 325.

9. See C. Mildred Thompson, *Reconstruction in Georgia: Economic, Social, Political, 1865–1872* (New York: N.p., 1915). Thompson regarded Akerman as the most talented attorney to participate in Georgia's 1868 constitutional convention. See also *New-York Tribune*, July 1, 1870, for a lengthy and effusive tribute by a fellow attorney and avowed secessionist to Akerman's expertise during the convention, his Republicanism, and his integrity.

10. See *Atlanta Constitution*, Feb. 5, 1869. Stephens and Akerman, as leading Democratic and Republican attorneys in Georgia, were asked for their opinions, and independently concurred, in a case involving payment of an antebellum debt owed by the state government.

11. See, for example, *Georgia Weekly Telegraph and Messenger*, Jan. 4, 1870. Terry was forced to send troops to protect tax assessors in the Georgia countryside from the Ku Klux Klan, but the U.S. Treasury Department would not pay for their transportation. Terry discontinued the protection and ordered weapons distributed to the assessors. The *Telegraph*'s final comment: "We shall hear next of an order to mount and arm the negro members of the Southern Legislatures. Those dreadful troubles!"

12. Rebecca Felton, "Hon. Amos T. Akerman, A Biographical Sketch," *Cartersville* (Ga.) *Courant*, Mar. 26, 1885. See also Hamilton," Amos T. Akerman," 46. Felton, a neighbor in Cartersville, interviewed Akerman's widow, Martha, on several occasions. See also chap. 5, note 28.

13. Felton, "Hon. Amos T. Akerman."

14. Hamilton, "Amos T. Akerman," 7.

15. Felton, "Hon. Amos T. Akerman," quotes Akerman in what appears to be an 1871 letter to his wife, Martha "Matty" Galloway.

16. Hamilton, "Amos T. Akerman," 10.

17. *Buffalo Morning Express and Illustrated Buffalo Express*, June 18, 1870.

18. Diary entry, Oct. 30, 1846, in Akerman, *Diaries 1846–1875*.

19. Hamilton, "Amos T. Akerman," 12.

20. Ibid.

21. Ibid.

22. Ibid., 15. See also McFeely, "Amos T. Akerman," 395. Akerman's lack of ambition is examined in some detail.

23. Hamilton, "Amos T. Akerman," 15.

24. Ibid., 17–34.

25. Diary entry, Sept. 20, 1846, Akerman, *Diaries 1846–1875*.

26. Ibid., June 22, 1855.

27. Hamilton, "Amos T. Akerman," 19.

28. Diary entry, Feb. 23, 1874, in Felton, "Hon. Amos T. Akerman."

29. Diary entry, July 24, 1861, Akerman, *Diaries 1846–1875*.

30. Diary entry, June 12, 1861, ibid.

31. Mrs. Alexander Akerman to Mrs. Albert Menard, July 31, 1946, in Akerman, Biographical Notes.

32. Hamilton, "Amos T. Akerman," 38–39.

33. Akerman to Matty, June 1, 1864, in Akerman, Civil War Letters.

34. Ibid. See also Hamilton, "Amos T. Akerman," 40.

35. Diary entry, Feb. 23, 1874, in Felton, "Hon. Amos T. Akerman."

36. Akerman to "My Dear Sister," July 17, 1870, in Akerman, Letters to Family.

37. Akerman to James Jackson, Nov. 20, 1871, in Akerman, Akerman Letter Books, 1871–76.

38. Hamilton, "Amos T. Akerman," 43.

39. *Atlanta Constitution*, Aug. 7, 1868.

40. Akerman to Matty, Feb. 9, 1868, in Felton, "Hon. Amos T. Akerman."

41. Akerman to Jackson, Nov. 20, 1871, in Akerman, Akerman Letter Books, 1871–76.

42. *Chicago Tribune*, June 18, 1870.

CHAPTER 4. DISORDER IN THE UPCOUNTRY

1. U.S. Congress, *Report of the Joint Select Committee*, vol. 3, 227–28 (Richard Carpenter). Hereafter in this chapter's notes: *Joint Committee*.

2. Current, *Those Terrible Carpetbaggers*, 224. See also *Joint Committee*, vol. 5, 1716 (Andy Tims).

3. U.S. Census Bureau, *Ninth Census of the United States: Statistics of Population* (Washington, D.C.: GPO, 1872), 88.

4. *Joint Committee*, vol. 5, 1753 (John Moroso).

5. For background on the Union Leagues, see Foner, *Reconstruction*, 283–85.

6. *Joint Committee*, vol. 3, 207 (Joseph Herndon).

7. For a description of rituals, grips, and ceremonies of the Union League in York County, see Hall, *A Shell in the Radical Camp*.

8. *Joint Committee*, vol. 5, 1753 (Moroso).

9. *Charleston Daily News*, Sept. 15, 1870.

10. Ibid., Aug. 1, 1870.

11. Ibid., Aug. 23, 1870.

12. *Joint Committee*, vol. 3, 229, 237 (Carpenter).

13. See Reynolds, *Reconstruction in South Carolina, 1865–1877*, 104–10. Scott won with 75 percent of the votes cast in 1868. The legislature had 135 Republicans and 20 Democrats, 88 blacks and 77 whites.

14. U.S. Census Bureau, *Ninth Census of the United States: Statistics of Population* (Washington, D.C.: GPO, 1872), 88.

15. Current, *Those Terrible Carpetbaggers*, 214–17.

16. *New York Times*, Apr. 25, 1871.

17. Current, *Those Terrible Carpetbaggers*, 215.

18. Ibid., 214–22.

19. *Joint Committee*, vol. 3, 243 (Carpenter).

20. *The Constitution of the State of South Carolina.*

21. Scoggins, *The Armament of Jim Williams' Militia Company in 1871*. See also Richard Zuczek, *State of Rebellion*, 75.

22. *Joint Committee*, vol. 3, 227, 236 (Carpenter).

23. For biographical details on James L. Orr, see Begley, "Orr, James Lawrence."

24. *Charleston Daily Courier*, Aug. 17, 1870.

25. *Joint Committee*, vol. 3, 238 (Carpenter).

26. Ibid., 227–28.

27. *Fairfield Herald* (Winnsboro, S.C.), Aug. 20, 1870.

28. *Joint Committee*, vol. 5, 1426 (Alexander Wylie).

29. See *Charleston Daily News*, Aug. 23, 1870, for a description of the Carmel Hill rally.

30. *Yorkville Enquirer*, Sept. 22, 1870. Italics in original.

31. *Joint Committee*, vol. 3, 244 (Carpenter).

32. *Joint Committee*, vol. 5, 1357 (J. Rufus Bratton).

CHAPTER 5. GRANT

1. See Downs, *After Appomattox*, 181–84.

2. Chernow, *Grant*, 635.

3. Ibid., 149–50, for Rawlins's devotion to Grant and concern about Grant's drinking problem.

4. Ibid., 634–38, for a comparison of the professionals and cronies.

5. See, for example, Nevins, *The Inner History of the Grant Administration*, 290–91, for a discussion of the misgivings of Hamilton Fish and others about Grant's choice of companions.

6. *Evening Telegraph* (Philadelphia), June 25, 1870.

7. Diary entry, Feb. 23, 1874, in Akerman, *Diaries 1846–1875*.

8. Terry to Grant, June 18, 1870, and Terry to DeRussey, June 21, 1870, in Department of the South, Letters Sent, U.S. Army, Part 1.

9. *New York Herald*, June 22, 1870.

10. *New York Times*, June 19,1870.

11. Ibid., June 21, 1870.

12. *Chicago Tribune*, June 25, 1870.

13. Ibid., July 8, 1870.

14. *Evening Telegraph* (Philadelphia) June 24, 1870, quoted in *New York Herald*, June 25, 1870.

15. *New York Herald*, June 25, 1870.

16. See Chernow, *Grant*, 660–65.

17. Cox, "How Judge Hoar Ceased to Be Attorney-General," 166.

18. Ibid., 162.

19. Ibid., 167.

20. See Nevins, *The Inner History*, 303–4. The rejection was "shocking."

21. Cox, "How Judge Hoar Ceased to Be Attorney-General," 162–73.

22. *Atlanta Constitution*, June 21, 1870.

23. Diary entry, June 17, 1870, in Fish, Diaries, Reel 1, Papers of Hamilton Fish.

24. *Chicago Tribune*, Feb. 14, 1871.

25. *Buffalo Morning Express and Illustrated Buffalo Express*, June 18, 1870.

26. *New-York Tribune*, July 1, 1870.

27. *Evening Star* (Washington, D.C.), Dec. 19, 1870.

28. Felton, "Hon. Amos T. Akerman." Felton, perhaps anachronistically, was well-known as both a staunch supporter of women's suffrage and a fierce advocate for white supremacy. Her memoir is laudatory in every respect but makes no mention of Akerman's civil rights record or his pursuit of the Ku Klux Klan.

29. Ulysses S. Grant, "First Annual Message, Dec. 6, 1869," in Richardson, *A Compilation of the Messages and Papers of the Presidents*, vol. 7, pt. 1, 28.

30. Butler, *Butler's Book*, 853. See also Nash, Howard P., Jr. *Stormy Petrel*, 250.

31. Butler, *Butler's Book*, 925.

32. See McFeely, *Grant: A Biography*, 362–364.

33. See, for example, Nevins, *The Inner History of the Grant Administration*, 585, for an outraged description of Butler's shortcomings.

34. Ulysses S. Grant, "Special Message, March 30, 1870," in Richardson, *A Compilation of the Messages and Papers of the President*, vol. 7, pt. 1, 56.

35. See "An Act to Enforce the Rights of Citizens of the United States to Vote in the Several States of this Union," Forty-First Cong., 2nd Sess., chap. 114, in *Statutes at Large and Proclamations of the United States of America*, vol. 16, *December 1869 to March 1871* (Boston: Little, Brown, 1871), 140–46.

CHAPTER 6. RACE RIOT

1. U.S. Congress, *Report of the Joint Select Committee*, vol. 3, 330 (Erastus Everson). Hereafter in this chapter's notes: *Joint Committee*.

2. See, for example, Leland, *A Voice from South Carolina*, 51.

3. *Joint Committee*, vol. 5, 1307, 1314 (William D. Simpson); *Charleston Daily News*, Mar. 7, 1871.

4. U.S. Census Office *Ninth Census of the United States: Statistics of Population* (Washington D.C.: GPO, 1872.

5. Leland, *A Voice from South Carolina*, 52.

6. *Joint Committee*, vol 5., 1303 (Simpson).

7. Quoted in *Charleston Daily News*, Apr. 26, 1870. Italics in original.

8. *Newberry Weekly Herald*, Aug. 10, 1870.

9. *Charleston Daily News*, Oct. 31, 1870. Italics and uppercasing in original.

10. *Joint Committee*, vol 3., 331 (Everson).

11. Ibid.

12. Ibid., 341–42.

13. Ibid. 344.

14. Quoted in *Anderson* (S.C.) *Intelligencer*, Oct. 27, 1870.

15. *Joint Committee*, vol. 3, 331 (Everson).

16. Ibid., 332.

17. Ibid., 332, 334.

18. Ibid., 332.

19. Leland, *A Voice from South Carolina*, 58. See also David T. Corbin to George Williams, Nov. 9, 1872, in Source Chronological Files for South Carolina, General Records of the Department of Justice. A federal grand jury indicted Leland for conspiracy and murder in the October 20, 1870, Laurensville riot. He spent five weeks in jail, was released on $5,000 bail, and was never tried.

20. *Joint Committee*, vol. 3, 332 (Everson).

21. Quoted in *Anderson* (S.C.) *Intelligencer*, Oct. 27, 1870.

22. *Joint Committee*, vol. 5., 1303 (Simpson). See also ibid., 1326 (B. W. Ball).

23. Leland, *A Voice from South Carolina*, 58.

24. *Laurensville Herald*, quoted in *Anderson* (S.C.) *Intelligencer*, Oct. 27, 1870. See also *Joint Committee*, vol. 5., 1306 (Simpson), 1326 (Ball).

25. *Joint Committee*, vol. 3, 332–33, 336 (Everson).

26. Leland, *A Voice from South Carolina*, 60. Italics in original.

27. *Joint Committee*, vol. 5, 1327 (Ball). See also *Anderson* (S.C.) *Intelligencer*, Oct. 27, 1870.

28. *Joint Committee*, vol. 5, 1306 (Simpson).

29. *Joint Committee*, vol. 3, 332–34, 336 (Everson).

30. Leland, *A Voice from South Carolina*, 63–64.

31. *Charleston Daily News*, Mar. 7, 1871.

32. Quoted in *Camden* (S.C.) *Journal*, Nov. 24, 1870.

33. Ibid.

34. Leland, *A Voice from South Carolina*, 67.

35. *Joint Committee*, vol. 3, 336–37 (Everson).

36. *Yorkville Enquirer*, Nov. 10, 1870. See also *Joint Committee*, vol. 5, 1312 (Simpson); Trelease, *White Terror*, 352.

37. *Joint Committee*, vol. 5., 1315 (Simpson).

38. Leland, *A Voice from South Carolina*, 63.

39. *Charleston Daily News*, Oct. 25, 1870.

40. *Charleston Daily Courier*, Dec. 14; *Daily Phoenix* (Columbia, S.C.), Dec. 15, 1870; *Buffalo Morning Express*, Feb. 24, 1871.

41. Leland, *A Voice from South Carolina*, 89.

42. *Daily Phoenix* (Columbia, S.C.), Feb. 22, 1871.

43. Leland, *A Voice from South Carolina*, 89.

44. *New National Era* (Washington, D.C.), Feb. 2, 1871.

CHAPTER 7. SWIMMING WITH SHARKS

1. See "An Act to Establish the Department of Justice," in U.S. *Statutes at Large and Proclamations of the United States of America*, vol. 16, 41st Cong., 2nd Sess., June 22, 1870, 162–65.

2. *Evening Star* (Washington, D.C.), July 27, 1870.

3. Downs, *After Appomattox*, 232.

4. Akerman to E. C. Camp, U.S. Attorney, Knoxville, Sept. 26, 1870, in Letters Sent, Instructions to U.S. Attorneys and Marshals, 1870–1877.

5. See Shugerman, "The Creation of the Department of Justice," 121.

6. Ibid., 122–23.

7. U.S. House of Representatives, "Letter from the Attorney General of the United States Transmitting His Annual Report to Congress," in *Annual Report of the Attorney General*, 41st Cong., 3rd Sess., H. Exec. Doc. 90, Feb. 1, 1871.

8. Ibid.

9. Diary entry, Jan. 12, 1872, in Fish, Diaries, Reel 1, Papers of Hamilton Fish.

10. Trelease, *White Terror*, 205.

11. Ibid., 212–13.

12. *Daily Standard* (Raleigh, N.C.), Mar. 22, 1870.

13. *Semi-Weekly Raleigh Sentinel*, July 20, 1870. Italics in original.

14. See U.S. Congress, *Appendix to the Congressional Globe*, 41st Cong., 2nd Sess., 576–78.

15. For a broad denunciation of the Butler-Bullock plan, see, for example: *Congressional Globe*, 41st Cong., 2nd Sess., 1708–10.

16. See, for example, Rufus Bullock to Butler, March 5, 1870, in Butler, "General Correspondence," container 52.

17. *Courier-Journal* (Louisville), July 27, 1870.

18. Quoted in *Chicago Tribune*, Aug 11, 1870.

19. *Brooklyn Union*, Aug. 5, 1870.

20. *Sun* (New York City), Aug. 11, 1870; *New York Herald*, Aug. 11, 1870.

21. *Atlanta Constitution*, Aug. 12, 1870.

22. *Evening Star* (Washington, D.C.), Aug. 13, 1870.

23. *Buffalo Courier*, Aug. 15, 1870.

24. *Atlanta Constitution*, Aug. 12, 1870.

25. *New York Times*, Aug. 13, 1870.

26. *Buffalo Morning Express and Illustrated Buffalo Express*, Aug. 16, 1870.

27. *Atlanta Constitution*, Sept. 2, 1870.

28. *New York Herald*, Oct. 10, 1870.

29. *Atlanta Constitution*, Sept. 20, 1870.

30. *New York Herald*, Sept. 24, 1870.

31. Ibid.

32. *New York Herald*, Oct. 15, 1870.

33. *New York Herald*, Sept. 23, 1870.

34. For endorsements of Bristow, see, for example, A. J. Ballard to Akerman, Sept. 16, 1870; J. F. Buckner, Collector of IRS, Louisville, to George S. Boutwell, Secretary of the Treasury, Sept. 16, 1870; Gresham to Grant, Sept. 17, 1870; Eli H. Murray to Akerman, Sept. 17, 1870; and Bland Ballard to Grant, Sept. 21, 1870, all in Bristow, Papers of Benjamin Helm Bristow, Box 1, 1839–Dec. 1870.

35. Bristow to Harlan, Oct. 30, 1870, in Harlan, Papers of John Marshall Harlan, Box 35, Reel 18.

36. Klein, *Union Pacific*, 273–74.

37. *Sun* (New York City), Aug. 2, 1870.

38. *Brooklyn Daily Eagle*, Oct. 26, 1870.

39. *New National Era* (Washington, D.C.), Oct. 13, !870

40. *New York Herald*, Nov. 4, 1870.

41. *New York Herald*, Nov. 26, 1870.

CHAPTER 8. HARRIET ROUNDTREE

1. U.S. Congress, *Report of the Joint Select Committee to Inquire into the Condition of Affairs in the Late Insurrectionary States*, vol. 5, 1549–50 (Harriet Roundtree). Hereafter in this chapter's notes: *Joint Committee*.

2. West, *The Reconstruction Ku Klux Klan in York County*, 61.

3. *Joint Committee*, vol. 5, 1862–65 (Shaffer Bowens).

4. Ibid., 1545–48 (court records).

5. Ibid., 1545.

6. Quoted in *Charleston Daily News*, Dec. 12, 1870.

7. See *Joint Committee*, vol. 5, 1356 (J. Rufus Bratton). Bratton submitted the *Enquirer* article to congressional investigators during his testimony.

8. Ibid., 1547–48 (court records).

9. Ibid., 1505 (I. D. Witherspoon).

10. Ibid.

11. Ibid.

12. Ibid., 1551 (court records).

13. Ibid., 1550 (court records).

14. Ibid., 1551 (court records).

15. Ibid., 1551, 1552 (court records).

16. Ibid.

17. Ibid., 1504 (Witherspoon).

18. Ibid., 1552 (court records).

19. Ibid., 1524 (Witherspoon).

20. Ibid., 1550 (court records).

21. Ibid., 1504–8, 1556 (court records).

22. See ibid., 1355 (Bratton)

23. Ibid., vol. 3, 211 (Joseph Herndon).

24. Ibid., vol 5, 1547 (court records).

25. See ibid., 1472 (Lewis Merrill); and Trelease, *White Terror*, 364. Both sources cite the Roundtree case as the likely reason why blacks never again sought redress in York County's local courts.

26. *Yorkville Enquirer*, Feb. 2, 1871.

27. *Anderson (S.C.) Intelligencer*, Mar. 9, 1871.

28. *Daily Phoenix* (Columbia, S.C.), Mar. 10, 1871.

CHAPTER 9. FALSE HOPES

1. *New York Times*, Dec. 19, 1870.

2. *Buffalo Commercial*, Dec. 15, 1870. See also *Evening Star* (Washington, D.C.), Dec. 17, 1870.

3. *Atlanta Constitution*, Dec. 17, 1870.

4. *Buffalo Commercial*, Dec. 20, 1870.

5. Akerman to Terry, Nov. 18, 1871, in Akerman, Akerman Letter Books, 1871–76.

6. *Daily Columbus* (Ga.) *Enquirer*, Dec. 16, 1870.

7. Thompson, *Reconstruction in Georgia*, 270–71.

8. *New-York Tribune*, Dec. 26, 1870.

9. Quoted in *Selma* (Ala.) *Weekly Times*, Jan. 7, 1871.

10. *New York Herald*, Jan 5, 1871.

11. *Cincinnati Enquirer*, Jan. 14.

12. Ackerman, "Union Pacific Railroad Company," 360–69.

13. Ibid., 362.

14. Ibid., 363.

15. Klein, *Union Pacific*, 143.

16. Ibid., 274.

17. *Nashville Union and American*, Feb. 5, 1871.

18. *New York Herald*, Feb. 9, 1871.

19. Ibid., Feb. 16, 1871.

20. Quoted in *Buffalo Courier*, Feb. 15, 1871.

21. *Daily Atchison* (Kan.) *Patriot*, Feb. 23, 1871.

22. U.S. Congress, Senate, *Union Pacific Railroad*, 4.

23. Ibid., 5.

24. Ibid., 4.

25. Klein, *Union Pacific*, 276.

26. *Buffalo Weekly Courier*, Mar. 1, 1871.

27. U.S. House of Representatives, "Letter from the Attorney General of the United States," 1871, 2.

28. Akerman to A. Stirling, Oct. 4, 1870, in Letters Sent, Instructions to U.S. Attorneys and Marshals, 1870–1877.

29. U.S. House of Representatives, "Letter from the Attorney General of the United States," 1871, 7.

30. Ulysses S. Grant, "Second Annual Message," Dec. 5, 1870, in Richardson, *A Compilation of the Messages and Papers of the Presidents*, vol. 7, pt. 1, 96.

31. *Charleston Daily News*, Feb. 15, 18, 20, 1871. See also Trelease, *White Terror*, 357–58.

CHAPTER 10. BAR FIGHT

1. West, *The Reconstruction Ku Klux Klan in York County*, 46.

2. *Yorkville Enquirer*, Mar. 9, 1871.

3. U.S. Congress, *Report of the Joint Select Committee*, vol. 5, 1470 (Lewis Merrill). Hereafter in this chapter's notes: *Joint Committee*. See also ibid., 1288–98 (David Russell).

4. Ibid., 1294.

5. *Yorkville Enquirer*, Jan. 26, 1871.

6. *Daily Phoenix* (Columbia, S.C.), Feb. 1, 1871.

7. Ibid. See also *Yorkville Enquirer*, Feb. 2, 1871.

8. *Joint Committee*, vol 5., 1290 (Russell).

9. Ibid., 1298.

10. *Charleston Daily News*, Jan. 29, 1871.

11. *Yorkville Enquirer*, Feb. 2, 1871.

12. Ibid.

13. Ibid.

14. *Joint Committee*, vol. 5, 1465 (Merrill).

15. *Yorkville Enquirer*, Feb. 16, 1871. See also Trelease, *White Terror*, 365.

16. *Joint Committee*, vol 5., 1370 (William K. Owens). See also *Yorkville Enquirer*, Feb. 23, 1871.

17. Hall, *A Shell in the Radical Camp*, 10, 57–58.

18. *Joint Committee*, vol. 5, 1288 (Russell).

19. See ibid., 1725 (John Caldwell), for an unequivocal statement of Avery's status. He was the subject of innumerable denunciations, indicted as the leading defendant in cases of conspiracy and murder, and named repeatedly as a Klan leader by fellow members, informants and federal authorities.

20. Ibid., 1293 (Russell).

21. Ibid., 1292.

22. Ibid., 1291.

23. Ibid.

24. Ibid., 1395 (Owens).

25. Ibid., 1367, 1368, 1395.

26. Ibid., 1367.

27. Ibid., 1289–90 (Russell).

28. Ibid., 1367–68 (Owens).

29. Ibid., 1556–59 (James Porter).

30. Ibid., 1368 (Owens).

31. Ibid., 1558 (Porter).

32. Ibid., 1290 (Russell).

33. *Edgefield* (S.C.) *Advertiser*, Mar. 9, 1871.

34. *Charleston Daily News*, Mar. 2, 1871. See also *Joint Committee*, vol. 5, 1465–66 (Merrill).

35. *Charleston Daily News*, Mar. 4, 1871.

CHAPTER 11. RUNNING OUT OF PATIENCE

1. Ulysses S. Grant, "Special Message to the Senate," Jan. 13, 1871, in Richardson, *A Compilation of the Messages and Papers of the Presidents*, vol. 7, pt. 1, 117.

2. U.S. Senate, Message of the President of the United States," 1871.

3. See, for example, diary entry, Feb. 24, 1871, in Fish, Diaries, Reel 1, Papers of Hamilton Fish. See also Nevins, *The Inner History of the Grant Administration*, 290–91.

4. Downs, *After Appomattox*, 181.

5. *Courier* cited in *Norfolk Virginian*, Jan. 31, 1871.

6. For Pool's role in promoting the Secret Service in the Justice Department, see Lane, *Freedom's Detective*, 149–54.

7. Akerman to C. Cole, Jan. 23, 1871, in Letters Sent, General and Miscellaneous Letter Books, July 13, 1869–July 15, 1871. See also Hamilton, "Amos T. Akerman and His Role in American Politics," 70.

8. Feb. 11, 1871, Akerman to John A. McInnes, Feb. 11, 1871, in Letters Sent, Instructions to U.S. Attorneys and Marshals, 1870–1877.

9. Ibid.

10. U.S. House of Representatives, A Bill to Amend an Act Approved May Thirty-One, Eighteen Hundred and Seventy, 41st. Cong., 3rd Sess., H.R. 2634, Jan. 9, 1871.

11. *Charleston Daily News*, Feb. 15, Feb 18, 1871.

12. U.S. Congress, *Congressional Globe*, 41st Cong., 3rd Sess., 1274.

13. Ibid.

14. Ibid.

15. Ibid., 1271.

16. Ibid., 1277.

17. Ibid., 1285.

18. Ibid., 1655.

19. U.S. House of Representatives, A Bill to Protect Loyal and Peaceable Citizens of the United States in the Full Enjoyment of Their Rights, Persons, Liberty and Property, 41st Cong., 3rd Sess., H.R. 3011, Feb. 13, 1871.

20. Ibid.

21. Ibid.

22. *Congressional Globe*, 41st Cong., 3rd Sess., 1871, 1185–86.

23. U.S. House of Representatives, A Bill to Protect Loyal and Peaceable Citizens.

24. U.S. House of Representatives, To Protect Loyal and Peaceable Citizens of the United States, 41st Cong., 3rd Sess., H. Rep. 37, to accompany H.R. 3011, Feb. 20, 1871.

25. *Congressional Globe*, 41st Cong., 3rd Sess., 1871, 1762.

26. *Public Ledger* (Memphis), Mar. 1, 1871.

27. *Alexandria* (Va.) *Gazette*, Mar. 2, 1871.

28. Diary entry, Feb. 24, 1871, in Fish, Diaries, Reel 1, Papers of Hamilton Fish. For Hubbard report, see Williams, *The Great South Carolina Ku Klux Klan Trials*, 37.

CHAPTER 12. LYNCHING

1. U.S. Congress, *Report of the Joint Select Committee to Inquire into the Condition of Affairs in the Late Insurrectionary States*, vol. 5, 1706 (Charles Foster). Hereafter in this chapter's notes: *Joint Committee*. See also West, *The Reconstruction Ku Klux Klan in York County*, 42.

2. "Aristocrats" and "minors": U.S. Congress, *Joint Committee*, vol. 5, 1367 (William K. Owens).

3. Ibid., 1686–87 (Kirkland Gunn). Many versions of the oath can be found in a number of sources. All are similar. This one, entered as evidence by prosecutors at the U.S. Circuit Court trials in 1871–72, is cited here because it was the version widely used in York County. See also ibid., 1735–37 (Elias Ramsay), for the description of the March 5 ritual.

4. Ibid., 1735–37 (Ramsay).

5. U.S. Congress, *Joint Committee*, vol. 5, 1719 (Gadsden Steel).

6. Ibid., 1737 (Elias Ramsay).

7. Scoggins, *A Brief History of Historic Brattonsville.*

8. Carroll, handwritten memoir. See also *Yorkville Enquirer*, Feb. 18, 1921.

9. *Joint Committee*, vol. 5, 1727 (John Caldwell); 1737 (Ramsay).

10. Ibid., 1720–21 (Rose Williams). Williams's widow's given name is variously written as Rosy (Joint Committee); Rosa (pension application); and Rose (plantation documents). See also Carroll, handwritten memoir.

11. *Joint Committee*, vol. 5, 1720–21 (Williams).

12. Carroll, handwritten memoir.

13. *Joint Committee*, vol. 5, 1737 (Ramsay).

14. Ibid., 1727 (Caldwell).

15. Ibid., 1738 (Ramsay).

16. Ibid., 1713 (Andy Tims).

17. *Joint Committee*, vol. 4, 709–10 (Thomas M. Graham).

18. Ibid. See also *Charleston Daily News*, Mar. 15, 1871.

19. *Joint Committee*, vol. 5, 1428 (Andrew Wylie); 1583 (Benjamin Gore).

20. Ibid., 1429 (Wylie); 1582–83 (Gore).

21. Ibid., 1430–31 (Wylie); 1580–81 (Gore).

22. Ibid., 1431 (Wylie).

23. Ibid., 1431–32 (Wylie); 1581 (Gore).

24. Ibid., 1581–82 (Gore).

25. Ibid., 1433 (Wylie); 1583–85 (Gore). See also *Charleston Daily News*, Mar. 13, 1871; *Daily Phoenix* (Columbia, S.C.), Mar. 14, 1871. U.S. Army captain John Christopher, stationed in Yorkville, at first had his men surround the York County jail to protect the militiamen from what he thought were marauding Klan gunmen riding the surrounding countryside during the night. It later became apparent that the sheriff had put the militiamen in jail as a protective measure. Many of the horsemen were quite likely Klansmen, but they were not marauders. They were riding sentry duty with the rifles that Andy Tims had turned in to Avery earlier in the day.

26. *Joint Committee*, vol. 5, 1578–91 (Benjamin Gore).

27. Ibid., 1424–55 (Alexander Wylie).

28. *Daily Phoenix* (Columbia, S.C.), Mar. 7, 1871; *Charleston Daily News*, Mar. 7, 1871.

29. *Winona* (Minn.) *Daily Republican*, Mar. 10, 1871.

30. *Joint Committee*, vol. 5, 1446 (Andrew Wylie).

31. Telegram, Governor Robert Scott to President Grant, March 9, 1871, in U.S. Department of Justice, Source Chronological Files for South Carolina.

32. *Yorkville Enquirer*, Mar. 16, 1871.

33. Ibid., Mar. 9, 1871. Emphasis in original.

34. Ibid.

CHAPTER 13. "UNLAWFUL COMBINATIONS"

1. *New York Evening Post*, Mar. 7, 1871.

2. *New York Herald*, Mar. 8, 1871.

3. *Chicago Tribune*, Mar. 7, 1871.

4. Grant to James G. Blaine, Mar. 9, 1871, in Grant, Letterbooks, 1869–77.

5. *New York Herald*, Mar. 11, 1871. See also U.S. Congress, *Congressional Globe*, 42nd Cong., 1st Sess., 53.

6. Grant to A. G. Cattell, March 11, 1871, in Grant, Letterbooks, 1869–77.

7. *Buffalo Commercial*, Mar. 6, 1871.

8. Akerman to A. W. Shaffer, U.S. Commissioner, Raleigh, Apr. 4, 1871, in Letters Sent, General and Miscellaneous Letter Books, July 13, 1869–July 15, 1871.

9. *Richmond* (Va.) *Dispatch*, Mar. 11, 1871.

10. Akerman to Gov. Scott, Mar. 11, 1871, in Letters Sent, General and Miscellaneous Letter Books, July 13, 1869–July 15, 1871.

11. D. H. Chamberlain to Akerman, Mar. 16, 1871, in Source Chronological Files for South Carolina.

12. U.S. House of Representatives, A Bill Authorizing the Employment of the Land and Naval Forces of the United States in the Enforcement of the Laws.

13. *Congressional Globe*, 42nd Cong., 1st Sess., 18–19.

14. Ibid., 116.

15. Ibid.

16. Ibid., 116–17.

17. Ibid., 117.

18. Ibid.

19. Ibid., 123.

20. Ibid.

21. Ibid., 124.

22. Ibid., 124–25.

23. Ibid., 125.

24. Ibid., 127–28.

25. Ibid., 128.

26. Ibid., 128–29.

27. Ibid., 131.

28. U.S. Senate, A Bill for the Protection of Persons Resident within the United States against Unlawful Combinations and Conspiracies.

29. U.S. Senate, A Bill More Fully to Enforce the Fourteenth Amendment to the Constitution of the United States.

30. U.S. Senate, A Bill to Amend an Act Approved February Twenty-Eighth Seventeen Hundred Ninety-Five, and to Authorize the President, at His Discretion to Declare Martial Law in Certain Cases.

31. U.S. House of Representatives, A Bill to Protect Loyal and Peaceable Citizens of the United States in the Full Enjoyment of Their Rights, Persons, Liberty and Property.

32. U.S. House of Representatives, A Bill to Secure to All Persons within the Jurisdiction of the United States the Equal Protection of the Laws within the Several States.

33. U.S. House of Representatives. *Journal of the House of Representatives*, 42nd Cong., 1st Sess., 1871, 109.

34. U.S. Congress, *Congressional Globe*, 42nd Cong, 1st Sess., 1871, 244, 249.

35. Ulysses S. Grant, "Proclamation," March 24, 1871, in Richardson, *A Compilation of the Messages and Papers of the Presidents*, vol. 7, pt. 1, 133.

36. *Charleston Daily News*, Mar. 25, 1871.

37. *New York Times*, Mar. 25, 1871.

38. *Yorkville Enquirer*, Mar. 30, 1871.

CHAPTER 14. BRATTON'S "PEACE"

1. *Daily Phoenix* (Columbia, S.C.), Mar. 3, 1871. Emphasis in original.

2. *Yorkville Enquirer*, Mar. 16, 1871.

3. *Buffalo Courier*, Mar. 8, 1871.

4. *South Kansas Tribune* (Independence, Kans.), Mar. 8, 1871.

5. Quoted in *Yorkville Enquirer*, Mar. 16, 1871.

6. *Charleston Daily News*, Mar. 18, 1871.

7. Ibid.

8. *Daily Phoenix* (Columbia, S.C.), Mar. 19, 1871.

9. *New York Herald*, Mar. 20, 1871.

10. *Charleston Daily News*, Mar. 25, 1871.

11. Ibid.

12. Quoted in ibid.

13. Quoted in ibid., Mar. 28, 1871.

14. *Yorkville Enquirer*, Mar. 30, 1871.

15. Martinez, *Carpetbaggers, Cavalry and the Ku Klux Klan*, 76, 83.

16. Ibid., 97–101.

17. U.S. Congress, *Report of the Joint Select Committee to Inquire into the Condition of Affairs in the Late Insurrectionary States*, Vol. 5, 1482 (Lewis Merrill). Hereafter in this chapter's notes: *Joint Committee*.

18. Ibid., 1497 (I. D. Witherspoon).

19. Ibid., 1482 (Merrill).

20. For a detailed description of Merrill's techniques, see ibid., 1464–81 (Merrill).

21. *Yorkville Enquirer*, Mar. 30, 1871.

22. Ibid., Apr. 6, 1871.

23. Ibid.

24. *Joint Committee*, vol. 5, 1353–54 (J. Rufus Bratton).

25. *Yorkville Enquirer*, Apr. 6, 1871.

26. Ibid.

CHAPTER 15. ENFORCEMENT

1. *Yorkville Enquirer*, Mar. 30, 1871.

2. U.S. House of Representatives, A Bill to Enforce the Provisions of the Fourteenth Amendment to the Constitution of the United States, and for Other Purposes.

3. *Congressional Globe*, 42nd Cong., 1st Sess., 1871, 317.

4. U.S. House of Representatives, Amendment in the Nature of a Substitute to the Bill (H.R. 320).

5. *New York Herald*, Dec. 2, 1870.

6. U.S. House of Representatives, Amendment to the Bill (H.R. 320) to Enforce the Provisions of the Fourteenth Amendment to the Constitution of the United States, and for Other Purposes.

7. *Congressional Globe*, 42nd Cong., 1st Sess., 1871, 351–52.

8. Ibid., 391–92.

9. Ibid., 395. Rainey quoted Shakespeare's *Julius Caesar*.

10. *Harrisburg Telegraph*, Apr. 3, 1871; *Pittsburgh Commercial*, Apr. 8, 1871.

11. *Congressional Globe*, 42nd Cong., 1st Sess., 1871, 522.

12. Ibid., 709.

13. *Urbana* (Ohio) *Union*, Apr. 19, 1871.

14. Sanger, *The Statutes at Large and Proclamations of the United States of America from March 1871 to March 1873*, Vol. 17, 13–15.

15. *Daily Phoenix* (Columbia, S.C.), Mar. 21, 1871.

16. *Sumter* (S.C.) *Watchman*, Mar. 29, 1871.

17. *Yorkville Enquirer*, Apr. 20, 1871.

18. Ulysses S. Grant, "Proclamation," May 3, 1871, in Richardson, *A Compilation of the Messages and Papers of the Presidents*, vol. 7, pt. 1, 134–35.

19. *New York Herald*, June 23, 1871.

20. Pool to Akerman, Mar. 31, 1871, in Letters Received, Senate, January 1871–May 1871, Source Chronological Files, 1871–1884.

21. Akerman to Pool, Mar. 31, 1871, in Letters Sent by the Department of Justice to Executive Officers and to Members of Congress, 1871–1904. See also Lane, *Freedom's Detective*, 151–52.

22. Scott to Grant, June 8, 1871, in Letters Received, President, Jan. 1871–Dec. 1871, Source Chronological Files 1871–1884.

23. U.S. House of Representatives, *Affairs in Alabama*, 43rd Cong., 2nd Sess., 1875, 1021.

24. Bristow to Joseph Hester, June 10, 1871, in Letters Sent, General and Miscellaneous Letter Books, July 13, 1869–July 15, 1871.

25. Alum File David Corbin, Class of 1857, Rauner Special Collections Library, Dartmouth College, Hanover, New Hampshire.

26. Post, "A 'Carpetbagger' in South Carolina," 72,78.

27. Akerman to J. H. Laville, chief clerk of the Treasury Department, Oct. 22, 1870; Akerman to Henry L. Dawes, chairman of House Appropriations, Jan. 19, 1871, both in Letters Sent by the Department of Justice, General and Miscellaneous Letter Books.

28. See, for example, Akerman to Wm. H. Wisener, Shelbyville, Tenn., Nov. 5, 1870, in Letters Sent, General and Miscellaneous Letter Books. Requests continued for several months.

29. Bristow to Harlan, Apr. 25, 1871, in Harlan, *Papers of John Marshall Harlan*, Box 35, Reel 18.

30. Delano to Akerman, May 5, 1871, in Letters Received, Jan.–May 1871, Source Chronological Files, 1871–1874; Akerman's reply: Akerman to Delano, May 9, 1871, in Letters Sent by the Department of Justice, General and Miscellaneous Letter Books.

31. See "Central Branch, Union Pacific Railroad Company," in Bentley, *Official Opinions of the Attorneys General of the United States*, vol. 13, 430–39. See also Hamilton, "Amos T. Akerman and His Role in American Politics," 97–101.

32. Bristow to Boutwell, June 20, 1871, in Letters Sent by the Department of Justice to Executive Officers and to Members of Congress, 1871–1904.

CHAPTER 16. "A BAD STATE OF AFFAIRS"

1. See Terry to Adjutant General, June 11, 1871, in Letters Received, Adjutant General, U.S. Army headquarters.

2. U.S. Congress, *Report of the Joint Select Committee to Inquire into the Condition of Affairs in the Late Insurrectionary States*, vol. 5, 1747–1749 (Dick Wilson). Hereafter in this chapter's notes: *Joint Committee.*

3. Ibid., 1565 (Hampton Hicklin).

4. In Terry to Adjutant General, June 11, 1871, Letters Received, Adjutant General.

5. *Joint Committee*, vol. 5, 1947–48 (Abraham Brumfield); 1948–49 (Emeline Brumfield); 1949–50 (Sam Sturges); 1951–52 (Harriet Postle); 1952–55 (Isaac Postle).

6. Quoted in Terry to Adjutant General, June 11, 1871, Letters Received, Adjutant General.

7. *Joint Committee*, vol. 5, 1406–16 (Elias Hill).

8. Ibid., 1485 (Lewis Merrill).

9. In Terry to Adjutant General, June 11, 1871, Letters Received, Adjutant General.

10. *Yorkville Enquirer*, May 18, 1871.

11. In Terry to Adjutant General, June 11, 1871, Letters Received, Adjutant General. Both the telegram and the letter are here.

12. Ibid.

13. *Joint Committee*, vol. 5, 1500 (I. D. Witherspoon).

14. See Trelease, *White Terror*, 373.

15. In Terry to Adjutant General, June 11, 1871, Letters Received, Adjutant General.

16. *Joint Committee*, vol. 5, 1503–4 (Witherspoon). See also Martinez, *Carpetbaggers, Cavalry and the Ku Klux Klan*, 138–39.

17. *Joint Committee*, vol. 5, 1485–88 (Merrill).

18. Terry to Adjutant General, June 11, 1871, Letters Received, Adjutant General, Emphasis in original.

19. Ibid.

CHAPTER 17. THE LONG HOT SUMMER

1. *New York Herald*, June 23, 1871.

2. *Evening Telegraph* (Philadelphia), June 23, 1871.

3. *Cincinnati Enquirer*, June 28, 1871.

4. *Intelligencer Journal* (Lancaster, Pa.), June 7, 1871.

5. Quoted in *Times-Picayune* (New Orleans), June 11, 1871.

6. *New York Herald*, June 25, 1871.

7. Ibid.

8. *Buffalo Commercial*, June 27, 1871.

9. *New York Times*, June 1, 1871.

10. *Buffalo Commercial*, June 27, 1871.

11. *New York Herald*, June 25, 1871.

12. *Buffalo Weekly Courier*, June 21, 1871.

13. *New York Times*, June 1, 1871.

14. *Buffalo Weekly Courier*, June 21, 1871.

15. *Charleston Daily News*, June 16, 1871.

16. *Chicago Tribune*, July 4, 1871.

17. *Buffalo Commercial*, June 27, 1871.

18. Akerman to Grant, July 1, 1871, in Letters Sent by the Department of Justice to Executive Officers and to Members of Congress, 1871–1904.

19. *Republican Banner* (Nashville), July 4, 1871.

20. *Sun* (New York City), Nov. 13, 1871.

21. See Lane, *Freedom's Detective*, 158.

22. Akerman to H. C. Whitley, June 28, 1871, in Letters sent, General and Miscellaneous Letter Books, July 13, 1869–July 15, 1871.

23. *New York Herald*, July 27, 1871. See also, for example, Akerman to McInnis, Montgomery, Ala., July 7, 1871, in Letters Sent, Instructions to U.S. Attorneys and Marshals, 1870–77.

24. Akerman to D. H. Starbuck, June 6, 1871, in ibid.

25. Akerman to John H. Caldwell, July 22, 1871, in ibid.

26. Ben Butler to Akerman, July 29, 1871, in Letters Received, House of Representatives, April 1871–November 1871, Source Chronological Files, 1871–1884.

27. Akerman to Benjamin F. Butler, Aug. 9, 1871, in Akerman, Akerman Letter Books, 1871–76.

28. Akerman to E. P. Jacobson, Jackson, Miss., Aug. 18, 1871, ibid.

29. See *Charlotte* (N.C.) *Democrat*, July 18, 1871, to view the entire convention bill.

30. *Chicago Tribune*, July 20, 1871.

31. *New-York Tribune*, July 24, 1871.

32. *Chicago Tribune*, July 20, 1871.

33. *Tri-Weekly Era* (Raleigh, N.C.), July 25, 1871.

34. *New-York Tribune*, July 24, 1871.

35. *Sun* (New York City), July 29, 1871.

36. *Public Ledger* (Memphis), Aug. 24, 1871.

37. *Christian Advocate* (Raleigh, N.C.), Aug. 23, 1871.

38. Akerman to S. C. Pomeroy, Aug. 11, 1871, in Letters Sent by the Department of Justice to Executive Officers and to Members of Congress, 1871–1904.

39. See B. R. Cowen to Akerman, Aug. 30, 1871, in Letters Received, Interior, March–May 1871. See also Hamilton, "Amos T. Akerman and His Role in American Politics," 103.

40. Akerman to Delano, Sept. 5, 1871, in Letters Sent by the Department of Justice to Executive Officers and to the Members of Congress, 1871–1904.

41. Hamilton, "Amos T. Akerman and His Role in American Politics," 106.

42. Akerman to Matty, Aug. 30, 1871, in Felton, "Hon. Amos T. Akerman, a Biographical Sketch."

CHAPTER 18. BEARING WITNESS

1. U.S. Congress, *Report of the Joint Select Committee to Inquire into the Condition of Affairs in the Late Insurrectionary States*, vol. 5, 1564–74 (Hampton Hicklin). Hereafter in this chapter's notes: *Joint Committee*.

2. Merrill to Akerman, Nov. 29, 1871, and Merrill to Akerman, Nov. 29, 1871, in Source Chronological Files for South Carolina, Jan. 1871–Oct. 1872.

3. *World* (New York City), July 10, 1871. Quoted in *Charleston Daily Courier*, July 21, 1871.

4. *Joint Committee*, vol. 3, 449–69 (James Chestnut).

5. *San Francisco Examiner*, Aug. 1, 1871.

6. Quoted in *Yorkville Enquirer*, July 20, 1871.

7. *Daily Phoenix* (Columbia, S.C.), July 16, 1871.

8. Quoted in *Charleston Daily News*, July 19, 1871.

9. *Daily Milwaukee* (Wisc.) *News*, July 29, 1871.

10. *Joint Committee*, vol. 3, 400 (William Moss), 412 (Elias Thomson).

11. *Yorkville Enquirer*, July 20, 1871.

12. Trelease, *White Terror*, 393.

13. See, for example, *Philadelphia Inquirer*, July 31, 1871, for the basic dispatch. For "semi-official," see *New York Herald*, July 31, 1871.

14. West, *The Reconstruction Ku Klux Klan in York County*, 30–31.

15. *New York Times*, July 30, 1871; *New-York Tribune*, July 31, 1871; *Chicago Tribune*, Aug. 1, 1871; *Yorkville Enquirer*, Aug. 3, 1871.

16. *Yorkville Enquirer*, July, 27, 1871. See also Martinez, *Carpetbaggers, Cavalry and the Ku Klux Klan*, 142–43.

17. *New-York Tribune*, July 31, 1871.

18. Ibid.

19. *Charleston Daily Courier*, July 21, 1871.

20. *Joint Committee*, vol. 4, 1268 (John Tomlinson).

21. Ibid., 1278–82 (Rufus McClain).

22. Ibid., vol. 5, 1284–88 (John Hunter).

23. Ibid., 1342–62 (J. Rufus Bratton).

24. Ibid., 1362–1402 (William K. Owens).

25. *Yorkville Enquirer*, July 27, 1871.

26. *Chicago Tribune*, Aug. 1, 1871.

27. *Joint Committee*,. vol. 5, 1463–87 (Lewis Merrill).

28. Ibid., 1564–74 (Hicklin).

CHAPTER 19. NINE COUNTIES

1. *New York Herald*, Sept. 2, 1871.

2. Scott to Grant, Sept. 1, 1871, in Letters Received, President, Jan. 1871–Dec. 1871, Source Chronological Files 1871–1884; .

3. *New York Herald*, Sept. 2, 1871.

4. Taylor to Merrill, Aug. 4, 1871, Department of the South, Letters received, 1868–1883.

5. Scott to Grant, Sept. 1, 1871, in Letters Received, President, Jan. 1871–Dec. 1871.

6. Diary entry, Sept. 1, 1871, in Fish, Diaries, Reel 1, Papers of Hamilton Fish.

7. *New York Herald*, Sept. 2, 1871; *New York Times*, Sept. 2, 1871.

8. Major Reno to Senator Scott, Sept. 6, 1871, in Source Chronological Files, January 1871–October 1872.

9. *New-York Tribune*, Sept. 8, 1871.

10. *New York Herald*, Sept. 9, 1871.

11. *New York Times*, Sept. 12, 1871. See also Scott to Akerman, Sept. 10, 1871, in Letters Received, Senate, January 1871–May 1871, Source Chronological Files 1871–1884.

12. *Charlotte Democrat*, Sept. 19, 1871. See also Corbin to Akerman, Dec. 5, 1871, Source Chronological Files, January 1871–October 1872. Corbin, at Akerman's request, submitted a bill for expenses in Raleigh and Yorkville, suggesting a $50 per diem. See also Corbin to Akerman, Dec. 27, 1871, Source Chronological Files, January 1871–October 1872. Corbin had received $1,200 for services rendered in both Raleigh and Yorkville ("this is entirely satisfactory to me").

13. U.S. Congress, *Report of the Joint Select Committee to Inquire into the Condition of Affairs in the Late Insurrectionary States*, vol. 2, 417–18 (James M. Justice). Hereafter in this chapter's notes: *Joint Committee*. See also *Charlotte Democrat*, Sept. 26, 1871.

14. *Wilmington* (N.C.) *Journal*, Sept. 22, 1871.

15. Pool to Bristow, Oct. 2, 1871, in Letters Received, Senate, January 1871–May 1871.

16. See, for example, *Joint Committee*, vol. 2, 422–23 (J. R. DePriest), 427–28 (M. M. Jolly). Samuel Phillips later served as U.S. solicitor general under four presidents.

17. *Tri-Weekly Era*, Sept. 21, 1871.

18. *Elberton Gazette*, Jan. 3, 1871, quoted in McKintosh, *The Official History of Elbert County*, 122.

19. Akerman to Bristow, Oct. 20, 1871, Bristow, Papers of Benjamin Helm Bristow, Box 1, 1839–Dec. 1870.

20. *Joint Committee*, vol. 5, 1687–96 (Kirkland Gunn).

21. Terry to Akerman, Sept. 26, 1871, Department of the South, Letters Received, 1868–1883.

22. *Yorkville Enquirer*, Sept. 28, 1871. Emphasis in original.

23. *Joint Committee*, vol. 5, 1600 (Lewis Merrill).

24. Ibid. See also West, *The Reconstruction Ku Klux Klan in York County*, 88.

25. *Joint Committee*, vol. 5, 1600 (Merrill).

26. *Yorkville Enquirer*, Oct. 5, 1871.

27. *Charleston Daily News*, Oct. 9, 1871.

28. *Joint Committee*, vol. 5, 1601–2 (Merrill).

29. *New York Herald*, Oct. 4, 1871.

30. Akerman to Bristow, Oct. 10, 1871, in Letters Received, Justice, June 1871–August 1871, Source Chronological Files, 1871–1884.

31. Ibid.

32. Adjutant General to Department of Justice, Oct. 10, 1871, in Letters Received, War, Source Chronological Files, 1871–1884.

33. See ibid.

34. Bristow to Harlan, Apr. 25, June 22, 1871, in Harlan, Papers of John Marshall Harlan, Box 36, Reel 19.

35. Harlan to Bristow, Sept. 27, 1871, Bristow, Papers of Benjamin Helm Bristow, Box 1, 1839–Dec. 1870.

36. Bristow to Harlan, Apr. 25, 1871, and June 22, 1871, in Harlan, Papers of John Marshall Harlan, Box 36, Reel 19. Emphasis in original throughout.

37. Bristow to Harlan, Oct. 14, 1871, ibid.

38. Ulysses S. Grant, Proclamation, Oct. 17, 1871, in Richardson, *A Compilation of the Messages and Papers of the Presidents*, vol. 7, pt. 1, 136–37.

39. *Joint Committee*, vol. 5, 1602 (Merrill).

40. Grant, Proclamation, Oct. 17, 1871.

CHAPTER 20. THE HAMMER FALLS

1. Myers, "Prelude to Little Bighorn," 60–64. See also U.S. House of Representatives, *Report of the Secretary of War*, vol. 1, 42nd Cong., 3rd Sess., 85–91.

2. Diary of Winfield Scott Harvey, quoted in ibid., 73, 74.

3. Terry to Merrill, Oct. 12, 1871, in Department of the South, Letters Sent, U.S. Army, Part 1.

4. U.S. Congress, *Report of the Joint Select Committee to Inquire into the Condition of Affairs in the Late Insurrectionary States*, vol. 5, 1602 (Lewis Merrill). Hereafter in this chapter's notes: *Joint Committee*.

5. *Charleston Daily News*, Nov. 23, 1871.

6. *Joint Committee*, vol. 5, 1602–93 (Merrill).

7. *Yorkville Enquirer*, Oct. 26, 1871.

8. *Fairfield Herald* (Winnsboro, S.C.), Oct. 25, 1871.

9. Reprinted in *Charleston Daily News*, Oct. 25, 1871.

10. *Anderson* (S.C.) *Intelligencer*, Oct. 19, 1871.

11. *New York Herald*, Oct. 21, 1871.

12. *New York Daily Herald*, Oct. 19, 1871.

13. U.S. Army Adjutant General to Department of Justice, Oct. 20, 1871, in Letters Received, War, Source Chronological Files, 1871–1884.

14. Akerman to Bristow, Oct. 20, 1871, in Bristow, Papers of Benjamin Helm Bristow, Box 1, 1839–Dec. 1870.

15. Merrill to Maj. G. H. Taylor (adjutant), Oct. 27, 1871, in Department of the South, Letters Received, 1868–1883.

16. Merrill to Terry, Oct. 28, 1871, in ibid.

17. *Joint Committee*, vol. 5, 1604 (Merrill).

18. *New York Daily Herald*, Oct. 21, 22, 1871; *Chicago Tribune*, Nov. 4, 1871.

19. Post, "A 'Carpetbagger' in South Carolina," 44.

20. See, for example, Harlan to Bristow, Oct. 11, 1871 and G. C. Wharton to Bristow, Oct. 16, 1871, Bristow, Papers of Benjamin Helm Bristow, Box 1, 1839–Dec. 1870. Bristow was careful not to openly express interest in the attorney generalship, but both Harlan and Wharton urged him to accept the job if it were offered. Wharton assured Bristow that Harlan had no desire to be named, and Harlan offered to come to Washington and lobby on Bristow's behalf.

21. See Akerman to Terry, Nov. 18, 1871, in Akerman, Akerman Letter Books, 1871–76.

22. *Chicago Tribune*, Nov. 4, 1871.

23. *Brooklyn Union*, Nov. 4, 1871; *New York Daily Herald*, Nov. 4, 1871.

24. Ulysses S. Grant, Proclamation, Nov. 3, 1871, in Richardson, *A Compilation of the Messages and Papers of the Presidents*, vol. 7, pt. 1, 139.

25. Merrill to Adjutant General, Nov. 9, 1871, in Letters Received, War, Source Chronological Files, 1871–1884.

26. Grant, Proclamation, Nov. 10, 1871, in Richardson, *A Compilation of the Messages and Papers of the Presidents*, vol. 7, pt. 1, 141.

27. Merrill to Akerman, Nov. 10, 1872, in Source Chronological Files, January 1871–October 1872. See also *Joint Committee*, vol. 5, 1679–80 (Lieutenant Godfrey).

28. See Williams, *The Great South Carolina Ku Klux Klan Trials 1871–1872*, 50–53.

29. Corbin to Akerman, Nov. 20, 1871, in Letters Received, Justice, June 1871–Aug. 1871, Source Chronological Files, 1871–84.

30. Akerman to Corbin, Nov. 23, 1871, in Letters Sent, Instructions to U.S. Attorneys and Marshals, 1870–1877. See also Akerman to Corbin, Nov. 24, 1871, ibid.

31. Corbin to Akerman, Dec. 12, 1871, in Letters Received, House of Representatives, April 1871–November 1871.

32. Corbin to Akerman, Nov. 23, 1871, in ibid. See also Akerman to Belknap, Nov. 23, in Department of the South, Letters Received, 1868–1883.

33. See *Charleston Daily News*, Nov. 14, 1871; *Yorkville Enquirer*, Nov. 16, 1871.

34. Quoted in Nevins, *The Inner History of the Grant Administration*, 148.

35. See Williams, *The Great South Carolina Ku Klux Klan Trials 1871–1872*, 55.

36. *Charleston Daily News*, Nov. 24, 1871.

37. Akerman, Akerman Letter Books, 1871–76.

38. Reprinted in *Yorkville Enquirer*, Nov. 16, 1871.

39. *New-York Tribune*, Nov. 16, 1871.

40. *Sun* (New York City), Nov. 16, 1871.

41. See Zuczek, *State of Rebellion*, 104–7, presents a detailed analysis of the decline in reported Ku Klux outrages as 1871 advanced.

42. Elias Hill himself, along with 167 of his followers, left York County on October 31, emigrating to Liberia. He took passage in Norfolk aboard the bark *Edith Rose*, chartered by the American Colonization Society. Hill died of malaria in his adopted country on March 28, 1872. See Farris, *Freedom on Trial*, 63–64. See also *Sumter* (S.C.) *Watchman*, Nov. 7, 1871; *Vermont Chronicle* (Bellows Falls), Nov. 11, 1871.

43. Akerman to B. D. Silliman, Nov. 9, 1871, in Akerman, Akerman Letter Books, 1871–76.

44. Akerman to Corbin, Nov. 10, 1872, in Letters Sent, Instructions to U.S. Attorneys and Marshals, 1870–1877.

45. Corbin to Akerman, Nov. 3, 1871, in Source Chronological Files, January 1871–October 1872.

46. Akerman to Corbin, Nov. 15, 1871, in Letters Sent, Instructions to U.S. Attorneys and Marshals.

47. Corbin to Akerman, Nov. 13, 1871, in Source Chronological Files, January 1871–October 1872.

48. *Charleston Daily News*, Nov. 24, 1871; *Daily Phoenix* (Columbia, S.C.), Nov. 28, 1871.

49. See Corbin to Akerman, Dec. 2, 1871 for the number of defendants; see First Lieutenant Whitehead to Akerman, Dec. 6, 1871 for the number of witnesses; see note 47 above for Corbin's determination that none but Yorkville cases would be tried in the upcoming term. All citations from Source Chronological Files, January 1871–October 1872.

CHAPTER 21. GREAT QUESTIONS

1. *Charleston Daily News*, Nov. 29, 1871.

2. Ibid., Nov. 27, 1871.

3. See "An Act to Enforce the Rights of Citizens of the United States to Vote in the Several States of this Union," in U.S. *Statutes at Large and Proclamations of the United States of America*, vol. 16, 140–46.

4. Corbin to Akerman, Nov. 13, 1871, in Source Chronological Files for South Carolina.

5. Akerman to Corbin, Nov. 15, 1871, in Letters Sent, Instructions to U.S. Attorneys and Marshals, 1870–1877.

6. U.S. Congress, *Report of the Joint Select Committee to Inquire into the Condition of Affairs in the Late Insurrectionary States*, vol. 5, 1620 (court proceedings). Hereafter in this chapter's notes: *Joint Committee.*

7. Ibid., 1774–76 (Amzi Rainey), 1481 (Lewis Merrill).

8. Corbin to Akerman, Dec. 6, 1871, in Source Chronological Files for South Carolina.

9. Ibid.

10. *Joint Committee*, vol. 5, 1621–25 (court proceedings).

11. See Williams, *The Great South Carolina Ku Klux Klan Trials 1871–1872* (Athens: University of Georgia Press, 1996), 61.

12. *Joint Committee*, vol. 5, 1629 (court proceedings).

13. Ibid., 1633–42.

14. Post and Pittman, *Proceedings in the Ku Klux Trials at Columbia*, 62.

15. Ibid., 63–64.

16. Ibid., 68–83, 86–87.

17. Ibid., 89–92.

18. Ibid., 96–111.

19. Diary entry, Dec. 1, 1871, Fish, Diaries, Reel 1, Papers of Hamilton Fish.

20. For Grant's entire presentation, see Ulysses S. Grant, "Third Annual Message," Dec. 4, 1871, in Richardson, *A Compilation of the Messages and Papers of the Presidents*, vol. 7, pt. 1, 142–55. For mention of the Ku Klux Klan, see 150.

21. *Buffalo Commercial*, Dec. 5, 1871.

22. *New York Herald*, Dec. 5, 1871.

23. *Richmond* (Va.) *Dispatch*, Dec. 6, 1871.

24. *Sun* (New York City), Dec. 12, 1871.

25. *New York Herald*, Dec. 5, 1871.

26. Akerman to B. D. Silliman, Nov. 9, 1871, in Akerman, Akerman Letter Books, 1871–76.

27. Diary entry, Nov. 24, 1871, Fish, Diaries, Reel 1, Papers of Hamilton Fish.

28. *Baltimore American*, Dec. 18, 1871, cited in Felton, "Hon. Amos T. Akerman, a Biographical Sketch."

29. Diary entry, Dec. 11, 1871, Fish, Diaries, Reel 1, Papers of Hamilton Fish.

30. Ibid., Dec. 13, 1871. See also Hamilton, "Amos T. Akerman and His Role in American Politics," 108.

31. *New-York Tribune*, Dec. 15, 1871.

32. Ibid. See also Grant to Akerman, Dec. 12, 1871, Grant, Letterbooks, 1869–77, vol. 1.

33. *Philadelphia Inquirer*, Dec. 15, 1871.

34. See, for example, Chernow, *Grant*, 739–51.

35. Akerman to Benjamin Conley, Dec. 28, 1871, in Akerman, Akerman Letter Books, 1871–76.

36. Akerman to Corbin, Dec. 15, 1871, in ibid.

37. *Intelligencer Journal* (Lancaster, Pa.), Dec. 23, 1871.

38. Felton, "Hon. Amos T. Akerman, a Biographical Sketch."

CHAPTER 22. "CRADLE TO GRAVE"

1. U.S. Congress, *Report of the Joint Select Committee to Inquire into the Condition of Affairs in the Late Insurrectionary States*, vol. 5, 1678 (court proceedings). Hereafter in this chapter's notes: *Joint Committee.*

2. Ibid., 1676, 1678. See also *New-York Tribune*, Dec. 21, 1871.

3. *Joint Committee*, 1680 (court proceedings).

4. Ibid., 1681, 1683–84.

5. Ibid., 1685–87.

6. Ibid. 1691.

7. Ibid., 1696.

8. Ibid., 1693.

9. Ibid., 1706.

10. Ibid., 1713.

11. *New-York Tribune*, Dec. 21.

12. *Joint Committee*, vol. 5, 1722 (court proceedings).

13. Ibid., 1717.

14. Ibid., 1727. For names of the raid defendants, see also ibid., 1726, 1733, 1735, 1740.

15. Ibid., 1738.

16. Ibid., p1729.

17. See Post, "A 'Carpetbagger' in South Carolina," 60. For the durability of this characterization, see, for example, Reynolds, *Reconstruction in South Carolina, 1865–1877*, 189–90. Reynolds describes Williams as a "bold and aggressive fellow, unquestionably a hater of the white race."

18. Despite the common surnames, there is no evidence that Amzi Rainey and Jim Williams (originally Rainey) were related.

19. *Joint Committee*, vol. 5, 1744–46.

20. Post and Pittman, *Proceedings in the Ku Klux Trials at Columbia*, 88. Post and Pittman (son of Isaac Pittman, the inventor of Pittman shorthand) were contracted by the Columbia *Daily Union* to provide a "real time" transcript of the court proceedings for immediate publication. Their version differs in some particulars from the official transcript and is used here to provide added depth to the official text.

21. Ibid., 289–91.

22. *Joint Committee*, vol. 5, 1752–57.

23. Ibid., 1756.

24. Ibid., 1758.

25. Ibid., 1771.

26. Ibid., 1789.

27. Ibid., 1790–1810.

28. Ibid., 1810–17.

29. Ibid., 1819–26.

30. Ibid., 1826–36. Emphasis in original.

31. Ibid., 1837.

32. Ibid., 1936.

33. Corbin to Akerman, Dec. 18, 1871, in Source Chronological Files, Jan. 1871–Oct. 1872.

34. *Buffalo Morning Express*, Dec. 20, 1871.

35. *New York Herald*, Dec. 25, 1871.

36. There is no indication that John W. Mitchell was related to Robert Hayes Mitchell.

37. *Joint Committee*, vol. 5, 1866–67 (court testimony).

38. Ibid. 1871–72, 1842–43.

39. Ibid., 1904–5.

40. Ibid., 1915–16.

41. Ibid., 1939.

42. Ibid., 1942.

43. Ibid., 1954, 1957.

44. Ibid., 1963.

45. Ibid. 1971.

46. Corbin to Akerman, Jan. 5, 1872, in Source Chronological Files, January 1871–October 1872. See also Williams, *The Great South Carolina Ku Klux Klan Trials, 1871–1872*, 100.

47. Akerman to Merrill, Jan. 8, 1872, in Akerman, Akerman Letter Books, 1871–76.

EPILOGUE. "NOT WITH A BANG BUT A WHIMPER"

1. Merrill to Akerman, Nov. 29, 1871, in Source Chronological Files, Jan. 1871–Oct. 1872, General Records of the Department of Justice.

2. Merrill to Akerman, Jan. 10, 1872, ibid.

3. *Yorkville Enquirer*, Aug. 1, 1872.

4. Miller, *A Century of Western Ontario*, 180.

5. *Ottawa Daily Citizen*, Jun. 8, 1872. See also Landon, "The Kidnapping of Dr. Rufus Bratton," 330–33.

6. *Ottawa Daily Citizen*, Jun. 8, 1872.

7. *Yorkville Enquirer*, Aug. 1, 1872.

8. *Missouri Republican* (St. Louis), Jun. 18, 1872.

9. Quoted in Williams, *The Great South Carolina Ku Klux Klan Trials 1871–1872*, 124.

10. Farris, *Freedom on Trial*, 197–200.

11. Chernow, *Grant*, 802–8.

12. *Wilmington* (N.C.) *Journal*, Jan. 6, 1872.

13. *New-York Tribune*, Jan. 1, 1872.

14. *Wilmington Journal*, Jan. 6, 1872.

15. U.S. House of Representatives, "Letter from the Attorney General of the United States Transmitting His Annual Report to Congress," 42nd Cong., 2nd Sess., Jan. 16, 1872.

16. *Yorkville Enquirer*, Mar. 28, 1872. See also Supreme Court of the United States, Case 6161, *United States v. James William Avery, Robert Riggins, et al.*, filed Jan. 5, 1872, dismissed Mar. 21, 1872.

17. *Yorkville Enquirer*, Mar. 28, 1872.

18. West, *The Reconstruction Ku Klux Klan in York County*, 101–2.

19. Farris, *Freedom on Trial*, 195–96.

20. Corbin to Williams, Feb. 20, 1872, in Source Chronological Files, January 1871–October 1872, General Records of the Department of Justice. Emphasis in original.

21. Corbin to Williams, Nov. 21, 1872, in ibid.

22. See *Norfolk Virginian*, May 11, 1892, for death notice.

23. Alum File David Corbin, Class of 1857, Rauner Special Collections Library, Dartmouth College, Hanover, New Hampshire.

24. Martinez, *Carpetbaggers, Cavalry and the Ku Klux Klan*, 221–35.

25. U.S. Census Bureau, *Ninth Census of the United States*; U.S. Census Bureau, *Tenth Census of the United States.*

26. *Yorkville Enquirer*, May 25, 1876.

27. Farris, *Freedom on Trial*, 278–80.

28. Akerman to Terry, Nov. 18, 1871, in Akerman, Akerman Letter Books, 1871–76.

29. Akerman to Merrill, Nov. 9, 1871, ibid.

30. Akerman to Merrill, Jan. 8, 1872, ibid.

31. Diary entry, Apr. 9, 1874, in Akerman, Diaries, 1846–1875.

32. Diary entry, June 2, 1874, ibid.

33. *Columbus* (Ga.) *Enquirer-Sun*, Dec. 24, 1880.

34. *Columbus* (Ga.) *Sunday Enquirer*, Sept. 5, 1875.

OFFICIAL U.S. GOVERNMENT RECORDS

U.S. Census Bureau. *Ninth Census of the United States: Statistics of Population.* Washington, D.C.: GPO, 1872.

U.S. Census Bureau. *Tenth Census of the United States: Statistics of Population.* Washington, D.C.: GPO, 1882.

U.S. *Statutes at Large and Proclamations of the United States of America*, 18 vols. Boston: Little, Brown, 1845–1873.

CONGRESSIONAL DOCUMENTS

U.S. Congress. *Appendix to the Congressional Globe*, 41st Cong., 2nd Sess. 1869–70.

———. *Congressional Globe.*

———. *Report of the Joint Select Committee to Inquire into the Condition of Affairs in the Late Insurrectionary States*, 13 vols.Washington, D.C.: GPO, 1872.

U.S. House of Representatives. *Affairs in Alabama.* 43rd Cong., 2nd Sess., H.R. 262/2, 1875, Serial 1661.

———. Amendment in the Nature of a Substitute to the Bill (H.R. 320). 42nd Cong., 1st Sess., H.R. 320, Mar. 31, 1871.

———. Amendment to the Bill (H.R. 320) to Enforce the Provisions of the Fourteenth Amendment to the Constitution of the United States, and for Other Purposes. 42nd Cong., 1st Sess., H.R. 320, Apr. 5, 1871.

———. A Bill Authorizing the Employment of the Land and Naval Forces of the United States in the Enforcement of the Laws. 42nd. Cong, 1st Sess., H.R. 7, Mar. 7, 1871.

———. A Bill to Amend an Act Approved May Thirty-one, Eighteen Hundred and Seventy. 41st. Cong., 3rd Sess., H.R. 2634, Jan. 9, 1871.

———. A Bill to Enforce the Provisions of the Fourteenth Amendment to the Constitution of the United States, and for Other purposes. 42nd Cong., 1st Sess., H.R. 320, Mar. 28, 1871.

———. A Bill to Protect Loyal and Peaceable Citizens of the United States in the Full Enjoyment of Their Rights, Persons, Liberty and Property. 41st. Cong., 3rd Sess., H.R. 3011, Feb. 13, 1871.

———. A Bill to Protect Loyal and Peaceable Citizens of the United States in the Full Enjoyment of Their Rights, Persons, Liberty and Property. 42nd Cong., 1st Sess., H.R. 189, Mar. 20, 1871.

———. A Bill to Secure to All Persons within the Jurisdiction of the United States the Equal Protection of the Laws within the Several States. 42nd Cong., 1st Sess., H.R. 224, Mar. 20, 1871.

———. *Condition of Affairs in Georgia.* 40th Cong., 3rd Sess., H. Misc. Doc. No. 52.

———. *Journal of the House of Representatives.* 42nd Cong., 1st Sess. 1871.

———. "Letter from the Attorney General of the United States Transmitting His Annual Report to Congress." In *Annual Report of the Attorney General.* 41st Cong., 3rd Sess., H. Exec. Doc. 90, Feb. 1, 1871.

———. "Letter from the Attorney General of the United States Transmitting His Annual Report to Congress." In *Annual Report of the Attorney General.* 42nd Cong., 2nd Sess., Exec. Doc. 55, Jan. 16, 1872.

———. *Report of the Secretary of War.* vol. 1. 42nd Cong., 3rd Sess., Exec. Doc. 1, Pt. 2, 1872.

———. *To Protect Loyal and Peaceable Citizens of the United States.* 41st Cong., 3rd Sess., H. Rep. 37, to accompany H.R. 3011, Feb. 20, 1871.

U.S. Senate. A Bill for the Protection of Persons Resident within the United States against Unlawful Combinations and Conspiracies. 42nd Cong., 1st Sess., S. 226, Mar. 16, 1871.

———. A Bill More Fully to Enforce the Fourteenth Amendment to the Constitution of the United States. 42nd Cong., 1st Sess., S. 243, Mar. 16, 1871.

———. A Bill to Amend an Act Approved February Twenty-eighth Seventeen Hundred Ninety-five, and to Authorize the President, at His Discretion to Declare Martial Law in Certain Cases. 42nd Cong., 1st Sess., S. 303, Mar. 23, 1871.

———. *Journal of the Executive Proceedings of the Senate of the United States of America, 1869–1871.*

———. Message of the President of the United States. 41st Cong., 3rd Sess., Exec. Doc. 16, Jan. 13, 1871.

———. *Union Pacific Railroad.* Committee on the Judiciary, (Union Pacific). 41st Cong., 3rd sess., S. Rep. 375, Feb. 21, 1871.

NATIONAL ARCHIVES AND RECORDS ADMINISTRATION

Department of the South, Letters Received, 1868–1883, U.S. Army, Record Group 393, National Archives, Washington, D.C.

Department of the South, Letters Sent, U.S. Army, Part 1, Entry 4091, Record Group 393, National Archives, Washington, D.C.

Letters Received, Adjutant General, U.S. Army headquarters, File 2051, Identifier 142810837, Record Group 94, National Archives, Washington, D.C.

Letters Received, House of Representatives, April 1871–November 1871, Source Chronological Files, 1871–1884, General Records of the Department of Justice, Box 530, Record Group 60, National Archives, College Park, Md.

Letters Received, Interior, March–May 1871, General Records of the Department of Justice, Box 357, Record Group 60, National Archives, College Park, Md.

Letters Received, January–May 1871, Source Chronological Files, 1871–1874, General Records of the Department of Justice, Box 505, Record Group 60, National Archives, College Park, Md.

Letters Received, Justice, June 1871–August 1871, Source Chronological Files, 1871–1884, General Records of the Department of Justice, Box 186–187, Record Group 60; National Archives at College Park, Md.

Letters Received, President, January 1871–December 1871, Source Chronological Files, 1871–1884, General Records of the Department of Justice, Box 1, Record Group 60, National Archives, College Park, Md.

Letters Received, Senate, January 1871–May 1871, Source Chronological Files, 1871–1884,

General Records of the Department of Justice, Box 505–506, Record Group 60, National Archives, College Park, Md.

Letters Received, War, Source Chronological Files, 1871–1884, General Records of the Department of Justice, Box 261, Record Group 60, National Archives, College Park, Md.

Letters Sent by the Department of Justice to Executive Officers and to Members of Congress, 1871–1904, General Records of the Department of Justice, National Archives Microfilm Publication, Microcopy 702, Roll 1, Volume A, February 16, 1871–September 21, 1872, Record Group 60, National Archives, College Park, Md.

Letters Sent, General and Miscellaneous Letter Books, July 13, 1869–July 15, 1871, General Records of the Department of Justice, National Archives Microfilm Publication, M699, Roll 13, Record Group 60, National Archives, College Park, Md.

Letters Sent, Instructions to U.S. Attorneys and Marshals, 1870–1877, General Records of the Department of Justice, National Archives Microfilm Publication, M701, Books A–G, 1870–1877, Record Group 60, National Archives, College Park, Md.

Source Chronological Files, January 1871–October 1872, General Records of the Department of Justice, M947, Roll 1, Record Group 60, National Archives, College Park, Md.

Source Chronological Files for South Carolina, General Records of the Department of Justice, National Archives Microfilm Publication, M947, Record Group 60, National Archives, College Park, Md.

OTHER PRIMARY SOURCES

Akerman, Amos T. Akerman Letter Books, 1871–76. Accession #1165, Albert and Shirley Small Special Collections Library, University of Virginia, Charlottesville.

———. Biographical Notes. Private collection held by Mark Akerman.

———. Civil War Letters. Private collection held by Mark Akerman.

———. Diaries, 1846–1875. Private collection held by Mark Akerman.

———. Letters to Family. Private collection held by Mark Akerman.

———. "Union Pacific Railroad Company." In *Official Opinions of the Attorneys General of the United States*, vol. 13, edited by A. J. Bentley, 360–69. Washington, D.C.: W. H. and O. H. Morrison, 1873.

Bristow, Benjamin Helm. Papers of Benjamin Helm Bristow. Manuscript Division, Library of Congress.

Butler, Benjamin F. *Butler's Book*. Boston: A.M. Thayer, 1892.

———. "General Correspondence." In Papers of Benjamin F. Butler. Manuscript Division, Library of Congress, Washington. D.C.

Carroll, Milus Smith. Handwritten memoir, 1924. Copy held by the Historical Center of York County, South Carolina.

The Constitution of the State of South Carolina. Charleston, S.C.: Denny & Perry, 1868.

Cox, Jacob Dolson. "How Judge Hoar Ceased to Be Attorney-General." *Atlantic Monthly*, August 1895, 162–73.

Felton, Rebecca. "Hon. Amos T. Akerman, a Biographical Sketch." *Cartersville* (Ga.) *Courant*, Mar. 26, 1885.

Fish, Hamilton. Diaries, Reel 1, Papers of Hamilton Fish. Manuscript Division, Library of Congress, Washington, D.C.

Grant, Ulysses S. Letterbooks, 1869–77, vols. 1–2, Ulysses S. Grant Papers, Series 2, Manuscript Division, Library of Congress, Washington, D.C.

Hall, S. B. *A Shell in the Radical Camp*. Charleston, S.C.: John C. Hundley and Brother, 1873.

Harlan, John Marshall. Papers of John Marshall Harlan, Boxes 35–36, Reels 18–19, Manuscript Division, Library of Congress, Washington, D.C.

Leland, John A. *A Voice from South Carolina*. Charleston: Walker, Evans and Cogswell, 1879.

Lester, J. C., and D. L. Wilson. *Ku Klux Klan: Its Origin, Growth and Disbandment, 1884*. New ed. New York: Neale Publishing, 1905.

Post, Louis F. "A 'Carpetbagger' in South Carolina." *Journal of Negro History* 10 (1925): 10–79.

Post, Louis F., and Benn Pittman. *Proceedings in the Ku Klux Trials at Columbia, South Carolina in United States Circuit Court, November term, 1871*. Columbia, S.C.: Republican State Printers, 1872.

Richardson, James D. *A Compilation of the Messages and Papers of the Presidents*, vol. 7, pt. 1, *Ulysses S. Grant*. New York: Bureau of National Literature and Art, 1907)(later edition).

NEWSPAPERS

South Carolina

Abbeville Press and Banner
Anderson Intelligencer
Camden Journal
Charleston Daily Courier
Charleston Daily News
Daily Phoenix (Columbia)
Edgefield Advertiser
Fairfield Herald (Winnsboro)
Laurensville Herald
Newberry Weekly Herald
Sumter Watchman
Yorkville Enquirer

Outside South Carolina

Atlanta Constitution
Brooklyn Daily Eagle
Brooklyn Union
Buffalo Commercial
Buffalo Courier
Buffalo Express
Buffalo Morning Express
Buffalo Morning Express and Illustrated Buffalo Express
Buffalo Weekly Courier
Cartersville (Ga.) *Courant*
Charlotte (N.C.) *Democrat*
Chicago Tribune
Christian Advocate (Raleigh, N.C.)
Cincinnati Enquirer
Columbus (Ga.) *Enquirer-Sun*
Columbus (Ga.) *Sunday Enquirer*
Courier-Journal (Louisville)
Daily Atchison (Kans.) *Patriot*
Daily Columbus (Ga.) *Enquirer*
Daily Milwaukee (Wisc.) *News*
Daily Standard (Raleigh, N.C.)
Evening Star (Washington, D.C.)
Evening Telegraph (Philadelphia)
Georgia Weekly Telegraph and Messenger (Macon)
Harrisburg (Pa.) *Telegraph*
Intelligencer Journal (Lancaster, Pa.)
Missouri Republican (St. Louis)
Nashville American
Nashville Union and American
New National Era (Washington, D.C.)
New York Evening Post
New York Herald
New York Times
New-York Tribune
Norfolk Virginian
Ottawa (Ont.) *Daily Citizen*
Philadelphia Inquirer
Pittsburgh Commercial
Pittsburgh Weekly Gazette
Public Ledger (Memphis)
Reading (Pa.) *Times*
Republican Banner (Nashville)
Richmond (Va.) *Dispatch*
San Francisco Examiner
Selma (Ala.) *Messenger*
Selma (Ala.) *Weekly Times*

Semi-Weekly Raleigh (N.C.) *Sentinel*
South Kansas Tribune (Independence, Kans.)
Sun (New York City)
Times-Picayune (New Orleans)
Tri-Weekly Era (Raleigh, N.C.)
Urbana (Ohio) *Union*
Vermont Chronicle (Bellows Falls)
Weekly Telegraph (Macon, Ga.)
Wilmington (N.C.) *Journal*
Winona (Minn.) *Daily Republican*
World (New York City)

SECONDARY SOURCES

Begley, Paul R. "Orr, James Lawrence." In *South Carolina Encyclopedia*, https://www.scencyclopedia.org/sce/entries/orr-james-lawrence.

Bradley, Mark L. *The Army and Reconstruction: 1865–1877*. Washington, D.C.: Center of Military History, United States Army, 2015.

Chernow, Ron. *Grant*. New York: Penguin, 2017.

Current, Richard Nelson. *Those Terrible Carpetbaggers*. New York: Oxford University Press, 1988.

Downs, Gregory P. *After Appomattox: Military Occupation and the Ends of War*. Cambridge, Mass.: Harvard University Press, 2015.

Farris, Scott. *Freedom on Trial*. Lanham, Md.: Rowman & Littlefield, 2020.

Foner, Eric. *Reconstruction: America's Unfinished Revolution 1863–1877*. New York: Harper & Row, 1988.

———. *The Second Founding: How the Civil War and Reconstruction Remade the Constitution*. New York: Norton, 2019.

Hamilton, Lois Neal. "Amos T. Akerman and His Role in American Politics." Master's thesis, Columbia University, 1939.

Groce, W. "John B. Gordon." New Georgia Encyclopedia, 2004. https://www.georgiaencyclopedia.org/articles/government-politics/john-b-gordon-1832-1904.

Hurst, Jack. *Nathan Bedford Forrest: A Biography*. New York: Alfred A. Knopf, 1993.

Klein, Maury. *Union Pacific: Birth of a Railroad, 1862–1893*. Garden City, N.Y.: Doubleday, 1987.

Knight, L. L. *A Standard History of Georgia and Georgians*, vol 2. New York: Lewis, 1917.

Landon, Fred. "The Kidnapping of Dr. Rufus Bratton." *Journal of Negro History* 10 (1925): 330–33.

Lane, Charles. *Freedom's Detective: The Secret Service, the Ku Klux Klan and the Man Who Masterminded America's First War on Terror*. Toronto: Hanover Square, 2019.

Martinez, J. Michael. *Carpetbaggers, Cavalry and the Ku Klux Klan: Exposing the Invisible Empire during Reconstruction*. Lanham, Md.: Rowman & Littlefield, 2007.

McFeely, William S. "Amos T. Akerman: The Lawyer and Racial Justice." In *Region, Race and Reconstruction: Essays in Honor of C. Vann Woodward*, edited by J. Morgan Kousser and James M. McPherson, 395–417. New York: Oxford University Press, 1982.

———. *Grant: A Biography*. New York: Norton, 1981.

McKintosh, John H. *The Official History of Elbert County, 1730–1935*. Atlanta: Cherokee, 1968.

Miller, Orlo. *A Century of Western Ontario: The Story of London*. Toronto: Ryerson Press, 1949.

Myers, Andrew H. "Prelude to Little Bighorn." In *Recovering the Piedmont Past: Unexplored*

Moments in Nineteenth-Century Upcountry South Carolina History, edited by Timothy P. Grady and Melissa Walker, 54–76. Columbia: University of South Carolina Press, 2013.

Nash, Howard P., Jr. *Stormy Petrel: The Life and Times of General Benjamin F. Butler, 1818–1893*. Rutherford, N.J.: Fairleigh Dickinson University Press, 1969.

Nevins, Allan. *The Inner History of the Grant Administration*. New York: Dodd, Mead, 1936.

Reynolds, John S. *Reconstruction in South Carolina, 1865–1877*. Columbia, S.C.: State Company, 1905.

Sanger, George P., ed. *The Statutes at Large and Proclamations of the United States of America from March 1871 to March 1873*, vol. 17. Boston: Little, Brown, 1873.

Scoggins, Michael. *The Armament of Jim Williams' Militia Company in 1871*. Pamphlet held by Historical Center of York County, South Carolina.

———. *A Brief History of Historic Brattonsville*. Rock Hill, S.C.: Yorkville County and Heritage Commission, 2004.

Shugerman, Jed Handelsman. "The Creation of the Department of Justice: Professionalization without Civil Rights or Civil Service." *Stanford Law Review* 66, no. 1 (2014): 121–72.

Thompson, C. Mildred. *Reconstruction in Georgia: Economic, Social, Political, 1865–1872*. New York: no publisher listed, 1915.

Trelease, Allen W. *White Terror: The Ku Klux Klan Conspiracy and Southern Reconstruction*. Westport, Conn.: Greenwood, 1971.

West, Jerry L. *The Reconstruction Ku Klux Klan in York County, South Carolina, 1865–1877*. Jefferson, N.C.: McFarland, 2002.

Williams, Lou Falkner. *The Great South Carolina Ku Klux Klan Trials 1871–1872*. Athens: University of Georgia Press, 1996.

Zuczek, Richard. *State of Rebellion: Reconstruction in South Carolina*. Columbia: University of South Carolina Press, 1996.

INDEX